ALEXANDER PHIMISTER PROCTOR
SCULPTOR IN BUCKSKIN

Alexander Phimister Proctor, about 1885

ALEXANDER PHIMISTER PROCTOR

SCULPTOR IN BUCKSKIN

AN AUTOBIOGRAPHY
BY ALEXANDER PHIMISTER PROCTOR

EDITED AND WITH A FOREWORD
BY HESTER ELIZABETH PROCTOR

INTRODUCTION BY VIVIAN A. PALADIN

UNIVERSITY OF OKLAHOMA PRESS : NORMAN

International Standard Book Number: 0–8061–0912–2

Library of Congress Catalog Card Number: 77–108803

Copyright 1971 by the University of Oklahoma Press, Publishing Division of the University. Composed and printed at Norman, Oklahoma, U.S.A., by the University of Oklahoma Press First edition.

TO MARGARET, MY BELOVED WIFE AND COMPANION

EDITOR'S FOREWORD

"It's a boy!" The doctor's announcement in a cabin in Bozanquit, Canada, on September 27, 1860, began a ninety-year life that was filled with hard work, high adventure, and notable achievement. Alexander Phimister Proctor was the boy, and this is his story.

Of pioneer stock on both his mother's and his father's sides, my father had a lifelong interest in pioneers, Indians, cowboys, and hunters—in their way of life, and especially in the animals that were part of that life. As a sculptor of living things, he always portrayed what he saw in what is called photographic style. Whether sketching in pencil or modeling in three dimensions, he was in every sense of the word a realist.

Dad's early years were spent in Canada and Colorado, where people were rugged and wildlife was plentiful. He studied and drew what he saw, even on the pages of his schoolbooks. When he went hunting, he made sketches and took careful measurements of the animals he shot. His ability to observe and record stood him in good stead later, when he modeled animals of all species and sizes, from rabbits to cougars to elephants.

Dad's father, my grandfather, was a poet and a dreamer. Recognizing Dad's talent, he encouraged the young artist and arranged for him to receive art lessons.

But Dad's youth was not a sheltered, reclusive one. During his early years in Colorado he hunted and fished, for fun and food. He set out trap lines and prospected, as did most youngsters of that time. In 1885 Dad sold a homestead and with the proceeds went to New York to study art. Each fall, however, he returned to the West to hunt and study animals. One year as he was returning from his annual western visit he received a commission to sculpture several animals for the World's Columbian Exposition in Chicago in 1893. He worked long and hard and created many pieces that helped establish him as an artist. Before the fair ended, he met Margaret Daisy Gerow, who shortly afterward became his wife.

The newlyweds went to Paris on a Rinehart

Scholarship. During their years in Europe, two children were born to them, the first of a family of eight boys and girls, a healthy, happy brood who still recall with joy the years they accompanied Dad from city to city all across the country, wherever Dad had a commission. One brother expressed the feeling of all of us when he said, "I would rather belong to this family than to have been born a prince."

Alexander Phimister Proctor knew that he was a good artist, but withal he was humble before the talent which had been given to him, and he deferred to the expert judgments of his wife, who was his best, though a loving, critic. He had a wonderful sense of humor and a delightful twinkle in his eye. He could always be counted on to say yes to requests our mother (Mody, as everyone called her) had refused us—sometimes, I must confess, because his mind was on other things and he did not listen carefully. To all of his children he was consistently kind, generous, and affectionate.

To his friends he was an endless source of tales and anecdotes, tall and otherwise. His early adventures and escapades were many and exciting, and they lost nothing in the telling.

He was active all his life. Once he considered joining Teddy Roosevelt's Rough Riders, and he even thought of going with Roosevelt on an African safari. A steadily growing family kept him from accepting either invitation, but the urge to be up and doing every minute was a manifestation of his impatience with unproductiveness and indecision. In later years, when the depression came and commissions slowed, he had periods of leisure that were not easy to fill and did not fit his temperament.

One such time arose in the winter of 1936, when Dad's statue of Robert E. Lee was being cast. He and Mody were wintering in Sarasota, Florida. Dad fished, sketched, painted, and made dry points, but nothing kept him occupied for long. Finally Mody dug out a collection of scraps of paper she had been saving over the years. They were records of trips and notes on Dad's earlier days. Finally acceding to the repeated urgings of family and friends, he began writing about his adventurous life. Again in 1943 he found himself with nothing to do. Bronze, a critical metal in wartime, was unavailable for sculpture. Out came the writing once more.

After Mody died, life was pretty empty for Dad, and we had to find some way to keep his spirits up. I persuaded him to go back to work on his autobi-

EDITOR'S FOREWORD

ography. I typed anecdotes during the day and read them to friends at night. They were well received, and Dad was encouraged to stay with his writing.

One day after Dad's death, Mrs. Vivian Paladin, editor of the Montana Historical Association, wrote to me asking for an article about him. Her interest gave me the incentive to put the finishing editorial touches on the work which was started by Dad long ago and which is now being published after he has gone. In this effort I have been assisted by a good friend, Jack McDowell.

No one could be more grateful than I to these people and to all the others who have helped see Dad's story into print. The recognition of his contribution to American art and the interest expressed in his life have been most rewarding, and the whole Proctor family—now forty-six strong—will always be grateful for all the encouragement along the way.

HESTER PROCTOR

Palo Alto, California
May 15, 1970

CONTENTS

Editor's Foreword		*page* vii	
Introduction by Vivian A. Paladin		xv	
Chapter	I.	My Bear Tree	3
	II.	Early Memories of Denver	5
	III.	At Home in the Open	12
	IV.	Early Art Training	20
	V.	Learning to Hunt	26
	VI.	Colorado Indians	42
	VII.	Friends and Fights at Grand Lake	47
	VIII.	The Grand County Feud	59
	IX.	California and Yosemite	75
	X.	New York at Last	82
	XI.	Lone Camp in the Flat Tops	89
	XII.	The Fawn and the Panther	94
	XIII.	Another Summer in the Mountains	99
	XIV.	Washington and the Cascades	108
	XV.	The World's Columbian Exposition	114
	XVI.	The First Trip to Paris	124
	XVII.	Horses for Saint-Gaudens	128
	XVIII.	The Rinehart Scholarship	135
	XIX.	A Try at Country Life	144
	XX.	Tigers, Ducks, and Rams	150
	XXI.	A Summer with the Cheyennes	158
	XXII.	Cowboys and Indians	163
	XXIII.	Back to Denver	173
	XXIV.	Between California and New York	178
	XXV.	*The Pioneer Mother*	184

XXVI.	General Lee and the Mustangs	191
XXVII.	Epilogue	201

A Gallery of Sculptures by Alexander
   Phimister Proctor   205

Appendix   The Major Sculptures of
                   Alexander Phimister Proctor   257

Index   261

ILLUSTRATIONS

Alexander Phimister Proctor — Frontispiece

Title-page etching for *Hands Up* — Page 24
Lynching of Musgrove (from *Hands Up*) — 25
Proctor at the Art Students' League — 87
Proctor and his family, 1897 — 138
Little Wolf, chief of the Cheyennes — 159
Gozo Kawamura pointing up the
   Robert E. Lee statue — 194

A GALLERY OF SCULPTURES
By Alexander Phimister Proctor

Fate — Page 207
Cub and Rabbit — 208
Stalking Panther — 209
Polar Bear — 210
Moose — 211
Dog with Bone — 212
Bronze Horse — 213
Arab Stallion — 213
General John A. Logan — 214
General William Tecumseh Sherman — 215
Puma — 216
Quadriga — 218
Trumpeting Elephant — 219
Lion (Frick Building) — 220
Griffin — 221
Louis Jolliet — 222
Decor for elephant house, Bronx Park Zoo — 223
McKinley Monument — 225
Tiger — 227
Princeton Tigers — 229
Lion (Pratt Institute) — 230
Tigers at entrance to Pratt Estate — 231
Pony Express — 232
Bear's Head (Boone and Crockett Club) — 233
Buffalo on Q Street Bridge, Washington, D.C. — 233
Tarpon — 234
William Hanley — 234
Indian Pursuing Buffalo — 235
Jackson Sundown — 237
Bronze cornerstone for Arlington Cemetery
   Bridge, Washington, D.C. — 238

Pioneer	239
Broncho Buster	240
On the War Trail	241
Model for *The Rough Rider*	242
The Rough Rider, ready for casting in bronze	243
The Rough Rider	243
The Circuit Rider	244
Til Taylor	245
The Pioneer Mother, Kansas City, Missouri	246–48
Indian and Trapper	249
Gifford Pinchot	250
Irving Hale	250
Pioneer Mother, University of Oregon	251
Model for *General Robert E. Lee*	252
General Robert E. Lee and Young Soldier	253
Working model for *Mustangs*	254
Mustangs	255

INTRODUCTION

BY VIVIAN A. PALADIN
Editor, *Montana: The Magazine of Western History*

Late in 1958 a reader of *Montana* wrote to our editorial offices at the Montana Historical Society in Helena, commenting that we or someone else in the field of western history and art ought to publish an article on Alexander Phimister Proctor, who was commonly regarded as "the greatest American sculptor of western horses (including mustangs), Indians, elk, deer, and buffalo."

The reader implored us, before it was too late, to ask the great Texas historian J. Frank Dobie to write such an article for us. Many years before, Dobie had chosen Proctor over every other eminent sculptor in America to create the awesome mustang group for the University of Texas in Austin.

At the dedication of this magnificent monument in May, 1948, Mr. Dobie had said: "As I behold these glorious creatures that Phimister Proctor has arrested in enduring bronze, they inspire in me a kind of release and elation. I am free with them and with the wind, in spaces without confines."

Clearly Mr. Dobie, who at the time was also southwest regional editor for *Montana*, was the person to write an article about Proctor. We at once wrote to Mr. Dobie, who replied by reiterating his enthusiasm for the sculptor and remarking that the seven-mustang group in Austin "is one of the finest pieces of bronze in America." He wished that "time and energy" permitted him to write the article and thus give him a chance to probe more deeply into the career which, to Mr. Dobie, had culminated in the mustang group.

But it was not to be. J. Frank Dobie died a few months after our exchange.

The matter would not rest. Correspondence began between our office and Hester Proctor, the sculptor's oldest daughter. Pictures of Proctor's works, of early humorous sketches and of the sensitive model of a timid fawn, of animal studies he did for the World's Columbian Exposition in Chicago in 1893, of the heroic equestrians of Theodore Roosevelt and Robert E. Lee, and finally of the seven plunging mustangs, reached our office. The humanity of the man began to emerge, too, even in the first materials we received.

As associate editor of the magazine at the time, I finally found the temerity to write the article, which was published in the January, 1964, issue of *Montana*. My courage was inspired entirely by the subject himself and by his children, particularly Hester.

In the weeks that I spent on the project A. Phimister Proctor became a good friend. I got to know, vicariously, his whole family—all eight of the children and the gentle, talented Mody who was their mother. I kept wishing that I could have joined the big family as it crowded into the car every year for the trip west. I wanted to visit the many homes and studios across the country where live animals had been kept for study and sketches before they were modeled and their counterparts pointed up and cast in bronze. Finally, I wanted to join the family circle that had formed in Seattle in the 1940's, enlarged with grandchildren, the aging Proctor reading aloud from Dickens at Christmastime, masking his grief at the loss of Mody with stories about his adventures as a hunter in the early West. In short, for me, writing and publishing that one article had resulted in a closer-than-usual attachment to the subject.

Throughout our correspondence Hester talked about her father's autobiography, begun at the urging of Mrs. Proctor in periods of restlessness between commissions and when wartime shortages of metals held up casting. After Mrs. Proctor's death the children had urged him to continue.

Not long after we published the Proctor article, Hester sent us the autobiography. As we read the manuscript, the excitement engendered by the article grew. Here, in Proctor's own words, was high adventure. There emerged from the narrative a remarkable tapestry of humor, danger, honesty, artistic striving, love.

The matter of publishing Proctor's own story became uppermost in our minds. Obviously the Montana Historical Society could not undertake the project. At Hester's suggestion, the manuscript, accompanied by sketches which Proctor had prepared especially for it, went off to the University of Oklahoma Press. Now, with the help of the Proctor children and many others, it appears in print, with an appended gallery of the sculptor's great works, which form a memorial to a remarkable life.

After a dozen years, my excitement in discovering Proctor the man remains undiminished. To try to kindle the same excitement in the reader of this book would be superfluous. The reader is captured in the first sentences of Proctor's story. To try to appraise Proctor as a sculptor would be presump-

INTRODUCTION

tuous. The artist emerges from his work, seen in splendid aspect from Washington, D.C., and New York to Kansas City, Denver, and Dallas. His legacy to his adopted country is some of America's greatest heroic statuary.

My personal conviction is that the reader will discern the overriding quality of A. Phimister Proctor: his enthusiasm. It was an enthusiasm that pervaded every aspect of his life and of his art. It embraced every member of his family and those within its circle. It is evident in every word that he wrote and in every line of bone and muscle in his immortal works of art.

ALEXANDER PHIMISTER PROCTOR
SCULPTOR IN BUCKSKIN

Above the Clouds.   A. Phimister Proctor

I.

MY BEAR TREE

"What is beauty?" I am often asked. First on my list is the baby, fresh from nature's hand. Next come the lovely woman and the physically perfect man. Last but not least are the animals, especially the wild ones.

The art of yesterday may not be appreciated today, but perhaps it will be at some time in the future. That is why art appraisal is so difficult. For instance, it is impossible for me to appreciate the so-called art of the modernists, as many do—or make believe they do. I often wonder when the younger generation will realize that fifty years from now they will be the graybeards and others will say to them, "Go up, Old Baldy, go up!"

It must be my misfortune that I cannot see the beauty in or appreciate the art of deformity as practiced now. Where the young get their models for the disgusting human beings they portray is an enigma to me. I can't believe that such art will last.

I don't contend that if you can recognize a statue it is good art, but it seems to me that it has a better chance than something that does not look like anything on or under the earth. God made man in his image, the Bible says, and I believe that God and nature know more about beauty than some of us human beings. It certainly takes nerve to think that one can improve on what God has made!

The Greeks, to my mind, reached the pinnacle of perfection in sculptured art. They used for models the highest physical types and most nearly perfect people, and the result is beauty in every form and line. There is a divine touch in Grecian art which I find lacking in the Roman copies. There is charm in the smallest modeled fragment of Greek sculpture that thrills my soul.

While at Olympus I went to see the Hermes by Praxiteles. There in what looked like a chicken coop stood one of the masterpieces of the world. I had seen pictures of the statue all my life, but when I was face to face with it the glorious creation was almost more than I could bear. A friend who was with me told me later that he thought I was going to faint. There wasn't another soul in the museum that day. Nearby was an old table, which I pushed against the box of sawdust that Hermes was standing in up to his knees; then I stood on the box to run my hands all over the contours of the figure. Feeling the marvelous modeling gave me a joy greater than that my eyes had given me. The back of the statue was in shadow and looked smooth, but my fingers told me it was far from smooth. During all this experience I kept wondering what a guard would think if he had entered, but I did not care.

In regions inhabited by bears there are what hunters call bear trees. They are the bears' daily, weekly, or monthly news records and advertising media. Bruin will mosey up to a tree and sniff to see whether friend or foe has been there. He may reach up with his paw and scratch a nasty gash in the bark. Then he will investigate the highest marks. They tell him if a bigger bear has ambled into his bailiwick. Getting close up against the tree, he'll stand on his hind legs, stretch to his full height, and bite a splinter out of the trunk. If his mark is the highest, he need not worry about newcomers; if not, he may look up a new country or prepare to fight the intruder.

I have made my mark on the tree of art as high as I possibly could. How high the mark is I am not sure, and I do not worry about it overmuch. But it is there for all to see.

II·

EARLY MEMORIES OF DENVER

Both of my parents were of pioneering stock. My paternal grandfather and great-grandfather were members of the Highland Black Watch, and my great-grandfather was with Wolfe and the British when they stormed the heights of Quebec.

My grandfather's regiment, the Forty-second Highlanders, was transferred to Canada to fight against the Yanks in the War of 1812, but his sympathies were with the colonials. When his regiment captured Captain Jonathan Smith of the Fourth New York Infantry, Grandfather took a liking to him and when they reached some woods looked the other way while Captain Smith escaped.

Grandfather John Proctor returned to Scotland with his regiment and married Anne Cantoch MacGregor. In 1822, in Cromarty on the Firth of Forth my father, Alexander Proctor, was born. In 1832, Grandfather returned to Canada with his family and settled in the wilds of Ontario.

ALEXANDER PHIMISTER PROCTOR

In the meantime, Captain Jonathan Smith had married, and in 1832 my mother, Tirzah Smith, was born. Several years later Captain Smith also moved to Ontario, Canada, and much to his surprise found his wartime friend living nearby. Mother began teaching school in Ontario, and shortly thereafter met my father. They were married in 1852 and had eleven children. I was the fourth child, and the last born in Canada.

The old doctor who rode herd on our neighborhood was used to napping as he traveled his rounds on horseback. On the day I was born, just as he reached the bridge over the creek near our house, the nag shied, and doctor, saddlebags, and horse were dunked in the creek. In my impatience I gave the doctor time only to throw off his wet cape and coat before hurrying to officiate at my appearance on life's stage.

The highlights of my memories of Bozanquit, Ontario, are the view of the pit where Father liked to dig up fossil fish and the wonderful floury smell of Father's mill, which still seems to linger in my nostrils. I remember boys fishing in the millrace, and the death of my oldest sister when she was about twelve years old.

One day when I was not quite four, my father took me out into the woods, where he cut down hickory trees, massive-looking to me, but probably six inches in diameter. I soon learned that the trees were to be bows for the top of a covered wagon that was to carry us from Canada to Clinton, Michigan. We stayed in Clinton only about a year and then auctioned off our house to move again, this time to Newton, Iowa.

Not long after we arrived in Newton, I saw my first Indians. I was standing on a pile of lumber when a band of Indians on horseback emerged from the woods and passed within a few yards of me. I can still see the chief riding solemnly along, followed by some fifteen or twenty braves. Behind them came the women with their papooses. I started to pull a silent sneak-away, but my first step made a board fall with a crash. All the Indians turned to look at me. Abandoning caution, I scrambled off the lumber and, to the great delight of the savages, fled, yelling at every step, just as fast as my legs would carry me.

Toys were scarce in our house, but my imagination carried me far. On the floor I would arrange realistic backgrounds for some little pewter deer and other animals which had come from someone's Noah's ark. Somewhere I had acquired the figure of a hunter with a gun, and I got as much excitement

from helping him creep up on the metal deer as I did years later stalking real ones myself.

About this time I found a stick that resembled a gun, and I carried it with me for a long time, even taking it to bed. In time I lost it, and though I searched everywhere I never found it. I suppose that was the beginning of my longing for a shooting iron.

In the summer of 1866 we moved from Newton to Des Moines, Iowa. During the early part of our stay there Father rented a farm on the Raccoon River. We boys were overjoyed, for that meant shooting in the woods.

I had gone to school for a few weeks in Newton, but my first real introduction to education was in Des Moines, in a little unpainted schoolhouse with a wood stove and hard wooden benches. Out-of-school hours were spent roaming the countryside or doing chores.

Life in Des Moines was certainly much like that of any middle western town, but it was full of excitement for small boys. Evangelists such as Moody and Sankey came to town to hold revivals, and I caught religion along with a few of the other children.

I think it was about 1869 that long-whiskered Horace Greeley made a speech at the Iowa State Fair, but the only thing I remember of his talk was his saying, "Go West, young man, go West." It was also at that fair that Edward Payne Weston, the famous heel-and-toe walker, gave an exhibition of his speed on the race track. Quite a group of walk experts competed with him, but all were left in the distance.

Sometime during 1869 we left the farm on the Raccoon River and moved into town. Father continued to talk much about the West, which delighted us boys, and I looked forward to the day when we might make a start in that direction. The stories of wonderful fishing and unlimited game fired my young imagination. About this time an unexpected circumstance speeded up the decision to move. The house that Father had built in town was nearly paid for, but the man who held the mortgage foreclosed when Father missed a small payment, and we lost everything.

In the spring of 1871 it was decided that we would move to Denver, Colorado, in the hope of bettering our condition. To be sure that this was the best move, Father preceded the family to the promised land. He set up a tailoring business there and several months later sent for us.

While we were waiting to hear from Father, a cousin of Mother's passed through town in a covered wagon drawn by mules. He stopped for a visit, and his tales of buffalo hunting, gold mining, and Indian scares were all any boy could wish for. I was too young to join in the discussions concerning the move, but old enough to look forward to adventure.

The train ride to Denver was uneventful except that we saw a few buffalo, some Indians, and many antelope. Denver, Colorado, which the Proctor family reached late in 1871 was not the beautiful city it was later to become. Trappers, cowboys, and dirty-clothed prospectors were familiar sights on the few sagging wooden sidewalks. Huge charcoal wagons with many yokes of oxen filled the streets. Covered wagons were to be seen at any time of day or night. Saloons and gambling halls flourished. Frequently herds of longhorns were driven through town. My brother George and I were on our way to school one morning when several men dashed around the corner of Fifteenth Street, shouting, "Run, you damn fools, run!" All of us flew for the alley fence and scrambled to the top just as a herd of longhorns stampeded past in a cloud of dust. Several struck the fence just below our feet with clattering horns.

When the danger appeared to be over, several men dropped to the ground, just as a lone steer bounded around the corner. The men fled down the alley, followed closely by the steer. Nearby I saw Detective Frank Smith, whose pistol had brought to dust more local desperadoes than that of any other officer, except perhaps Sheriff Dave Cook himself. Revolver in hand, Smith dropped to the ground in front of the longhorn, fired at his head, and leaped aside as the steer, making a clean hoof spring, fell dead right where Frank had been standing. George and I considered that we had a good excuse for being late to school that morning.

Father was superintendent of the Sunday school in our church. He arranged for George and me to join a class with a group of boys our own age. The other members included Wilbur Steele and Irving Hale, who became my best friends. Steele later became a cartoonist for the *Denver Post*, and Hale graduated from West Point and as colonel and later brigadier general distinguished himself in the Spanish-American War and the Philippine Insurrection.

We boys had always liked our Sunday-school teachers, and Miss Dorothy Lawson was no exception. She encouraged us to sign the pledge not to touch intoxicating liquors or tobacco. Several of us did so, and George and I kept our promise throughout our lives. Wilbur signed reluctantly and later took to tobacco, though not to drink.

About a year after I began attending the church, I was appointed chief engineer of the pumping system for the big organ. This high office carried a salary of two bits a Sunday and other valuable compensations, among them exemption from listening to the sermons. Since the pumping station was in an anteroom, it was convenient for my purpose of reading between hymns. But always at the most exciting point of a story, it seemed, the signal bell attached to the pump handle would clang furiously. I would "set fire" to the handle, filling the bellows with hot air and making the organ roar every time a key was touched, to the annoyance of the preacher, the rage of the organist, and the amusement of the congregation. Needless to say, the organist and I were rarely on good terms.

My early days in Colorado seem to have been marked by experiences of a more or less religious nature. One particularly memorable event occurred in Sage Brush Flats.

The women of the settlement had long prayed for someone to regenerate the place, which was served only by traveling preachers. One afternoon, as if in answer to their prayers, a sky pilot and his helper rode in to hold a meeting. Since there were no houses large enough to accommodate the expected crowd, Deacon Andrew's ranch yard was chosen for the meeting. Benches, boxes, and chunks of wood answered for chairs, and there was plenty of sitting room on the ground.

Sure enough, a large crowd, of which I was one, gathered. The preacher was a big man, redheaded, bewhiskered, and explosive. When he rose, all conversation ceased. Standing silently, he let his eyes move over the audience. When his gaze settled on anybody, the person felt that his innermost soul was being searched and that every sin he had ever committed was open to view.

"Men and women!" the preacher suddenly shouted, "The Day of Judgement is at hand!" Everyone jumped. "The Devil's hot on your trail! You got to repent, and I'm here to rope you and drag you into the fold of God. Right now I'm the range boss of the Lord!" "This 'ere cowboy," he said, pointing to his helper, "is 'ere to record your brand, so when you check your guns at the Golden Gate, the angel'll know who you is. You-all go prancin' around here totin' guns and shootin', gamblin', and drinkin' whisky. You got to come right up standin' now! All you repenters come 'ere!"

Half a dozen listeners, including me, went forward, and there was great rejoicing among the womenfolk. The preacher went on haranguing us for what seemed hours. Finally the celestial soul herder asked where the pool was, "to baptize these mavericks." All the creeks were dry that year, but something had to be done before we slipped back into our state of sin, and Deacon Andrew's sheep-dip tank was chosen as a baptistery. Now all of us knew what sheep dip was, and when the preacher said that we must be tried by fire, we knew that we would be!

The preacher let himself down into the tank, slowly and solemnly uttering a prayer to heaven for the unruly sinners and for those about to be saved for the Kingdom. To us about to join him in the tank the hell-fire he had predicted was real and imminent. As each of us was plunged down, the ladies broke into a verse of the hymn "Sinners Plunged Beneath the Flood," which helped smother the coughs and sounds of choking. Most of us forgot to breathe until we were submerged and came up spluttering. All of us had to be revived in the shade of the only tree in the vicinity. Even the preacher had a dose, for I pulled him under with me, and we nearly drowned each other in our struggles to get out. There is nothing like sheep dip to pull off a baptism and make it stick!

"Hey, kids!" yelled little Johnny Taylor, as he raced by the ball grounds where we were playing. "They're lynchin' a guy on Cherry Creek Bridge! Come a-runnin'!" As we approached the bridge, we saw a crowd of armed men and spectators circling the execution area in the creek bed. In the center was an express wagon with a horse hitched to the front and a barrel standing on the rear end. On this impromptu execution trap stood the condemned, L. H. Musgrove. Musgrove, a notorious outlaw, had been captured in Wyoming and taken to the Denver jail. Around his neck was a rope suspended from a beam of the bridge. All was ready except for Musgrove. He was slowly smoking the cigar which had been his last request.

"Hurry up, Musgrove!" shouted someone from the crowd. "We can't hang around here all day!"

Musgrove waved his hand and replied, "What the

hell's the hurry? I'll swap my job of hangin' for yours of waitin'."

Finally the cigar began to burn his fingers, and the leader of the party asked, "Musgrove, do you have anything to say?"

Musgrove, throwing away the cigar butt, said, "Nothin'," and before the horse could jerk, he jumped high in the air, away from the barrel and into eternity.

A cowboy remarked, "Them's the last acrobatics Musgrove'll promulgate in this 'ere vale of tears."

III.

AT HOME IN THE OPEN

The nomadic strain in our family kept us continually wandering. Whether it was handed down from my father's early Scottish ancestors or from my mother's adventuresome colonial forebears I don't know. No sooner had we settled in Denver than we began to think of camping in the Rocky Mountains. For the first two vacations Father sent the family by hired wagon to Bradford Junction, about forty miles from Denver. It was there that we heard of a wonderful country over a range called Middle Park, at the upper end of which was Grand Lake.

Early in the spring of 1873, Father, my brother George, and I began to haunt the many corrals of old West Denver, in the vicinity of Blake and Wazee streets, looking for horses, a wagon, and some riding ponies. We finally found what we wanted.

One fine day in June the entire family set out for a vacation at Grand Lake. That first evening I rode

ahead of the wagon to explore the country. About camping time, while I was waiting for the wagon to catch up with me, a wagonload of Missourians passed. I asked whether they had seen our wagon and, if so, how far back. The driver answered, "Oh, about two whoops, a yell, and a go-by back yonder." We camped that night on Bear Creek, not far from Morrison, a small town tucked among the rocky cliffs of Bear Creek Canyon where it emerges onto the plains.

In those days the roads were rough indeed, and there was little opportunity for jockeying in the hills. A wagon road usually went up "right now." After days of slow and difficult travel, we passed over the main range of the Rockies, and for the first time in our lives we held snow in our hands in June.

One Saturday afternoon found us slowly dropping down the densely timbered western slope of the Continental Divide. The old Ute trail, by then a rough road, wound snakelike down the steep grade, and we often had to set our screeching brakes to prevent a too-rapid descent. Toward evening Father found a lovely meadow for the horses and a perfect place to pitch our tent. We had to hurry to gather wood and cook enough food to carry us over Sunday. Father and Mother believed strongly that the Sabbath should be a day of rest and religious observance.

After several days of leisurely travel, we reached the old Grand River Ford. There we found five or six wagons camped along the river bottom waiting for the spring flood to subside. The river bed was covered with smooth round boulders, about the size of a man's head and as slick as glass. The only place that the wagons could attempt a crossing was at a riffle, and, to make it safer for the teams, the boulders had to be moved from the creek bed. It was a difficult and risky job. Several men would rope themselves together, about ten feet apart, so that if one slipped the others could keep him from being carried downstream. Equipped with poles about seven feet long and forked at one end, a group of men would enter the water and push the boulders downstream, working as long as they could stand the icy water. When they came ashore to have their legs rubbed, another group continued operations.

Waiting at the ford were two men with a four-horse team pulling a big freight wagon. They were hauling supplies to a mining camp in the mountains. They chafed over the delay and finally, against all advice, decided to take a chance on crossing. As they swung their broncos into position in front of the ford, the horses backed and started to tremble and snort. Several times the leaders got their hind feet over the tugs, and it took a couple of our party to hold them in line.

Just as they were about to start across, we heard a shout downstream, and a pack train appeared. With the outfit was a young man named Warren, probably in his twenties, clad in well-worn buckskins. His weatherbeaten face showed determination and courage. Quick of movement and sinuous, he was the real hunter and rider type. His stiff-brimmed sombrero, dented on four sides, sat on his head at a devil-may-care angle. Antelope Jack, as Warren's companions called him, sat in the saddle and surveyed the scene with a knowing glance. He took his pipe from his mouth and, after knocking out the ashes against the stock of his rifle, which was balanced across the saddle in front of him, put it in the pocket of his coat. He drew his right foot out of the stirrup, patted his right trouser leg, pulled out a plug of tobacco, bit off a piece, and returned the plug to its place.

The driver of the four-horse team sat calmly on the wagon seat, reins and whip in his hands, his foot on the brake. When all was ready, he called, "Cut 'em loose, boys!" The broncos, feet gathered under them, started with a jumping half buck toward the river, only a rod away. The two leaders balked at the take-off, but a light touch of the whip sent them plunging in. Then, as the wagon lunged forward into the current, the wheelers dropped down, holding back on their breeching. The icy water splashing against the horses' bellies made them all the more frantic. Halfway across, the nigh-leader fell, scrambled to his feet churning water, fell again, and was swept under the off-leader's feet. Down they went together.

At that instant Antelope Jack handed me his rifle, put spurs to his horse, and dashed into the river, undoing his lasso as he rode. Nearing the floundering team, he whirled over his head a small loop such as Texas cowboys use. When the nigh-leader's head emerged from the water for an instant, a well-directed throw dropped the loop over it. Jack's horse, Kino, turned upstream and put all his weight on the rope, which Jack had turned around his

Antelope Jack Warren

saddle horn several times. The team made a wild lunge, and Kino was pulled off balance just as the rope broke.

Losing the support of the rope, the team swung downstream. The off-wheeler fell, dragging the others with him. The front wheels cramped under the wagon as the struggling horses swung around. Then, to our consternation, the big freight wagon turned over, and men, horses, and wagon went tumbling downriver. Kino regained his footing, and Jack started after the helpless team. The water, halfway up Kino's sides, made him difficult to handle. Regardless of danger, Jack went right up to one of the struggling horses, trying to grab a bridle and help the animal to his feet. Jack had kept part of the broken rope, and he tossed one end to the driver, who seized it in both hands and thus was dragged out of the seething mass. Meanwhile, Kino was twisting and turning to keep his feet. Pulling the man to him, Jack gripped him and headed for the nearest shore, which happened to be the opposite one. They had now drifted into deep water, and Kino had to swim for it, landing them a couple of hundred yards below us.

In the meantime all available horsemen were engaged in trying to rescue the second man and the horses. They rode out into the dangerous water and lassoed projections on the wagon, the horses' legs, and anything else above water. Finally the men were able to drag the wagon ashore, but by the time they got it back all the horses were dead. There was nothing to do but remove the harness and let the beasts drift downriver.

The rescuers had hoped that the second man might still be in the wagon, but when it was righted, it was empty. Nothing was left of the ton of food and mining materials. A search of both banks was commenced, and before long the poor chap was found dead about a mile downstream.

In my boyish eyes Antelope Jack was a great hero, and I was proud to have been able to help him. He was acting as guide to a hunting party which included Sir Gordon Cummings, the great English hunter Sir Henry Hussey Vivian, and others. Since the swollen stream did not offer the hazards to a pack train that it did to a wagon, the hunters crossed the river with no difficulty and headed for the Yellowstone.

Several days passed before the water receded enough to allow the wagons to cross safely. Teams were doubled on each wagon, everybody turning in to help his neighbor. Since many of the boulders had by now been pushed out of the way, the crossing was easier.

Leaving the Grand River, we set out on a wagon trail (it couldn't by any stretch of the imagination be called a road) which wound up a considerable incline through rocky sagebrush flats, bogs, and timber. It had first been used by Ute Indians, then by trappers, hunters, and prospectors whose duffel (grub and pelts) was carried on pack animals. Turns were so short that we had to back and twist constantly. The wheels were everlastingly being snagged on trees, and mudholes were so deep that the wagon couldn't be pulled through until everybody got out and carried the load by hand to the other side.

Luckily we found horse feed and water everywhere. There was also plenty of fish and small game to replenish the larder. On one of the flats through which the road wound, we saw our first band of elk; there were seven of them.

Going around Table Mountain, we encountered a steep, rocky foothill which our horses couldn't navigate. George and I pulled out a lot of our baggage and packed it up the hill to lighten the load, while the rest of the family climbed up on foot. Just as we were ready to bring up the wagon, three elk hunters rode up. Two of them fastened their lariats to the wagon tongue and, turning the other ends around their saddle horns, lined up ahead of the horses, who were scrambling and pulling with all their might. George ran alongside driving the team, using whip and voice freely. They gained ground slowly, with many rest stops. My job was to run along behind with a chunk of wood to block a wheel when the horses stopped, to prevent the wagon from slipping back downhill. Though we feared that a tug might break or a horse might fall and plunge the outfit down the mountain, we made it up safely.

Three miles from the lake there was another ford,

but since it was sandy and not so deep and dangerous as the first, it gave us little trouble. Leaving open country, we entered a fringe of thick timber and emerged on the west shore of the beautiful sheet of water that white men called Grand Lake and the Indians called Meteor Lake.

The ground just behind the sandy beach was reasonably flat. About 150 yards to the right of us were a couple of knolls, and beyond them loomed heavily timbered South Mountain. Nearby were two log cabins and a dugout inhabited by three men, J. L. Westcott, Jack Baker, and "Old Avery" (no one knew his real name). The land had been partly cleared of trees to make room for camping places and provide wood for cabins, firewood, and rafts. While we were deciding where to pitch our tent, a grouse flew into a tree close by, and I shot him for our first meal. That was the spot where I was to spend much of my time for the next twelve years, for we returned again and again in the summer, and when we grew older, my brother George and I went back in the winter to trap and hunt.

It was readily evident that Grand Lake had been a favorite Indian camping ground because of the numbers of flint arrowheads we found among the pines and, after storms, on the shores. My sister once turned up seven beautiful points in one small hole that she dug with a stick. Five miles below the lake Grand River dashed through a gorge. Huge boulders were stacked all over the canyon, and it was among these rocks, on that first trip to the lake, that I found a pile of flint arrow chips. In the same boulders were

Old Avery

many holes in which Indians had apparently pounded food.

During the summer of 1873, the Proctors were about the only "outsiders" on the lake, though from the time we arrived George and I considered that we belonged.

On the Fourth of July miners, hunters, and trappers came to the lake to celebrate. About noon a pack train arrived from Georgetown. That meant "tanglebrain" for everybody, and one hell-roaring jamboree it would be. Before the men began to whoop it up, a sober fellow was sent to ride herd on our camp to prevent any tanked-up celebrant from annoying the family. Our guard that evening had been with General Custer in some of his early campaigns, and he filled us boys with stories of Indian warfare on the frontier.

One of the joys of Grand Lake was to be there when a bunch of trappers or hunters floated into camp on their way to or from the outside for grub. Then everyone would gather at one of the cabins. On these occasions no one seemed disposed to play cards. The men simply sat around the fireplace, which of necessity was kept burning brightly, since it was the only source of light. Little liquor was drunk, probably because it was difficult to come by.

We were seventy-five miles from the outside—"outside" meaning over the main Rocky Mountain range. A drink or two may have been taken on these occasions, but the effects were not noticeable. The evenings were chiefly given over to "waw-waw," much talk.

IV

EARLY ART TRAINING

A couple of years after we arrived in frontier Colorado, my father decided that I would benefit from instruction in art. He took me to a Dutch artist who had recently arrived in Colorado. When we entered his studio, he was sitting at an easel, working on a crayon portrait. As he rose slowly and unfolded his long, gangling figure, I wondered whether he would ever reach his full height. He was about forty years old. His thin figure was entirely draped in black. Dark, soulful eyes peered at me from under shaggy brows with a kindly look that offered assurance that at least he wouldn't eat me. A scanty black mustache draped his thin, sensitive mouth. From under the broad-brimmed hat, which he apparently wore to shade his eyes, black hair fell over thin shoulders and down his back. His shiny Prince Albert reached his knees, while his trousers were tucked into high-heeled boots.

EARLY ART TRAINING

My lessons cost fifty cents each and took place on Saturdays and holidays. This arrangement was not entirely to my liking because it interfered with baseball and rabbit hunting. While I studied with this artist, whose name I regret that I have forgotten, I spent most of my time copying pictures in pencil, an experience which at the time I doubted would advance my artistic education to any noticeable degree.

The next artist whose trail I cut was J. Harrison Mills, originally of Buffalo, New York, who had established quite a reputation in Denver. Mills had found, however, that in Colorado art was not equal in value to a gold mine. Since wood engraving had begun to come into vogue for newspaper work and advertising, Mills decided to start a wood engraving plant on a small scale. On the north side of Larimer Street, between Fifteenth and Sixteenth streets, stood the dingy *Rocky Mountain News* building. Under the roof, on a third floor reached by rickety stairs, was an attic. Mills rented the whole floor. The ever-present odors of paper, printing ink, and pipe-tobacco smoke pervaded the place. In the rear was a rather sizable room with a small skylight, which Mills used as his engraving studio. During slow seasons in the engraving line, Mills worked on nature scenes and also occasionally painted a portrait on commission.

There, on Saturdays and during vacations, I began to learn the art of wood engraving. My father, knowing from his reading that artists had difficulty making a living, decided that I should take up engraving as a trade, hoping that it would afford me a livelihood while I studied art. I followed his advice and during subsequent winters usually made enough money at engraving to finance summer sketching trips to the mountains.

Thus a good deal of my early art training came to me while I was working on engraving blocks. It was Mills's habit to talk art while we worked. I can see him still, his eyes close to the magnifying glass, watching his graver as he pushed it through the wood. Whenever a chip would stick to the graver point, he would rub it off on his stiff mustache. One day he explained to me that saltpeter, which was supposed to be used in the curing of tobacco, was responsible for the little explosions that were taking place in his pipe. I responded with manifest seriousness, although I knew that they were caused by the grains of gunpowder I had added to his tobacco.

Mills had spent a couple of years in the wild Middle Fork and Hans Peak region, studying landscapes and wild animals. He believed in the naturalistic school, as did most artists of the time, and felt strongly that an artist should live the life he intended to depict. He was a true outdoors painter.

At one time Mills was painting a large canvas entitled *Through Fire and Flood*, depicting a buck deer bounding from a flaming background right out of the picture over a cascade which dashed down a rocky cliff. To make a careful and realistic study of the deer, Mills hung a frozen buck in a cold back room. Unfortunately, the buck in his picture looked as stiff as the dead one.

Mills's studio had become a rendezvous for hunters and prospectors of Middle Park, and I met many interesting characters there. Among the locally famous people who visited the studio was the scout Jim Baker, who sat for his portrait. When Jim was in the studio, I spent most of my time listening in openmouthed wonder to his tales of the early frontier West, of Indian fights, and of bears. All these stories were related in a matter-of-fact way, with much detail. Jim's eyes glittered as he described a close call with an Indian tomahawk or an angry grizzly. His weatherbeaten, storm-seamed face was as wrinkled and tough as rhinoceros hide, with not a square inch of smooth surface. He was colorful and authentic—a product of the frontier mountains and plains.

My friend Antelope Jack, whom I had met at the Grand River Ford, came down from the mountains to spend a couple of winters and pose as a model for western characters. His arrival in buckskins, with rifle, cartridge belt, and hunting knife, interested the populace very much. Jack batched in a room behind

Jim Baker

EARLY ART TRAINING

the studio, and we often cooked our lunches there together. Afterward we shot cap boxes or other small objects out of each other's fingers with a .22 rifle. This fool play might easily have resulted in the loss of fingers, but luckily there were no accidents.

Jack first arrived in Denver after a long summer and fall hunt, and he turned in his clothes to a Chinese laundry for a badly needed washing. As it happened, when his clothes were returned, there were several people in the studio, among them Edward Drake, Richard Watson Guilder, and Ernest Ingersoll, all of *Century Magazine*. When Jack objected to the price for the washing, the laundryman said, "Me no charge too many. Me heap washee, washee. Clothes heap dirty. Plenty graybackee [fleas]." The laugh that ensued made Jack blush, and he paid off in a hurry.

Frederick Delenbaugh, then a young man, drifted into town and took up engraving for amusement. He had recently accompanied Major John Wesley Powell on the geologist's trip through the Grand Canyon. Delenbaugh's tales of that voyage through fearful waterfalls, whirlpools, and the like were hair-raising. Delenbaugh had studied art in Munich. He took a mild interest in my endeavors and suggested that I go to Europe to study. The thought came to my mind, "How can I go to Europe to study when I can hardly stay where I am?" Certainly my work at that time did not show sufficient merit to call forth such a suggestion, but in those days young aspirants to the world of art were scarce, and maybe Delenbaugh saw a shadow of hope beyond what I could envision.

Another friend, the Reverend Bayard Craig, pastor of the First Christian Church, took an interest in me and encouraged me in my art. Whenever my family was away, I stayed at his home. Craig often sold my small works or induced people to commission portraits. Through him I met many interesting people, including former Governor John L. Routt and Senator Thomas M. Patterson, whom I often visited.

Before I was twenty, I received a commission that paid what seemed at the time a great deal of money. I was to do about twenty illustrations, of which I was also to make the engravings, for a book called *Hands Up*, by Sheriff Dave Cook, the most noted peace officer in Colorado at the time.[1] Cook had

---

[1] The engravings appear in the Western Frontier Library edition of General D. J. Cook, *Hands Up; or Twenty Years of Detective Life in the Mountains and on the Plains* (introduction by Everett L. DeGolyer, Jr.), (Norman, University of Oklahoma Press, 1958).

killed a good many men and wanted to cash in on his adventures by writing a book.

During the several months I worked on the illustrations, I frequently went to Cook's Gilt Edge Saloon on Lawrence Street near Fifteenth, to consult with him about drawings or subjects for the pictures. As far as I remember, there was no special opposition in town to the sheriff's owning and running a saloon.

If Cook's knowledge of art had been equal to his ability to handle a gun or track a murderer, he undoubtedly would not have chosen a youngster like me to illustrate his book. I have often wondered how, with my meager knowledge of both drawing and engraving, I had the nerve to tackle the assignment. I was quite proud of myself at the time, but in later years I lost many hours' sleep, fearing that my early work would find me out.

About 1880 an artist named David McClusky, who had studied in Cincinnati and New York, turned up in Denver and began holding art classes. I didn't have private lessons with him, but I joined the art society that he founded. We held exhibits in a room in the Tabor Block, where we also drew from plaster casts at night. McClusky gave us much information about how advanced art students were trained in

Title-page etching for *Hands Up*

EARLY ART TRAINING

Lynching of Musgrove (from *Hands Up*)

New York, where he had worked with the Art Students' League. This made me more eager than ever to go to New York City.

As much as I enjoyed my art work, whenever spring came and the rocks began to show through the snow of Longs Peak and Pikes Peak, I became restless. Art materials, ammunition, and fishing tackle began to appear in my war bag. Knife and gun scabbards were patched up or renewed. My family and friends knew what was coming. At last the saddle and bridle were pulled out and cleaned. Finally I went out to the ranch where Turk, my saddle pony, had been wintered, and brought him in.

Although I was happy working with paints and paper and brushes and pencils, town life irked me and I was ever lured by the great outdoors.

V.
LEARNING TO HUNT

One of my boyhood ambitions was to be a great hunter, as well as a productive sculptor and painter. Consequently I spent as much time as I could hunting jack rabbits with brother George near Denver. On one occasion we were taking turns shooting a single-barrel, muzzle-loading shotgun. George had just shot. I was loading and was just tamping the powder home, when a rabbit came tearing toward us like a whirlwind. Crazy with excitement and without pulling the ramrod from the barrel, I poured in shot directly on top of the brass nubbin of the rod, which of course wedged it tight.

The rabbit was heading straight for us. I hastily put the cap on the nipple. The rabbit was within twenty yards of me before he saw me and turned. I aimed excitedly and pulled the trigger. The recoil was terrific. I got to a sitting position just in time to see the ramrod hit the ground just behind the

LEARNING TO HUNT

jack rabbit. If he had been scared before, he was wild with fright then. The ramrod gave a whirling bounce and landed in front of the rabbit with a noise like a runaway wheelbarrow. The rabbit's next frantic leap carried him ahead of the ramrod, which, flying end over end, followed hard on the rabbit's tail for several yards until it finally gave up the race. I have always believed that that rabbit kept up his licks until he died.

Shooting rabbits was fun for a while, but in time I yearned for bigger game. One day in 1874 I had been hunting in the mountains near camp but had had no luck. Toward evening I struck a nice trout stream and decided to have a go at fish for supper instead. I cut a willow stick and attached to it a line and fly which I always carried. Leaning my rifle against a tree, I started fishing. The trout were greedy, and I wandered farther and farther from my artillery. Finally I hooked a nice spirited fish under a steep bank, but as I was playing him, out of the corner of my eye I noticed something move. Thinking it was one of the boys from camp, I turned to ask if he'd had any luck. My blood froze, for just above me and only fifteen feet away was what looked like the biggest grizzly in the woods—or perhaps in the West.

Mr. Cuffy looked first at me and then at the trout. He seemed puzzled. I was standing with hand extended, holding the rod, and the trout was putting up a stiff fight. Being only fourteen years old, I didn't have sense enough to drop the rod. Suddenly the fish jumped clear of the water, right under Bruin's nose. He took it for a hostile act on my part. His hair went straight up—and so did mine. He let out a hell-shattering "woof," and made a jump toward me. I too went into the air and landed running for my gun.

The creek curved, but I didn't have time to go around—I sloshed right on. I was sure I could feel the old boy's breath on my neck, and each instant I thought I was a goner. I grabbed my gun without stopping and, cocking it as I ran, turned to shoot. There wasn't a thing in sight! Finally getting my breath, I sneaked back to look for my bear. He had vanished, and the trout was flopping around in the brush. Cautiously climbing the bank to where the bear had stood, I found that he had made one short hop toward me and then had wheeled and torn gravel in the opposite direction. As I looked at his tracks, I wondered how such a whale of a bear could have such small feet.

In August of the same year, 1874, fishing was poor in Grand Lake, and George and I decided that we needed a hunting and fishing trip down Grand River. We had plenty of fishing tackle but lacked weapons for shooting deer. J. L. Westcott, who lived in one of the cabins at the lake, had a collection of the most disreputable guns ever gathered together, and he was happy to lend me anything he owned, even to his antique pound-and-a-quarter zinc watch.

"Sure, boss," as he always called me, "jes take any of them critters ye wants. 'Ere's ol' Jezebel. If ye can pack her, ye sure can kill anything that wears hair." Jezebel was a double-barrel, muzzle-loading shotgun, five feet long and eight bore. "She eats nails, slugs, and bolts. Right 'ere's old Henry. He only shoots on rainy days an' Sundays. That pizen old reptile thar killed the feller that invented it" (and it looked as though it would do exactly that).

'Ere's what ye want—old Satan. He stands six feet in his shimmy, an' he drops the steelyards at ten pounds. He's good for half a mile backwards and forwards, mostly back. Satan has changed his style as much as a woman does her hats. First he's a matchlock, then a flintlock, then he turns cap an' ball, an' now he's a breech-loader, an' God knows what he'll change to next. That ole devil's plumbin' ain't too good, an' he has a helluva back draft when he busts off. Ye ain't awful big fer yer size, so before ye shoots ye wants to pick a good place to fall inter, for Satan will sure stomp on ye when he gits ye down. Oh, don't try to look through the barrel. It'd take a man a hull day to do that. . . . Yes, ye'll need the two-pound ramrod."

In spite of its lurid history, I decided to take Satan. It was probably the most ancient piece of artillery in America. Five feet long, it was a .65-caliber rim-fire with cartridges the size of an oil can. Its muzzle velocity was about twenty-five feet a minute. The bullet never did catch up with an animal running away from it, but when it did hit anything there was certainly hell to pay. It went through a critter like a cyclone loaded with stumps and fence posts. Only the hooves, tail, ears, and outer fringes of hide were left. After a long search in boxes of old

LEARNING TO HUNT

scrap iron, bolts, and nuts, we found seven cartridges.

"Now, boss," warned Westcott, "be careful of them critters. They're powerful as Jersey lightnin'. When a varmint gits one of them slugs cavortin' around in his innards, he knows that hell's a poppin' in thar. Old Satan is hard to rile, but oncet he's mad, he's pizen."

Early the next morning George and I packed our roan pony with duffel and were off on foot down the river trail. Nothing would do but that I must tote Satan myself. Before long its weight had my tail dragging, and I regretfully lashed it to the pack. Then the usual thing happened when a gun is stowed away—a handsome buck jumped into view sixty yards away and stood looking at us. Frantically I pulled at old Satan, but the more I yanked, the tighter the knots drew. By the time I was ready to shoot, the buck had bounded off. From then on I staggered under the weight of the old cannon but, of course, saw nothing.

Toward nightfall we prepared camp some miles from Grand Lake. While I was rustling for our beds, George, an expert fisherman, caught a mess of fine trout for supper. In the meantime, I had also pitched the tent and gathered wood for a fire. After supper we indulged in what was and still is to me one of the most enjoyable experiences of life—just sitting, back against a log or bedroll by a campfire in the wilds, discussing tomorrow's hunt and the prospects of finding game. That night old Satan received more loving care than it had probably had since its youthful days when it was a new flintlock. I even tucked it into my bed, but it stuck out a foot at both ends.

I was wakened that night several times by real or imaginary noises. Just before dawn a grizzly came close to camp and let out a blood-freezing "Woof." But before I could unscramble my blunderbuss from the bedding, he was gone.

Breakfast over the next morning, George moseyed upstream, fishing. I shouldered Satan and, followed by my dog, Shine, rambled cautiously downriver with hopes running high. Half a mile below camp I stopped to scan the mountain opposite and saw two bucks halfway up the slope. I dropped quickly on hands and knees and sneaked into some fallen logs at the water's edge. Appearing in open spots and vanishing again in thick timber, the deer trailed along the mountainside about a quarter of a mile away. Suddenly, for no reason that I could see, they stopped directly opposite me. My heart began to pump. Would they go on, or would they turn down-

hill my way? I was in an agony of suspense. Shine sensed my excitement. Finally they turned down the mountain toward me.

My heart pumped faster and faster, and my teeth began to chatter. Down, down they came, closer and closer. On the opposite bank, a hundred yards away, they stopped. Should I shoot? It seemed too far. They stepped into the swift water. I was suffocating with excitement, and so was Shine. One of the bucks scrambled over the slippery boulders in the water. I had heard that one could control buck fever by biting the fingernails. I tried it until my fingers bled, but with no effect, for the rifle still rattled against the log it rested on, and I couldn't keep track of the sight. I was sure the deer could hear my heart pounding against my ribs. I was shaking myself to pieces.

Both bucks stopped in the middle of the stream, only forty yards away. I finally managed to pull the trigger, and there was a terrific roar. One buck was hit—I saw him between my legs as I went over backward. Scrambling to my feet, I reloaded while both deer headed for the opposite bank. The first was evidently badly hurt, so I fired at the other. A heart shot sent him to the ground. Then I fired again at the wounded deer, and he went down in a heap. My ague turned to shivers of joy. Reloading the old piece, I jumped pell-mell into the water and forged across the slippery boulders. In my haste I must have run on top of the water because I didn't fall once. Two fine bucks with splendid antlers! Surely this was the greatest happiness that could come to any fourteen-year-old boy.

I ran upstream and found George, who had heard the shots but thought that I was hunting grouse. We cooked and ate some deer liver for lunch, and then I rode the pony across the river and packed the deer to Grand Lake. After I had made several sketches of the carcasses, we cut up the venison and divided it among the campers. I wouldn't have changed places with a king. It had been the most important event of my young life.

In the autumn of 1878, J. H. Mills, my current instructor in art and engraving, joined us at Grand Lake for a hunt. He had traded some of his portraits for two broncos, and George and I had two ponies. We proposed to pack one of our horses and take turns riding the other. But when we were ready to start, we found that one of the ponies had sprained a stifle joint and had to be led while George and I walked.

Stopping at Hot Sulphur Springs to lay in grub, the three of us slept on the floor over Ute Bill's saloon. Just as we were comfortably tucked in, the saloon doors downstairs crashed open and a gang of roistering toughs stormed in, their guns barking. Bullets tore through the floor, missing us but scattering splinters. We heard Ute Bill bawl, "Hell, I've got boarders up there!" The fireworks ceased. Bill, chagrined, came up to explain the situation. Texas Charley and his gang were on the rampage for the night, and so, Bill advised, we had better carry our bedrolls to his cabin behind the saloon and sleep there.

After two days we moved on. In the meantime I had an itch all over, and by the time we left I was sure I had caught some kind of disease. Mills laughingly explained that the trouble was caused by graybacks, otherwise known as lice. As we were moving out of town, we met Sir Gordon Cummings, Sir Henry Vivian, and their party returning from a hunt on the Muddy River. Mills had a letter to Sir Gordon, and while he was presenting it, George and I talked to the guides, packers, waiters, and roustabouts in the party, who numbered about fifteen. Among them was my old friend Antelope Jack. That night we camped at a deserted cabin on Troublesome Creek. The English party stopped there also, and one of the drivers gave us a good supply of meat from a buffalo that Sir Gordon had killed.

Deer were present in abundance. To the hide hunters of the early days it meant nothing to waste thousands of pounds of meat. It wasn't possible to pack venison to a market three hundred miles away, and there wasn't a wagon road for fifty miles. Some hide hunters tanned the skins themselves to make buckskin clothing. Others, too lazy or lacking the skill to tan, simply sold the raw hides for a dollar or two. In those early days no one realized that the game animals wouldn't last forever.

Though I got no game on my first day's hunt on that trip, I did see tracks of buffalo, grizzly, elk, and deer. That very night Mills decided that he wanted to go to the high, snow-capped peaks fifteen miles from Grand Lake to shoot a grizzly that had broken into Len Pollard's cabin, south of the lake. I protested that there were probably twenty grizzlies where we were to one where Mills wanted to go, but my opinions didn't count, since I was the kid of the outfit. Now we must travel back what seemed to me a hundred miles through North Park without hunting that wonderful region. It had probably been the favorite hunting grounds of the Ute Indians for centuries. Right near our camp was a small fort built by trappers not many years before to stand off hostile Indians. Filled with regret and disappointment, I accompanied the others as they headed back in a roundabout way for home. By now our pony was well, and we were able to ride him, which was some consolation. Since the weather was fine and game plentiful, I really did enjoy the trip toward the Rabbit Ear Range.

At that time antelope abounded in North Park. All day as we traveled we saw bands of them numbering from five to fifty. On the second day of the return trip I shot my first antelope with old Satan, which we had again borrowed from Westcott. Laying my rifle on the ground, I rushed up to the buck in great excitement and grabbed the big boy by the horns to stick him. The instant I touched the buck, he was on his feet. A toss of his head knocked the knife out of my hand, and the battle was on. Charging back and forth, we plunged and twisted, falling over sagebrush and rocks. Sometimes I was down, sometimes the antelope. I didn't dare let go of his horns or he would disembowel me. Mills sat on his horse a hundred yards away, laughing his head off, but it was no laughing matter for me. Gradually I worked the animal over to my knife, grabbed it, and

LEARNING TO HUNT

stabbed him in the side, still holding one horn with the other hand, until he gave up the fight.

One day old Satan missed fire while George was using it. Peeved, he inserted the long ramrod in the barrel and then, angrily hauling back, was about to give the offending bullet a nasty whack. Mills, who was sitting on his horse alongside George, yelled, "Point that damn gun up!" George did, and sure enough, when that rim-fire cartridge hit the block, off she went. Fire blasted from muzzle and breech. The ramrod tore into the air with a screech reminiscent of the time I shot one at a rabbit, scaring the daylights out of George. That night when I was trying to sleep it dawned on me how narrowly he had missed Mills and what a job it would have been for us kids to pack a dead man on horseback through those high mountains.

As we ascended the Rabbit Ear Range, the going grew rougher and steeper, and one day toward evening we ran into snow so deep that the map Len Pollard had given Mills was useless. Mills was leading, but he became confused and, leaving us, forged ahead to scout the trail. Although we had little faith in his mountaineering, we waited. Mills was warmly clad, but we weren't. We hadn't expected to climb to such a high altitude, and during

the six-week trip there had been no opportunity to replenish our supplies. Our boots were worn out, our socks nearly gone, and I had no gloves. My coat, with buttons gone and armholes ripped, flapped about, giving little protection to my body. George was not much better off.

We waited and waited and then plugged ahead alone. The snow became deeper until it was halfway up our horses' sides. A ten-foot drift filled the trail, forcing us to climb several hundred feet above the point where it crossed the ridge. We wallowed about in drifts, horses and boys stumbling over boulders. Clouds of snow blasted our faces, blinding us. By this time our clothes were so full of snow that we didn't try to shake it off. Night was pressing down when we finally and thankfully caught up with Mills.

Shortly afterward, George was leading our pack horse across a steep slide which ended three hundred feet below in a five-hundred-foot cliff. Suddenly to our horror an avalanche started around him. Horse and boy moved downward, and it seemed that nothing could save them. As they slid down, the snow filled in around them until they were half-covered. On, on toward the drop-off they headed. Suddenly, about nine feet from the edge, they stopped, while the avalanche surged by them and dashed over the precipice in billowing white waves. George, knees bent, stood braced.

I started to crawl down to help, but George called to me not to. He gave the mare's lead rope a flip, and she began the almost impossible climb back. Luckily she was sure-footed. Stumbling and slipping, she finally made it, and I grabbed her halter rope. All this time George had been crouching below, watching her, studying the lay of the land. Then, with cool courage, cautiously taking advantage of the few crevices and humps of rock, he made his way up.

We knew that part of the country pretty well, and we realized that Len's two old cabins, tucked away in the spruce, were but a mile from the avalanche area. But what a mile! We doubted whether we would be able to make it, but to stop where we were meant freezing to death, for all of us were numb with cold.

Then timber line at last—and the cabins. But as luck would have it, a grizzly had smashed in the four-inch-thick iron-bound door and devoured all the grub. Our hands were so numb and stiff that we couldn't untie our pack ropes or even get matches out of our pockets. Wood, scarce at any time and now covered with three feet of snow, was almost impossible to find. Finally George thawed out his fingers enough to start a fire. Mine were still useless. Even with the fire it was some time before we were warm enough to loosen our pack ropes. We found an old powder can, and in it we thawed some snow for water. When warmed, the water had a rancid odor, but we used it anyway. It is a wonder that we weren't all poisoned. In an hour we had coffee, and George made some biscuits, which, with antelope meat, were our supper. That night we slept three in a bed to keep from freezing. All the "feathers" had dropped from the hemlock boughs we used for a mattress, and I had to balance on one bare pole all night long. The next morning dawned bright and clear, and we made the lake without difficulty—needless to say, without Len's bear!

LEARNING TO HUNT

The winter of the same year was to hold more excitement. One day I was sitting on the dirt floor of Westcott's cabin at Grand Lake, using a gunny sack for a cushion. A few men were sitting around swapping stories. Outdoors the wind was making the pine and spruce trees rustle and creak, and the snow was falling fairly fast. Doc Porter opened the cabin door and looked out, letting a flurry of big flakes drift into the room. "Boys," he said, "thar's goin' to be a fine trackin' snow in the mornin'. Who's goin' out for meat? We shore need some in the fry pan. We can't be eatin' all that sowbelly, an' winter comin' on fast this-a-way."

I was close to the fire trying to fix up a sawed-off rifle. It was one of the muzzle-loaders that had been made into a needle gun after the Civil War. My brother had bought the old cast-off from Len Pollard the preceding spring. The story was that a hunter had wounded a grizzly with the rifle, which had then misfired. That would have been the end of the hunter if a friend hadn't shot the bear. The owner whanged the old thing against a tree and threw it into Lost Lake. A little later Len fished the relic from its watery grave. Len rarely had a good rifle, though he was one of the best hunters in the country. But this gun was too much even for him, and he sold it to my brother for three dollars. Unable to kill anything with it, George traded it to me for a seventy-five-cent hunting knife.

Eager to get the old gun in shape in time to take advantage of the tracking snow, I was wiring up the stock and making what other repairs I could. The front sight was missing, and it was a tough job filing the nickel that was intended to be used for that indispensable part of a rifle. The only tools I had were a saw, a file, and a hammer.

After a while the storm let up, and George and I stepped out into five inches of beautiful tracking snow, which augured well for tomorrow's hunt—that is, provided I could get my shooting iron together in time. As Studhorse Johnson started over to his camp, he warned George to be ready at four o'clock in the morning. I asked if I could go along.

"Not any a heap," he said. "We all's out for meat an' we don't want no kid stampedin' 'round with no old screech owl like that," he added, pointing to my treasure. "When you gits 'er so's ye kin see through 'er on a bright day, we'll think about it a hull lot." I was naturally disappointed, but George agreed with Studhorse, and, being older than I, he was the boss.

Early the next morning, after the hunters had gone, I resumed my repair job. The nickel was finally filed in two and dovetailed to the slot in the front-sight block, and the stock was properly wired. By nine o'clock my work was finished, and I had a usable gun.

I hit the trail to the south, knowing that George and the rest had gone across the lake. The snow was vanishing wherever the sun could reach it, and prospects for a successful hunt looked pretty slim. I reached an old log which years before had been hacked open by Indians with their tomahawks, probably in search of a squirrel. I stopped, kicked the snow off the log, and pondered.

"What's the use of going on?" I thought. "It's too late." Studying the log, I wondered why the Indians had spent so much time hacking a squirrel out of the log. They must have been very hungry. Then I thought, "I've started out to hunt.... I guess I'll go on."

I walked a couple of miles downstream, left the trail, and went over a burned ridge. There to my surprise I saw a herd of eight cow elks and one fine bull. The storm had driven them from the high mountains to the protecting gulch where I found them. An experienced hunter would have picked out the lead cow and shot her, for then he would have had the whole band at his mercy. Without their leader they would have become confused and stood still or milled about till several of them had been shot.

In my ignorance I elected to go for the bull, which was at the far side of the bunch. I began to sneak toward him. As I was crawling among the logs, a vigilant cow about twenty yards away saw me and started to run. At this the whole band broke into a trot and headed for the mountains. I blazed away at the bull just as he went running around a bush. It was a lucky shot and went home but failed to kill him. The elk ran about sixty yards and then stopped to look me over. I tried to reload, but the ejector wouldn't work. I tried to pry the shell out with my knife, but buck fever and my first experience at shooting an elk made me tremble with excitement. The band stood still, looking at me. I cut several willows, but they weren't long enough to use as ramrods. I drew back to break the fool gun against a tree, but just then I remembered that I had with me a bullet that belonged to George's .40-caliber Sharps. I dropped it into the muzzle and jounced it up and down furiously. Finally the shell loosened and came out. Still the elk stood watching me. I reloaded in a hurry and put the gun to my shoulder. At that the band started to run, and my second shot missed.

Following the tracks for half a mile up the mountain, I found that the wounded bull, unable to keep the pace toward the summit, had trailed off around the side. Wherever the tracks led onto hard ground I had difficulty following and had to make circles to pick them up in the snow. After about two hours of trailing, I followed the tracks to a little ridge, where the original forest had been burned over and a later stand of trees about thirty feet tall had also been swept by fire. A third crop of jack pines ten feet high was growing thickly among the dead second growth. Since the roots of the thirty-foot trees had rotted and a slight push would have sent the charred trunks to the ground, I avoided touching them. I crept carefully to the edge of the ridge and peered over. There, only fifteen yards from me, lay the elk, watching his back trail. In a jiffy he was up. Without much regard to the sight on the gun I blazed away again. The bull dashed into the trees. I followed him down the hill and ran plunk into him in a dense thicket. He whirled. I pulled the trigger, but nothing happened. I had forgotten to reload. Barely dodging the lightning smash of his antlers,

I took off for the jack pines like a scared rabbit, jumping right and left to avoid him.

While looking wildly back to avoid the bull's dashes, and at the same time watching out to miss the trees, I tried to reload the rifle. The elk was wounded in one hind leg, which made him run crooked. He kept hitting dead pines, sending them crashing to the ground and increasing my fright at every jump. Then, to my horror, I stumbled and slammed into a fallen tree. I ducked and dropped to the ground, pressing frantically against the thick branches which held me, just as the bull's antlers passed over my head. He rared back, made a lunge, and rattled his horns at my breastwork. I unscrambled my rifle, slipped a cartridge into the chamber, and fired. The old gun roared, and the bull crashed down, pinning me to the ground.

I lay quietly for a while, gasping for breath and wondering whether I was badly hurt. Finally I pulled my legs out from under the heavy load, relieved to find that no bones were broken. Trembling with exertion and excitement, I surveyed my prize with pride, feeling that downing that fine bull elk was quite an achievement for a kid.

The next thing to do, I decided, was to remove the head and carry it back to camp. The camp was a good five miles away, but that didn't seem far to me then. After an hour of hacking with a dull knife, I severed the head from the carcass. When I lifted it, I discovered to my regret that it weighed about a hundred pounds, and I realized that I could not bear my trophy in triumph to the lake. I stood admiring it for a long time, reluctant to leave.

I finally decided to carry the horns about a hundred yards from the carcass, to save them from the grizzlies that would come to eat the meat. Fifty yards away was a narrow gulch about ten feet wide and seven feet deep, and I decided to leave the head on the other side. The horns and rifle were some load, but I staggered to the gulch. The only way to get across was by walking over an old, slippery log spanning it. I carefully picked my way along that natural bridge, using my gun as a balancing pole. All went well until I reached the middle of the log, where the branches were rather thick. Teetering back and forth to keep my balance, I stepped on a limb, which broke, leaving a two-inch nubbin that caught me in the ribs close to my spine as I pitched downward. I landed in the ditch, and the horns and my rifle landed on top of me, doing everything to me that the bull had tried to do before he died.

I am not sure whether or not I fainted, but when

I realized what had happened to me, I found several points of the antlers sticking into me and the gun still lying on my head. I could hardly breathe, and what little breath I did take pained me so much that I could hardly stand it. So there I lay, weak and sore, thinking that I was going to die.

The thought that I wouldn't live long enough to reach camp with my trophy bothered me the most. In about half an hour I managed to drag myself out from under the horns and remove the points from my flesh and clothes. The wound in my back was the most serious, and the slightest movement caused me great pain. With difficulty I drew myself up the steep side of the gulch. I took another half hour to reach the top. The head stayed in the ditch, but I brought the rifle out with me. It was still another half hour before I was able to move on.

As I pulled myself painfully along, a large grizzly arose from a mudhole. Luckily I was in a deadfall of logs, and Mr. Cuffy didn't see me. He moseyed upstream, now and then digging up a root or turning over a rock for grubs. Dropping to my knees, I quickly pushed the barrel of the gun over a log. Then it occurred to me what might happen if I only wounded the old boy and the gun should again fail to eject the shell. That thought, together with my weakened condition and shaken nerves, made me hesitate. Should I shoot? The bear continued poking around, unaware of my presence. A minute seemed like an hour to me. I was trembling violently. The longer I looked at the bear, the bigger he got.

Then the thought came to me, "You dang fool! You've been bragging about wanting to kill a bear. Here he is. If you let him pass, you'll never forgive yourself!" I took careful aim and banged away. At the crack of the gun Bruin fell with a bawl. In an instant he was biting at his side. He smashed at a big log with a front paw, knocking huge splinters from it.

Then the grizzly stood up to find me. Frantically I tried to get the front sight on him again. Just as the gun went off, Cuffy saw me. With another roar he went down and then started straight for me. I pushed another cartridge home and fired—a clean miss! The bear ran toward me, diving into a hollow, tearing up the ground in my direction, jumping over logs. The thought flashed through my mind, "Will the gun throw the shell?" It did, and another loaded cartridge took its place.

The bear was taking long leaps, his right foreleg swinging like a windmill at every jump. I saw a red spot on his right side and one on his right shoulder. I hurriedly aimed at his "sticking place" and blazed away at a twenty-foot range. The cloud of smoke shut him from my view. There was no time for another shot. I jumped to my feet—to run, I suppose —though in my crippled condition I don't think I could have cleared the timber that was piled three and four feet high around me. The smoke quickly cleared away, and ten feet from me I saw the end of his somersault as Bruin fell.

I suppose it would be impossible for a person not born among hunters to appreciate my satisfaction as I stood gazing at my second prize of the day. In those days a good part of our food had to be got with guns, and to be a good shot was almost a necessity. But this was big game. I left the old boy with regret and slowly and painfully headed back to camp.

It was a Saturday evening, and as usual quite a gang of men was gathered about the post office, waiting for the mail. What a setting for my news! Soon my brother and Studhorse rowed to shore from their hunt across the lake.

"What luck?" I asked.

"Some nice fat grouse," said George. "And you?"

"A fawn," I said.

"Haw! I wouldn't give our grouse for your damn

LEARNING TO HUNT

fawn!" bawled Studhorse. The laugh that broke from the crowd burned up the husky giant. When he heard how I had beat him for game, he refused to believe it.

That night I slept at Westcott's. The next morning Westcott said that I had fought the battles over again all night and that he had had to wake me several times to keep me from killing him. The next day Father, Antelope Jack, George, and I took two ponies and Westcott's two jacks and brought in the meat and antlers.

VI⸴

COLORADO INDIANS

The Indians who lived in central Colorado were Utes and Arapahos. The Utes were usually friendly to white men, but factions within the tribe frequently meant trouble for the settlers and prospectors around Grand Lake.

In the spring of 1879 a small Indian outbreak threw the people of Grand Lake into a panic, and they stampeded across the main range to safety. Though our family moved out, George and I remained at the lake, along with about fifteen hunters, trappers, and miners. On the evening of the third day after the scare most of us were sitting in front of Westcott's cabin cleaning our guns and loading cartridges for our rifles. My armament consisted of a cap-and-ball rifle, a revolver, and a bowie knife. Suddenly three horsemen leading two pack animals loped into the clearing. Their appearance gave us a shock. If they had been Indians, we'd have been goners right there. We knew one of the men, Rebel Stokes, from Hot Springs. The other two were strangers, but we soon learned that they were Big Frank and Kentucky Johnny.

Big Frank was about thirty-two years old. In my eyes he was a veritable knight of old. As straight and free of movement as an Indian chief, he was six feet four and had long brown hair swirling about his broad shoulders. He wore tanned buckskins, the fringe swinging with every movement of his body. Hanging from his saddle pommel was a long-barreled, .50-caliber Sharps rifle. Around his waist were two belts, one for his rifle and the other for his revolver cartridges and bowie knife. His bridle was wide and beautifully stamped, and his silver- and gold-mounted Spanish spade bit was an impressive work of art.

After supper we gathered at Baker's cabin to hear the news. There I had a chance to study Frank's face up close. It was the face of a killer, but not the murderous type. When talking, he looked straight at you with a calm born of conscious strength. His tanned, rugged face was of the kind weathered only in the West, where dangers and hardships were the order of the day. Big Frank settled himself comfortably in a homemade elk-horn chair near the fireplace and lit his pipe. Then he told us about the recent Indian scrap.

It seemed that Pierre, a renegade Ute chief, had ridden up from White River country to have a good time and to buy arms and ammunition, ostensibly for the fall hunt. It afterward turned out that the munitions were intended for an uprising that Pierre was planning. About fifty Indians had camped on the Billy Cousins ranch at the edge of Middle Park where the Berthoud Pass Road entered the big timber belt, at the beginning of the Front Range of the Rocky Mountains.

Cousins, I later learned, was a well-known character in the mining country around Central City and Boulder. He had come up against the law on many occasions. Then he was made sheriff, and that changed Billy. He cut out whisky and became one of the most efficient sheriffs of the mountain region. No killer was too dangerous for him to tackle, and few escaped him.

The Indians made themselves obnoxious on the Cousins ranch, and finally Pierre, the chief, went to Billy and said, "My braves heap hungry. You give 'em cow." Billy refused.

Pierre said angrily, "You no give cow, me kill 'em cow."

Billy calmly answered, "You no kill 'em *my* cow, Pierre."

The savage became threatening and ugly, but Billy remained obdurate. Finally Pierre said, "We kill 'em little cow."

Billy's temper rose, and he said, "Pierre, you kill 'em cow, me kill 'em Injun."

Pierre knew that Billy meant it, and he ordered his braves to pull down their tipis and move to the Anderson ranch, about six miles to the south.

Anderson was made of different stuff from Billy Cousins, and the Indians knew it. At his ranch they ran horse races in the oat fields, killed a two-year-old heifer, and generally raised hell. Finally Anderson sent to Sulphur Springs for Sheriff Marker and a posse, which included Big Frank. The sheriff tried to persuade the Utes to stop damaging Anderson's farm crops and finally threatened to arrest Pierre. The chief showed signs of resisting, and an Indian at his side pulled his rifle from its buckskin case. Just as the brave got his rifle clear, Big Frank sent a five-hundred-grain bullet through him.

Wild excitement broke out in the Indian camp. After a big powwow, Sheriff Marker finally persuaded the Utes to move down the Grand to Sulphur Springs, escorted by the posse. The Indians camped about a mile below town and held a war dance and ceremony of mourning for the dead Indian, whose body they had taken with them. The next day Pierre sent word to town that if Big Frank was not turned over to the tribe by a certain time he would massacre the whole outfit. Big Frank sent back word that he would fight the whole band of warriors, one at a time. The Indians didn't accept the challenge, and after a day's delay Frank came up to the lake and joined us.

Shortly after Big Frank and Kentucky Johnny had gone, a courier rode into camp with word of the Meeker massacre at the Indian agency on White River. The news created a lot of excitement, and things seemed more serious than ever. Our informant did not know whether or not the Indians had killed the women at the agency, and there was a call for experienced frontiersmen to join a rescue force. Len Pollard, Sandy Mellon, and half a dozen others started off on horseback for the White River.

Nathan Cook Meeker, of Greeley, Colorado, had been appointed agent for the White River Utes in 1877. Born in Ohio, he was a fine old gentleman, but he knew nothing about Indians. He thought that what was good for him was good for the savages. He wanted them to settle down and grow pumpkins and vegetables. The Indians had different ideas. They wanted to continue the seminomadic life they had lived for centuries. To stop them from racing horses, Meeker ploughed up their race track. In revenge the brother-in-law of Chief Ouray beat up the old man. Meeker asked for soldiers to protect him, and Captain J. S. Payne and a troop of buffalo (Negro) soldiers from Fort Garland were ordered to patrol the reservation and to join Major Thomas T. Thornburgh's command of 106th Cavalry.

Chief Colorow of the Utes

When Thornburgh reached Bear River, the Indians became excited and ordered Meeker to ask the troops to halt. Meeker wrote a letter to that effect and sent it by courier to Thornburgh. Thornburgh's orders were to proceed anyway, but he sent word for five Ute chiefs to meet him at Milk Creek for a council on September 29.

At ten o'clock on the morning of September 29, as they were passing through a narrow gulch, Major Thornburgh and his troops were ambushed by a large band of Utes led by Chief Colorow. In an attempt to regain his wagon train some distance in the rear, Thornburgh charged the Indians. He and fourteen of his men were killed. Captain Payne, who assumed command, reached the wagons, but not before forty men were wounded, including most of the officers. Breastworks were made by piling up dead men and horses and covering them with earth. Though the Indians set fire to the grass to burn them out, the soldiers managed to extinguish the flames with blankets. In the evening the Utes charged but were repulsed with a loss. That night a scout sneaked out, secured a horse, and rode 160 miles for help. The troops endured hell on earth for six days until General Wesley Merritt arrived with five hundred men after a forced march of seventy-two hours.

On the same day Thornburgh was ambushed, the Indians drove a barrel stave down Meeker's throat and, putting a log chain around his neck, dragged him about the agency. A dozen men and boys employed by Meeker were also murdered. All the women were captured and divided up among the Indian leaders.

Everybody anxiously awaited the outcome of the rescue efforts. A few weeks later we rejoiced to hear that all the women had been saved. I don't remember what part our boys played in the affair. Sandy Mellon told me about their sneaking up on the Indian camp. Luckily there was no fighting. If there had been, all the captives would have been murdered, according to Indian practice.

Early one autumn, several years after the trouble with the Utes in 1879, my friend Alden Sampson and I set out on a sketching and hunting trip through the White River Reservation. We followed trails that the Indians had used for many, many years. After a few weeks we found our grub running low and decided to head for the military post about fifty miles south. Eighteen inches of snow covered the ground, and camping and traveling were difficult. Following the river and bucking snow at every step, we arrived at a soldiers' camp twenty-five miles from the fort. We learned from a private on guard that it was a wood camp and that the sergeant in charge and the rest of the soldiers were away chopping wood to be floated down the river before it froze solid. From the questions he asked it was clear that the private was especially interested in us. Finally, not getting much satisfaction from our answers, he said, "Aw, hell, fellers, nobody's goin' to be chasin' around in this God damn snow country fer fun! What yer hidin' out fer? You can't fool me!"

The next day, after spending the night in a camp on the bank of White River a mile above the army post, we rode into the fort to buy provisions. The sullen-faced old warrior Chief Colorow was sitting outside on a small keg. A tipsy soldier was trying to engage the chief in conversation. He showed Colorow his left hand with the end of the thumb missing and said that he had lost it in the Thornburgh ambush.

The old chief, who had led the Utes in that battle, grinned and remarked, pointing to the soldier's heart, "Too damn bad we no get you there!"

VII.

FRIENDS AND FIGHTS AT GRAND LAKE

What historians have called the westward movement brought many men to the vicinity of Grand Lake. Some of them, like J. L. Westcott, Doc Parker, and Len Pollard, settled there to make a living hunting, trapping, or mining. Some, like Antelope Jack, drifted in and out of the camp.

A third group was made up mostly of men who stopped to pass a night or a week or to buy supplies before going on their way. That group included such men as Sir Henry Vivian and Sir Gordon Cummings, who came again and again to hunt the wildlife that was so abundant; the artist Alden Sampson and Henry L. Stimson, for whom the call of the West was real but who lived most of their lives in the East. In the time I spent at Grand Lake I came to know most of the men who frequented the region.

By and large they were strong men, rough and ready, and perhaps that is the reason I remember

Ike Adams, our only milkman, who did not fit the pattern. He must have been a miserable little runt in the eyes of any man, and to an adolescent, intolerant of the peculiarities of others, Ike was both despicable and funny.

Ike was the smallest, skinniest shrimp that ever trod a trail. Someone once remarked, "When Ike's dressed in his winter clothes and wears an overcoat, he might weigh thirty-five pounds." But I think that it would take the addition of a can of milk to make Ike tip the scales at that weight. Ike was all skin and bone, and there wasn't much of either, and his yellow hide had a hard time covering what there was. His face was so thin and his skin stuck so close to his skull that when he shaved he had to put his finger in his mouth and push out his cheek so the razor could reach his beard. The razor must have needed a new edge, for his face always looked as though he had shaved with a curry comb. His hair was long, each strand separate, and he usually kept it plastered with bear grease.

Ike's summer garb consisted of an undershirt and a pair of loose overalls that flapped about his skinny shins. The bottoms were tucked into boots so large that he shuffled for fear of losing them. Ike's only sport was chewing tobacco, which he did with evident gusto and satisfaction. On whichever side of his face his quid was parked, it gave that side the appearance of having the mumps. When he was carrying milk, he seemed to balance himself with his tobacco, for he wore his quid in the cheek opposite to the side he carried the milk. When he shifted his load, he shifted his tobacco.

Cowtit Ike, or Tits, as everybody called him, had a small place a couple of miles from Grand Lake, where he kept two or three old razor-backed cows. Of course, milk had its uses, but they were limited. After a week or two of a whisky diet, when a man's tripe was honeycombed and blistered, milk was useful in bringing it back to seminormalcy. Ike had poor pickings during ordinary times but made it up when the bunch was in from the mountains, the mines, or the trap lines. He demanded, and got, two bits a pint.

One day as I was returning from a sketching trip, I saw Ike make the only quick move he was ever known to put forth. It was one of those memorable days when Westcott and his neighbor, Avery, had another skirmish in their constantly stewing feud. I was following Ike when hell broke loose without the slightest warning. Avery blazed away with his old .50-caliber needle gun, and Westcott let go with

FRIENDS AND FIGHTS AT GRAND LAKE

Jezebel, his six-bore, double-barrel cap-and-ball shotgun. The latter was loaded with a handful of black powder and Westcott's special assortment of hardware. When the pine cones and branches began to fall, I hugged the ground. In front of me, Ike dropped his can of milk and bounded into the air. When his feet hit the ground, he was running like a deer. Bang! went Westcott's second barrel. Ike shed both boots and his hat and fairly flew out of range, yelling like an Indian.

When the battle was over, Ike crawled back. A couple of slugs had penetrated his milk can, and it had leaked dry. With furtive glances back and forth from Avery's dugout to Westcott's cabin, he collected his wardrobe and, looking ruefully at the spot where several gallons of milk had soaked into the ground, withdrew from the scene.

On my many trips to Grand Lake I sometimes stayed in our cabin and sometimes with Westcott or another friend. I remember one stay about 1878 with Antelope Jack, who was living in a cabin he had built for himself as a sort of headquarters.

It was a Saturday afternoon, and the clans were gathering for social chats, cards, and drinks. Among the crowd outside I happened to notice Al Coffin, a

Cowtit Ike

former cowboy turned prospector and miner. Coffin, I knew, had been spreading tales about Jack, and that had got under Jack's skin. I casually mentioned Coffin's arrival to Jack, who got up from his chair, took his pipe from his mouth, and looked out the window. Then he picked up his two .45 Colts and examined them carefully. He twirled the cylinders to see that they worked freely and put both guns under his belt. He glanced out the window again and remarked, as he bit off a chew of tobacco, "Yes, there's that coyote Coffin. He's been scattering stories about me. I'll go down and call his bluff. Phim, if you want to see the fun, come along."

Jack left the cabin and sauntered quietly up to the boys. He waved to different members of the group with a "Hello, Bill," to this one, and a "When did you stampede into town?" to another. The party was composed mostly of Coffin's friends, among them Bill and Mann Redmond, Al Clark, and several others, as well as Al's brother, Lon Coffin. All of them were gun toters, and a couple of them had a notch or two on their shooters.

Presently Jack walked up to Al and said in even tones, "Coffin, you've been saying I'm a coward and afraid to face a gun." Jack pulled both guns from his belt and held them, butt out, saying, "They're both loaded. Take your choice and we'll see who's the coward, right here."

Al's face turned the color of smoked buckskin as he tremblingly waved back the guns and said in a shaky voice, "It ain't as bad as that."

Whereupon Jack said, "Yes, it's just as bad as that. You take water right now an' tell the boys you're lyin' or get it, right here."

Al proceeded to do as he was told, and the affair was settled.

Not all the men that I knew in the mountains near Denver were westerners. It was there that I first met Alden Sampson and Henry L. Stimson. Perhaps I would never have met Sampson if it hadn't been for a howling blizzard that almost took the lives of two of my acquaintances.

In early December, 1879, I decided to leave Grand Lake and hit the trail for Denver. Judge Hoyt, our county judge, who had been at the lake, was going to Georgetown with a span of big mules and a bobsled, and I was to pay $2.50 to go with him. At noon the day before we were to start, a terrific blizzard blew in. Lon Coffin and Al Clark were expected in from the Grand River Ford, ten miles away, and toward evening, as the storm increased and the snow piled deeper and deeper, we began to worry. We were sure that if they had not started before the storm struck they would not go out in it, but we were anxious nevertheless.

The gale increased in violence, driving the snow horizontally along the ground. No one stirred from his fireplace unless it was absolutely necessary to bring in wood. Finally the men gathered in Westcott's cabin to discuss the situation. About nine o'clock Antelope Jack and Al Coffin decided to mount Hoyt's mules and strike out, leading a pony, which was the only other animal in camp. We waited anxiously one hour, two hours . . . still no one showed up. Another hour passed, and then we heard a shout. Donning coats and mittens, we struggled out into the snow. About two hundred yards away we found them. Lon Coffin and Al Clark were on the mules, while Al Coffin was riding the pony and Antelope

FRIENDS AND FIGHTS AT GRAND LAKE

Jack floundered along behind it, clinging to its tail.

Coffin and Clark had started out in clear weather, but were overtaken by the storm at Willow Creek, about six miles from the lake. They were then nearly halfway to the lake, and there was nothing to do but go ahead, for it would be fatal to turn back into the teeth of the gale. With the mail they were bringing to the lake were some newspapers, which they unrolled and put next to their underclothes for protection. Both Al and Lon considered that the newspapers had saved their lives.

After three days the blizzard subsided, and on the morning of the fourth day Hoyt and I started on the seventy-mile trip through the deep snow. Hoyt's powerful mules plowed along, sometimes belly-deep in drifts, and several times we had to dig a trail through the crusted snow. We made only ten miles the first day. For some reason Hoyt had to go to Sulphur, and we arrived in bitter cold a couple of hours after dark. After supper at the Gardner House we sauntered over to the general store.

In a few minutes Hoyt came to me and said that an "Englishman" had just come in from a hunt on Troublesome Creek and that he wanted to go with us. Hoyt asked me not to tell the man what I was paying for the trip, since he was going to ask him for a good deal more. Next morning the stranger came aboard the bobsled with his duffel, which seemed like a lot of truck to me, and we were off bright and early.

I didn't talk much and only answered yes or no when my traveling companion tried to make conversation. When we reached the top of the long divide and started down to Ten Mile, we all got off and walked to save the mules. As we followed in the trails cut by the mules and sled runners, Alden Sampson got me to talking a little, and I learned that he was from New York City, not England. He finally got out of me that I was studying art and that I hoped to go to New York someday and enter one of the art schools there. That seemed to interest Sampson, who was an artist himself. At Georgetown we parted company with Hoyt and took the train to Denver.

That was the beginning of a friendship which lasted until Sampson's death in 1925. A number of times we hunted together in Colorado. After I settled in New York, our hunting and fishing trips included one to Manitoba, several to New Brunswick and Quebec, a couple to Montana, one to Minnesota, and an extended one to California. We both belonged to the Boone and Crockett, Camp Fire, and Century clubs, and in time we were to share a studio on Fifty-first Street in New York City.

It had been Westcott's idea to build a town on his homestead at the lake. With that end in view he persuaded everyone he could to build a cabin on his land. About 1880 a man from the "outside" named Waldron took up a homestead on the northeast side of the lake. Waldron had been a scout in the Indian wars on the Plains under Custer and Miles and had a reputation for courage and initiative. The first thing he did was bring some relatives to help him build his own "town." Then he cut out a road to the north side, meeting the main road about five miles below the lake. He started his road in thick timber just where the main road made a quick turn, so that people who didn't know the country got the impression that his road was the direct one to the lake. Then he put up a sign indicating that his road went to the lake. That peeved Westcott, and he took a young fellow named Murphy down to the intersection, cleaned up his own trail, and threw logs across Waldron's road where it left his.

A couple of days later I was sitting on the shore near Westcott's place, sketching the north mountains, when I noticed a boat with two men in it coming our way. Westcott was cutting bait on the seat of his scow, and Murphy was hanging out a few articles of clothing he had washed. The skiff grounded on the beach. The first man to step out on the shore was Waldron. He greeted me with a smile as he handed his fourteen-shot rifle to his nephew, Charley Johnson. Walking up to Murphy, Waldron said, "Murphy, I see you've been throwing logs on my road down at the forks." Then he lit into the young man and gave him a severe knocking about. Murphy was taller and more powerful, but he didn't have a chance against the other's catlike movements and ferocity. Westcott, whose eyesight was very poor, could hear everything but could see nothing.

When Waldron decided he had given the young chap enough punishment, he turned, took the rifle from his nephew, stepped back into his boat, put the gun at his side, and took up the oars. An awkward silence followed the boat's departure. I pretended to be sketching. Westcott kept on cutting bait, occasionally squirting tobacco juice into the water. Murphy half-staggered to the lake to bathe his bruised face in the cooling water. We all knew that it was Westcott's licking but also that no one would hit him because of his poor eyesight.

FRIENDS AND FIGHTS AT GRAND LAKE

After that the contest for the townsite broke out in earnest. Our side of the lake was more picturesque and accessible than Waldron's, but Waldron was more businesslike and resourceful than Westcott.

One day Westcott brought in a barrel of whisky and put it in a shed. The stuff was a knockout, and while it lasted it was a wonder. Bill and Mann Redmond came in from the range and lined up for a round. Al Coffin joined them, and soon the hogshead was empty. As effective as the liquor was, it needed surroundings—something more than a hewn table and sawed-off chunks of wood for chairs and something better than a leaky shed with a dirt floor.

Waldron bought a sawmill, set it up on his side of the lake, and sold rough lumber for twenty dollars a thousand. Soon he had enough lumber to build a pretty decent saloon with a bar, a rail, real benches for chairs, and sawdust on the floor. A street was cut through the jack pines on Waldron's side, and shacks started to spring up among the trees and stumps. Then a hotel was added to the saloon.

At this critical time for "our side," old Ned Schafer died. Westcott offered a nice burial site at the edge of his sagebrush flat in the jack pines. He said that he would build a good fence and make a real grave corral, with a gate, too. The spot Waldron's side offered was in burned timber on a rocky hill. Our side won. Westcott built the fence and made a nice dead man's settlement.

Though Westcott did his best for three or four years, however, the Grand Lake settlement spread out more from Waldron's side than from ours.

January 1, 1883, dawned bright and clear. I was slowly pushing my skis over the frozen surface of the lake toward the village of Grand Lake, having some business to transact with Waldron, who was county commissioner. At the edge of the village I stacked my skis against a tree and footed it the rest of the way to the saloon. Waldron, who had always been very friendly to me, met me at the door with a pleasant New Year's greeting. He was obviously well tanked up, which gave me a turn, since I had never seen him drunk before. After letting me in, he was called out of the room.

A high-tempered Irish chap by the name of Mike Finn was drinking alone at the bar. Seeing me standing near the door, he motioned to me to come over and gave the sign of a hooked elbow. I shook my head. Finn had enough poison in him to make him uglier than usual, and he came toward me with a threatening air. Lon Coffin rose from a stool in the corner, came over, and tapped Finn on the shoulder, remarking, "Say, stranger, this boy don't drink with nobody. We never asks him. I'll say right now that if your dinero's burnin' yer jeans, I'll drink with you or fight you, whatever you say. Now which'll you take?"

Finn took in Lon's broad shoulders, stocky form, and large jaw and answered. "Well, have one on me."

Just then Waldron returned, followed by his small wife, who was pleading with him to go to bed. He'd been up all night superintending the dance room and bar. I decided to let my business wait and turned to leave. At the door I met Bob Plummer—a miner we all knew—coming in. I'd gone about fifty feet from the saloon when the door of Waldron's place burst open and a shot rang out. As I turned, I saw Plummer running across the street. There was another shot, and Bob fell in a heap in the snow. By the time I reached the spot, three or four other men had come up. Bob was dead—the bullet had gone through his heart from the back.

It turned out that when Bob entered the barroom Waldron's wife was still trying to persuade her husband to go to bed. Waldron started to beat her, and Bob tried to stop him. Waldron attacked Bob furiously. Bob, who was a husky giant, didn't want to fight a drunken man whom he knew well. He tried to hold Waldron off but, finding him too fierce, finally knocked him down. Waldron was up and at him again in an instant. Bob floored him a second time and turned to leave. Waldron jumped for his rifle. Someone yelled to Bob, and he ran, but to no avail.

Bob's body was carried into the nearest empty cabin, his blood streaking the snow. There it was laid on a table, covered with canvas, and left to freeze.

The funeral took place the next day in a howling blizzard. The ground in the graveyard was frozen to a depth of four feet, and it took hours of thawing with fires before the grave could be dug. The hearse, a horse-drawn bobsled, stopped at the door of the cabin, and the men carried the coffin into the cabin. Snow whipping through the cracks in the walls had covered the dirt floor and the body inches deep. The heavily muffled men stamped their feet and swung their hands against their shoulders to keep from freezing. Finally half a dozen of them put the body in the coffin, shuffled through the door, and shoved the box onto the bed of the improvised hearse. Then

Shooting of Bob Plummer

Bob Plummer's Funeral

they formed a procession behind the bobsled. The storm increased in violence as the marchers, bending low against the gale and holding their hands before their faces to fend off the stinging blast, walked on. The snow came down so thick that it wasn't possible for those of us at the back to see the people at the front end of the procession. By the time we reached the grave, it was filled with snow which had to be shoveled out before the coffin could be lowered.

There was no preacher, and so my old friend Ed Butler read a passage from his Bible in measured tones and offered up a prayer. While the dirt was being shoveled into the grave, the blizzard howled a solemn requiem for the remains of Bob Plummer.

Then arose the question of what to do with Waldron. There was no sheriff or deputy or any other county officer at the lake except Waldron himself. There was, however, a constable, Charley Johnson, Waldron's nephew, who forgot that it was his duty to make the arrest until Waldron himself reminded him of it. Among the civic improvements Waldron had made in his capacity as county commissioner was a jail, and there he was locked up. Johnson was made jailer, and he brought Waldron's meals every day from the prisoner's own hotel.

Waldron was kept in jail throughout the winter and the following summer until late fall. One night in October, 1884, Waldron sent his nephew to the hotel for a bottle of Jamaica ginger to treat a stomach-ache. As Johnson handed him the bottle, Waldron hit him on the head with a stone he had dropped into the toe of a sock. Johnson dropped to the floor, and Waldron walked out of the jail, where he was joined by a friend who had brought around a horse, saddled and bridled, with Waldron's rifle and revolver hanging on the saddle horn. A pack horse was also waiting, loaded with a camp outfit, blankets, and provisions. No one ever heard of Waldron again.

When I was twenty-four, I took up a homestead on the south side of the lake and built a log cabin on it. Then several more people located on our side. There were three married women at the lake, and finally an unmarried girl put in her appearance. All the fellows rode hard for her. Trails from every direction were worn to her home. It wasn't too long before Charley Hensell won out, and everybody set to to hold a bang-up wedding. When we thought that everything was about ready for the ceremony, someone reminded us that there was no preacher. Then a wise fellow suggested, "Here, let's form a district and elect a judge. We can't make no sky pilots, but we can manufacture a justice of the peace." The suggestion was followed, and Westcott was elected to the post. Then we discovered another hitch: there was no Bible for the ceremony. Both my father and Ed Butler had gone away on business, taking their Bibles with them. A rider was dispatched to Hot Sulphur for one. He returned with it two days later. Word was sent out that the wedding was to take place on a Saturday evening, and Judge Westcott's cabin was chosen for the event. Candles were rustled; benches, boxes, kegs, and logs were brought in for seats; and a table was improvised. Finally the bride- and bridegroom-to-be arrived.

When the ceremony commenced, the cabin was filled, and a bunch of men were standing outside looking in. Westcott's forehead was shining, and his long hair was puffed up about his head. He was so nearsighted that he had to hold his face within an inch of what he was reading and follow along the line with his finger, making out one word at a time. There were just a few candles in the cabin, and I could make out people only dimly. The darkness beyond the rays of the candles was impressive.

When the judge came to the words, "Who gives this woman away?" a chap near me said in a stage whisper, "I could, but I won't!" causing snorts of laughter in our part of the room.

As soon as the ceremony was over (in fact, before it ended), the celebration began. The judge soon began to show strong symptoms of overexcitement, and I sneaked his bottle away. He looked for it everywhere. He staggered around, cursing the scoundrel who had stolen his bottle. Finally he decided to row to the north shore for some redeye. But I had taken both anchor ropes out of his boat, tied them together to make a line two hundred feet long, and tied the loose end to a bush. Westcott pulled out to the end of the rope and began rowing, too befuddled to realize that he was anchored to shore. After he had hauled away for about twenty minutes, he turned back to see if he was going in the right direction. Then he went at the oars again and rowed ten minutes more, repeating curses on the man who had hidden his whisky. After he had rowed in the same spot for some time, I pulled him back to land.

The crowd kept on howling and yelling and shooting for hours, while George and I cracked bottles and hid guns. When the boys couldn't hold any more, they fell down right where they were and slept until morning. George and I had to get Westcott back to his cabin. By then he was in tears because I wouldn't find his gun so that he could shoot up his old enemy Avery.

Cabin at Grand Lake

VIII.

THE GRAND COUNTY FEUD

In the late 1860's, Hot Sulphur Springs, a settlement on Grand River in Grand County, had gradually grown into a village of trappers and prospectors. Later, stockmen, ranchers, and a few businessmen had drifted in. In the 1870's mining fever had broken out afresh in Colorado, and Leadville and Cripple Creek had boomed. Miners were digging, gambling, and shooting at each other all over Colorado—whisky and blood flowed in equal quantities. Everywhere plowshares were exchanged for picks and shovels. An acquaintance of ours at Grand Lake got gold fever, left his plow in the middle of a furrow, hitched his team to his wagon, drove to Leadville, and made a fortune. Another farmer, who lost his ranch by foreclosure, threw what little grub he had into his wagon, pulled out for the mountains, and came back rich. Many miners swarmed into the Rabbit Ear Range, fifteen miles north of Grand

Lake. The budding village of Grand Lake soon rivaled Hot Sulphur Springs, which up to that time had been the county seat. The discovery of ore in the northern end of the county gave Grand Lake a preponderance of votes, and the county seat was transferred there in 1878–79.

About that time another development occurred: the Grand Lake Mine began to turn out rich ore. One day a man named Webber stepped into the picture. No one knew his first name or when he actually arrived—he was just there. He foresaw that someday the area would be a pleasure spot for tourists, and his aim was to acquire title to the mine, as well as to Westcott's homestead and those belonging to the rest of us. Webber, who was reputed to be a lawyer, knew that titles to many of the mines and ranches had loopholes in them, and he set out to take advantage of the fact. To our surprise, some of the "best" people of Hot Sulphur became Webber's supporters.

In 1882, Webber went before an "outside" judge and somehow convinced him that the people of Grand Lake were outlaws. The judge deputized Webber and a number of his hired men and empowered them to arrest Mann and Bill Redmond, Al Coffin and his brother Lon, and several others, all of whom were part owners of the Grand Lake Mine.

Antelope Jack's cabin was the only two-story cabin at the lake. One day early in May, Jack and I were sitting by an upstairs window loading rifle cartridges in preparation for an elk hunt on Willow Creek. The winter had been a hard one, and elk and deer had begun to drift in from the south. Jack was looking out the window when he suddenly pulled his pipe out of his mouth and said, "What in hell's them birds pullin' guns for?"

I jumped to the window to see two of Webber's gang, Steve Morey and Dave Munger, standing with guns pointed, Morey's at a bunch of our boys and Munger's at Al Coffin. Jack grabbed his .40-90 Ballard and rushed downstairs. I took my Sharps and followed.

As I reached the edge of the hill, Jack dashed out from behind the donkey dugout just below. When he emerged, someone in the crowd fifty yards away yelled. Morey jumped behind a tree and turned his gun on us. Munger, whose gun was covering Coffin, stepped behind his prisoner, pushing his revolver over Al's shoulder, and also covered us. In an instant Jack's rifle was at his shoulder, and he pulled the trigger, but the gun misfired. At the same

THE GRAND COUNTY FEUD

moment I dropped to my knees behind a small stump. Taking hurried aim at Morey, I touched the hair trigger. Nothing happened. In my excitement I had forgotten to set it.

Jack darted behind the dugout, ejected the shell, reloaded, ran to the other side of the cabin, and came out covering the two men. I sat still, my rifle pointed at Morey, waiting. Then Mrs. Hoyt, the wife of our county judge, ran out and handed Al a revolver, whereupon our fellows flocked around with all kinds of shooting irons. When Jack and I joined the bunch, Morey and Munger were explaining that they had been made deputy sheriffs and had orders to arrest Al Coffin and one or two others. They were escorted to their horses and told to "git."

The next day I shot a fine buck and walked back to camp with the deer on my pony. I propped the buck in a somewhat natural position behind my cabin and was sketching him when I noticed a commotion over by the mess hall. There I found old Captain Dean, Jack McQuarry, Jim Stokes, and Webber himself, all armed with rifles and looking for Mann Redmond. In addition to a rifle Webber was armed with a revolver specially made to hold ten cartridges. He carried it in a gamebag, and I could see the gun in his hand inside the bag.

Mann was in the woods just a couple of hundred yards away, cutting logs for a cabin. We gave the "deputy sheriffs" a wrong steer about his whereabouts, and Stokes and McQuarry went off along the lake. When I saw Mann coming in through the pines, cocked rifle in hand, I slipped off to warn him, not knowing that Antelope Jack had already done so and had given him the gun. Mann walked behind the cabins and suddenly appeared at the end of the porch where Webber and Dean were waiting. Mann said, "Well, gents, I guess I'm the guy you're lookin' fer. Thought I'd come up and let you take me."

Dean had been a captain in the Union Army during the Civil War. He had plenty of courage, but he knew what a move would mean, and he was not about to tempt Providence. Webber was made of different stuff. He was a sneak and a coward, and he turned as white as a sheet.

"You damn ol' bastard," Mann went on, "why don't you take me? I've a notion to shoot the button off that cap you're wearin'. You're a fine bunch of deputy sheriffs. Where's them other two? Out there in the bushes tryin' to sneak up on me? I'll fight the whole lot of you polecats!"

Webber's face had taken on a greenish hue, and

he twitched as though he were having a fit of the ague. His right hand was still in his gamebag, and I knew the shooter was in his hand. I was pretty close to Mann and almost in the line of fire. Webber was shaking so much that I was afraid he might accidentally pull the trigger, so I carefully moved out of the way.

Mann's keen eye had missed nothing. He knew what was in the bag. Lowering the muzzle of his gun, he pointed it directly at Webber's belly.

"Why don't you pull the trigger of that newfangled scatter gun o' yours?" he snarled. "Just pull it, you yellow-livered son-of-a-bitch! I'd love to give you a good gut shot with these explodin' bullets and see you wallerin' around with your guts hangin' out and draggin' on the ground. That'd look purty. I'd get this young artist feller to paint a picture of it to hang over the pianner in my back-east mansion." Webber wasn't long withdrawing his hand from the bag.

Finally Webber and Dean were allowed to go, and our group gathered to discuss the affair. It was evident that Webber was going the limit to get possession of the Grand Lake Mine. We wondered what would happen next. As we were eating dinner, still discussing the events of the morning, guns stacked handy, a cowboy, Al Clark, dashed up on his horse. The Webber gang had captured Lon Coffin and Jake Gibson, two of the owners of the mine, and had taken them to the Coffee ranch, fifteen miles away at a ford across the Grand River.

Then and there we realized what Webber's plan was. Webber knew that Bill Redmond and his youngest brother, Frank, had been staying at the mine all winter, and by raiding our camp and capturing all the partners of the mine who were there, he could keep them from warning Bill or getting reinforcements to him. Then, early in the morning while the snow was still hard enough to bear a man's weight, he would rush a bunch of men over the mountain to the mine and seize Bill.

Clark's news threw the camp into great activity. Antelope Jack, Mann Redmond, and Clark armed themselves and started for the Coffee ranch to rescue Lon and Jake. The next question was to warn Bill Redmond. I volunteered to go to the mine, and a nice little mare was put at my service. Armed with my Sharps .40-70 and my Colt .45, I started up the trail.

At the North Fork bottoms the trail passed a wide-open space filled with willows and beaver dams. The Bowen and Baker Gulch trails forked here.

I knew that some of Webber's gang were camped at the north side of the swamp, and since there was no concealing my movements, I broke into a gallop with an eye for their horses in the meadow. As I had foreseen, several men rushed for their mounts and made a dash to head me off. The trail from the mouth of Bowen Gulch to the point where it met our trail to Baker Gulch was about three miles away. I figured that if I could beat them to the upper fork they would hardly dare follow me up far into the dark spruce forest. I had made up my mind to stop and kill a couple of horses if they pressed me. Luckily I beat them.

From there to the mine it was six miles, with the grade increasing fast. The snow had been much softened by the afternoon sun, and by then I was not worrying about my pursuers but about the difficulties ahead. My horse plugged along knee-deep in snow, and as we went on it got deeper and deeper. Soon the crust became strong enough to bear our weight, but only for a few steps at a time. I tried walking and leading my mount, but that was dangerous because when the horse pitched nose-first into the snow, she'd flounder and lunge forward, sometimes pawing me. I tried driving her, with no better success.

Night was falling, and I had still three miles to go, the last mile up a steep mountainside. I reached a hundred-yard slide that had been swept by an avalanche. Removing the saddle, I tied the mare to a snag. If she "cast" herself, she would be dead by morning, but it couldn't be helped. Falling, breaking through the crust to my armpits at times, I struggled on. I heard water rushing under the snow and crawled on my hands and knees for greater safety. Suddenly the crust gave way, and I found I was on the wrong side of the creek. I crawled downstream in the darkness, feeling my way with my rifle butt. The creek was too wide to jump—a miss in that swift water would be fatal. Poking my rifle into the stream as a staff, I cautiously waded in. I could hardly keep my footing but finally made it across and found the trail. After several hours of climbing, I reached Bill Redmond's cabin. Too tired to eat, I gave him the news and fell into bed.

The next morning Bill was up at dawn and had a fire going and coffee made. Frank, Bill's youngest brother, was still asleep as I stuck my nose out from under the stiff, frosty blankets, dreading to put my feet on the icy hewn-log floor. Soon the odor of salt pork greeted my nostrils. I had hoped there would be bacon, but in a hunting or mining camp that

THE GRAND COUNTY FEUD

commodity had always disappeared by midwinter. As I lay there, aching in many spots and with the edges of my ears rubbed nearly raw by the hard blanket I had used for a pillow, my mind ran over the events of the previous day and the two brothers whom I had risked my life to help. Bill Redmond, six foot four and as powerful as a bull moose, was the oldest of the four Redmond brothers and the recognized leader. Frank was a fiddler and unlikely to kill anything except a tune on his violin. The other brothers protected Frank, holding his talent in awe.

I was thankful that a good deal of the frost had been driven out of the cabin through the loose mud-and-moss chinking by the time Bill announced, "Chow's ready. Excavate yourself from them coverin's and come chaw."

When I shiveringly "excavated" myself, I realized how stiff I was, for I nearly fell. My body was covered with bruises. Suddenly it dawned on me that there was serious work ahead.

The prospect of greasy sowbelly, unsugared black coffee from an equally black pot half full of grounds from weeks back, and dough bread minus baking powder, butter, or even lard was not so tempting. That was all there was, however. When breakfast was over, Bill and I hitched our sidearms to our hips and, rifles in hand, started up the ridge to the mine. My legs were pretty stiff at first, but they limbered up as we climbed. All was peaceful at the shaft. When we realized that the snow was too soft to bear a man's weight, we knew that the Webber gang would not arrive that day. As we were returning to the cabin, the strains of a well-known waltz were wafted to us from Frank's violin. The strange incongruity of place and music did not strike me at the time. Frank appeared lazy, but he did have the energy to stoke the fire—if someone else brought in the wood (he had to keep his fingers warm so that he could paw his fiddle).

After dinner I started down the snowy trail heading back to the lake. I crossed the stream several hundred yards above where I had fallen the night before. A whinny from the mare just as I came in sight told me that she was all right. Just after passing Webber's camp, I met Captain Dean, who merely gave me a short nod.

As I was moseying through the open meadow of Macy Park, ahead of me I spotted a man on a white horse. When he saw me, he dashed out of the big timber, down a steep pitch, and into the brush. "That means trouble," I thought. In the fracas of a couple of days before, Dave Munger, who would stop at nothing to harm our bunch, had been riding a white horse, and I knew of no other in the region.

A hundred yards ahead of me the trail forked. The new one, to the left, went directly to the lake; the old one was longer and not as good. Though either would do, I didn't want to fight that low-down cuss, Munger. Which trail to take? I pulled the mare to the left, slipped my six gun out of the holster, cocked it, and hid it behind my right leg. My rifle lay across the saddle in front of me. I rode along carelessly, as though I had seen nothing, but I kept a sharp eye on the brush.

Suddenly a man jumped out, and my shooter was on him. Much to my relief, it wasn't Munger. By the man's expression I knew he was as scared as I was, which made me bolder. He had thought he had the drop on me.

There was an awkward pause, and then I asked, "Well, what's it all about?" I was still holding my gun on him, resting my arm against the saddle horn to keep it from wobbling. I made him drop his revolver and move away from his rifle, which rested against a bush.

"It's this way," the stranger said. "Them damn gunmen from over the range in the Webber gang allowed they'd burn my shack and run me out of here if I didn't throw in with 'em. Say, pard, would you mind pointin' that God damn Gatlin' away from my belly button? It's givin' me chilblains!" I shifted the muzzle, knowing that I could crumple him before he could grab his artillery.

He must have noticed that I was looking at his horse, and he hastened to explain that it belonged to Gid Thompson, a gambler from Sulphur Springs. The stranger went on to tell me that he and two of Webber's henchmen had been sent to guard the trail after I had gone by the day before. Thompson had ridden up with Bud Redmond on their way to the mine, and both had been captured and taken to the Webber camp.

"The Webber bunch was at dinner when we brought 'em into camp," the stranger continued. "Cap says, 'Charley, you guard 'em while they're picketin' their critters.' Bud was terrible particular where he tied his horse and went way out in the meadow. When we get behind the bush, Bud hands me one on the chin, and I goes out. When I come to, the cayuses was mired down and the boys had skedaddled afoot. That's Bud's six-shooter and Gid's rifle."

Deciding that my prisoner wasn't dangerous, I

put my revolver in the holster, and we got quite chummy. Finally he said, "Say, why don't you take Thompson's cayuse and the shootin' irons to the lake, and I'll go back afoot and tell the gang you held me up."

Arriving at the lake, I tied the horse in the thick pines which bordered the partly cleared ground surrounding the cabin and then sneaked up to see if all was well before going into the open. When I saw Mrs. Hoyt hurrying to her cabin, I went forward, gun cocked, and cautiously opened the door of Garrison's cabin. A conference was being held inside. Bud Redmond was relating the experiences of his capture and escape. Gid had not yet returned, and they feared he had been recaptured.

In a few words I reported on my trip to the mine and my encounter with the stranger. Then I went out to put up the horses. A short way from the cabin Mrs. Hoyt rushed up and asked, "Did you shoot the hold-up man?" I was turning to reply when a figure scrambled out of the bushes close by and started to run. My six-shooter was on him in an instant. Mrs. Hoyt fled for the nearest cabin, screaming all the way.

The man stopped and yelled, "For God's sake, don't shoot!"

I ordered him to come forward. He came, hands up, shaking all over, and I saw that he was only a shorthorn who had been hanging around the camp for some time.

After putting up the horses, I moseyed back to the Garrison cabin to hear the news. While I was at the mine, Antelope Jack and Mann Redmond had rescued Lon Coffin and Jake Gibson from the Coffee ranch. Riding up to Coffee, who was guarding our men, Mann had said, "Well, we've come to take our boys away."

Coffee answered, "You'll do it over my dead body."

"All right, have it your own way," said Redmond, and handed each of the prisoners a rifle. The boys mounted, wheeled, and just rode away.

"I've a damn good notion to shoot!" Coffee shouted, as he jumped forward and pointed his gun.

"Go ahead, old man, begin shootin' as soon as you want to!" was Mann's answer, as they disappeared.

There wasn't much sleep that night, for we expected the Webber gang to raid us any minute. The next morning we decided that it was our turn to move. We sent word to Sheriff Charley Royer at Hot Sulphur Springs that we needed his help. He swore in a posse of ten men, and they arrived at the lake about noon. Nearly every man in camp who could carry a gun was sworn in. After lunch nineteen men, including the sheriff, were ready to start. Royer was a thickset man of about thirty-five. He had a strong jaw and keen eyes.

"Well, boys," he said, "them fellers are at the mouth of Baker's Gulch, and we have to git right in among 'em before they know it."

I was without a horse, but I rustled around and found a man who had one in pasture. He told me if I could catch the horse I could borrow him. The horse had no idea of letting me put my hands on him, and by the time I had caught and saddled the nag the posse had gone.

Securing my revolver and my rifle and carrying two belts of cartridges, I set out fast after the party. Riding past the others up to the sheriff, who was in the lead, I told him that I wanted to go and asked him to swear me in.

He looked at me and said, "No, son. This ain't goin' to be no ladies' party. There's liable to be some shootin'." Seeing the disappointment in my face, he asked, "Do you think you can stand it?" Assured that I could, he said, "Well, I've got to arrest some tough characters up there, so I deputize you to go along." That was what I had hoped for. If there was going to be any shooting, I wanted the law on my side.

When we reached Webber's cabin, we closed in, but the gang was not there. Royer found out from the saloonkeeper that the outfit had put out pickets, who had warned Webber of our approach. The sheriff had warrants for Hawkeye Bill, Dead Bill, and Phil Rogers, the last being an outsider brought in as a fighter. Royer ordered Jim Kinney to take three men and fetch Hawkeye Bill and Rogers, who had gone up Bowen Gulch. Jim chose Antelope Jack and Gid Thompson, and while he was looking around for another man, Jack edged over to him and whispered something, whereupon Jim threw a quick glance at me and said, "What, that kid? He's too young for this job." But Jack talked earnestly with Jim, who finally beckoned to me and said I could go.

As we mounted higher and higher up Bowen Gulch, the trail grew rougher and rougher. It had been dug out of the snow, which had been piled up on either side as high as our heads on horseback. Finally we reached the edge of the ragged clearing surrounding the half-dozen cabins which made up the camp. Instead of riding straight in, we dismounted and tied our horses and then worked up

the stream bed, out of sight of the cabins, with our six-shooters convenient.

Just as we emerged into the clearing, who should by passing but Hawkeye Bill and Phil Rogers, the men we were after. They were surprised, to say the least, to face four guns so suddenly.

Jim Kinney read the arrest warrants to the prisoners. They didn't want to surrender, saying that they weren't going to take a chance on being shot by our outfit. Jim told them that he was a deputy sheriff and would see that nothing happened to them.

After considerable argument back and forth Kinney said, "It's getting dark. We got to get out of here damned fast." Since there were no extra mounts, Antelope Jack and Gid Thompson offered the prisoners their horses. Jim pulled out handcuffs and secured each of the men to their saddle horns by one hand. It was pitch dark in the heavily wooded canyon, and our horses plunged, slipped, and tumbled in every direction.

We made a wide detour around the headquarters of the Webber outfit, arriving back at Grand Lake about midnight. Sheriff Royer and his party had already arrived. Dead Bill had secreted himself in a commanding position in a log barn and swore he would not be taken alive. He had been involved in the feud a long time and didn't trust our outfit. After an hour's parley, however, Royer persuaded him to give himself up.

The next day court was assembled in the dining room of the boardinghouse. There were no real lawyers, but Webber's man Stokes acted as attorney for the defendants. A farmer who knew about as much about the law as a jack rabbit served as judge. They wrangled for a couple of days, and finally the prisoners were turned loose with an admonition to "be good."

After the election of 1882, Hot Sulphur Springs claimed that it had regained the county seat. Grand Lake disputed the claim. On July 4, 1883, the contest ended abruptly. Early in the morning my mother was busy in our cabin when she heard a shot. Looking out, she saw three men—Captain Dean, the county treasurer, Barney Day, the county commissioner, and Webber—leave Young's Hotel and start toward the village, a mile around the lake. In a few minutes, there were two more shots together and then four more, followed by several others. But it was Independence Day, and Mother didn't think much about them.

THE GRAND COUNTY FEUD

It wasn't too long before we found out what had happened. It seems that as Dean, Day, and Webber reached Dick Anderson's cabin, about a hundred yards from the hotel, four masked men, heavily armed, burst out from behind a clump of jack pines. They covered the three men and barked, "Hold up your hands!"

Webber wheeled and broke for the hotel with all speed. One of the masked men dropped to his knee and fired, and Webber pitched forward with a bullet through his lungs. At that instant Barney Day blew out the masked man's brains. The other three attackers rushed forward, and a general melee broke out. Captain Dean was felled by several shots in the body and one between the eyes, besides being hammered on the head with a revolver barrel. Meanwhile, Day had run behind the cabin, followed by one of the masked men. Their revolvers cracked: Barney Day pitched headlong into the lake with a bullet in his heart, and the masked man got a shot in the groin.

When the shooting was over, three of the attackers—one badly wounded—escaped on horses they had hidden in the woods. Day and one masked man, who proved to be Commissioner Mills, of the Grand Lake faction, lay dead. Webber died that night, but Captain Dean lived for several weeks. He pleaded for a gun so that he could shoot two men who came to see him daily. He was sure he recognized them as members of the masked gang.

The wounded attacker turned out to be Bill Redmond. I don't remember how we found out, but I learned that Redmond's friends took him to my empty homestead cabin around the corner of the lake. Bill's wife went out every day to "gather flowers." At any rate, when she left the house, she carried a basket covered with a napkin, and when she came back, the basket was filled with flowers. After some weeks she stopped collecting flowers, and I went up to look at the cabin, but there was no one in it. The carpet had been taken up and folded in a corner, evidently for a bed, and it was caked with dry blood.

A reward of five thousand dollars was offered for Bill dead or alive, but we never saw him again.

Sheriff Charley Royer was suspected of being one of the masked men. One rancher reported that he had seen him galloping like mad toward Hot Sulphur the day of the shooting. The governor, not satisfied with the way Royer had handled the case, requested him to come to Denver and explain. Len Pollard accompanied Royer. At Georgetown, where the stage line connected with the train for Denver, they stopped overnight in a hotel, taking separate rooms. The next morning Len knocked on Charley's door but got no answer. Crawling along a shed, he looked through a partly opened window. There was Charley Royer, slumped in a chair with his left arm and head lying on a table. He was dead. His right arm hung down, and on the floor lay a double-action revolver. In Royer's left hand was a letter from his mother, and on the table lay a half-written letter from him to her. Beside him was an open trunk, on the tray of which were several other letters from his mother and sister. In his forehead, according to Len, "there was a pretty little thirty-two-caliber hole." It was believed that Charley had been one of the four masked men who had attacked the Webber party and that while reading over the letters from home he had been so overcome by remorse that he committed suicide.

From the Hot Sulphur people we got another version of the affair. According to them, Sheriff Royer had been ordered to Denver to explain matters. He had decided to confess his part in the shooting and expose all those connected with it. To prevent him from doing so, Len Pollard was chosen to go out with Charley, kill him on the way, and make it look like suicide. Knowing Len as I did, it was difficult for me to believe that he committed the deed. I felt that he knew the affair at Grand Lake was to come off because the Redmond brothers and he had interests in some of the mines Webber was trying to jump.

Still another version of Royer's death was circulated, to the effect that Captain Dean's two sons shot him. It was said that the Dean brothers were seen hastily riding out of Georgetown the day Charley was killed. One report that came out after the killings was that the Grand Lake attackers wanted only Webber (a hangman's rope was found where they had hidden it before the attack) and that no harm was intended to Day and Dean. When Webber broke and ran, Mills, afraid that he would escape, shot him. Then Day, though covered with three guns, killed Mills, and that changed the whole situation.

Two members of the Grand Lake faction—Gil Martin and Lon Coffin—were suspected of taking part in the fracas. They were apprehended and put in our county jail, where we visited them to help pass the time until they were released for lack of evidence. At the lake feelings between the two factions ran high for some time, but with Webber gone

THE GRAND COUNTY FEUD

things gradually settled down. Since practically every major county officer was either dead or wounded, it was necessary to hold a special election before Grand County business could resume.

IX

CALIFORNIA AND YOSEMITE

Late in 1883, after a good summer and fall of sketching at Grand Lake and Flat Top Mountain, I pointed my horses' heads toward Denver. I had taken a studio on Laramie Street preparatory to a winter's work of engraving and painting and was about ready to put out my shingle when Alden Sampson, my New York artist friend, dropped in. He was planning a sketching and hunting trip and invited me to join him. My prospects of making a living that winter were exceedingly slim, and I eagerly accepted the invitation. Since it was December, the Rockies were out of the question, and Mexico was infested with bandits in those days. We finally decided on California. Loaded with sketching and hunting outfits, we boarded the Santa Fe train for Los Angeles.

In those days Los Angeles was a picturesque, semi-Mexican town. Its streets were ankle-deep in mud. We stayed at a hotel with a patio filled with tropical fruits and flowers, a striking contrast for us who had just come out of the Rockies where the snow was several feet deep.

We bought five horses: Spider, Buck, Pinto, Pink, and Rattlesnake. As soon as we had assembled our paraphernalia, we left Los Angeles, spending our first night out in Pasadena. We had decided to go up the Wilson Trail until the rainy season was over.

Shortly after leaving Pasadena, we found out that our ponies were neither pack horses nor mountain animals. Not being used to the top loads, they fell over at the least provocation. The trail ran along the ridge of a hogback, and the falling was equally good on either side. They took turns flopping off the trail and rolling down the slopes. Once they all went over in chorus, doing a free-for-all rough-and-tumble for fifty feet. Since none of them could get up with his pack on, we had to unpack each pony, lead him up to the trail, and then carry the equipment up the steep mountainside, just to repack for another fall.

Rattler damaged a foot in one of his falls, so we put the riding saddle on him and put his pack on another bronc. We had just about covered the worst part of the trail when Rattler took a last slide. Down he went, sideways and end over end. Sometimes he was ten feet off the ground. His longest plunge was approximately forty feet, and at the peak of his tumble he struck a small tree and left the saddlebags hanging on a limb. I had to climb the tree to get them, and then we proceeded down the slide to take the saddle off Rattler. As we got near the bottom of the canyon, we found that he had landed in a clump of bushes and then skidded fifteen feet more. When we finally reached him, his head and neck were wedged under a fallen log. As we lifted it off, we would have taken five dollars for him, so sure were we that he was dead. But when the log was off his neck, he slid to the bottom of the gulch and began munching grass.

In spite of our prize pack horses, in six months we traveled fifteen hundred miles through California to Yosemite. One day Sampson and I were standing on Hanging Rock at the top of Glacier Point, gazing down into wonderful Yosemite Valley.

"Yes, sir," came a voice next to us, "it's over three thousand feet from this 'ere point down inter that valley, an' ye can spit clear to the bottom in one spit!"

Turning, I saw a fine old man with long fuzzy hair and whiskers standing at Sampson's side. He proved to be no less a person than the valley's oldest inhabitant, Galen Clark, who pointed out to us all the interesting places visible from where we stood, including Half Dome.

As we looked at the peak, Clark told us how a sailor named Anderson had put a rope on the top fifteen hundred feet of Half Dome and charged a dollar to anyone who wanted to make the ascent. Anderson had died several years before, and a snowslide the preceding winter had torn down the cable. Since then many parties had attempted to scale the mountain and replace the rope, but all had failed,

and now the valley was waiting for a group of Swiss climbers to do the trick. My blood tingled, and I decided right then that no Swiss would do the job until after I had at least given it a try. Sampson felt the same way.

We camped half a mile from Glacier Point for some days, enjoying the wonderful views and riding around the valley. Finally we set up camp in Little Yosemite, the nearest approach to Half Dome. A day or so later we were standing at the bottom of the granite pitch of Half Dome. The only side that looked remotely possible to climb appeared to be as smooth as writing paper. At our feet lay the remains of the sailor's rope cable.

As we studied the face of the mountain, we saw how Anderson had accomplished his work. He had climbed up the steep grade as far as he could go, using the slightest toe hold. Then, when he could go no farther, he reached up and drilled a six-inch hole into which he worked a half-inch-diameter bolt, whose end was bent into a ring. This pin stuck out from the rock about two inches. When a pin was well secured in the granite, he attached the cable to the ring with a smaller rope. His cable had been fashioned by stringing together a number of bale ropes until the diameter was about three inches. To keep the cable from tangling, he bound it every foot with heavy twine.

Wherever it was possible to climb (and he was a master at that game), he took advantage of the toe holds. When the rock became too smooth and steep, he put in another pin, fastening the cable as he went. Anderson had built a cabin at the nearest spring, a mile away, where he had lived and kept a forge for making the bolts.

Sampson and I returned to camp after our tour of inspection, to prepare to tackle Half Dome in the morning. We gathered all the pack and picket ropes that we could spare, and both of us looked forward to the attempt with considerable excitement. We intended to use the sailor's cable, fastening it to the pins with our rope.

Early the next morning we started the ascent, climbing the first couple of hundred feet and hauling up and fastening our rope and the cable. Then we tried every expedient we could think of to negotiate the smooth, steep rock, but no matter how hard we tried we kept slipping back. Forty feet or so above our heads a rock jutted out. If we could only reach it! But there was no way. Fortunately, we had not given anyone a hint of our intentions, and no one but ourselves would know if we failed.

That was some comfort, but a mighty small one.

"I'll lasso it!" I yelled. Luckily I was a pretty fair hand with the lariat. Tying a loop on a lash rope, I made a throw. After several false pitches I finally got the range. The knot caught in a crack of the rock and stuck. It didn't look too secure to us, but I started up the steep slope, supporting my weight on the rope. Just before I could grab the projection, the knot slipped down and I slid twenty feet. While I was collecting my scattered nerves, Sampson climbed up and secured the cable. I soon followed.

We found that the slide not only had carried away almost all of the sailor's cable but also had torn out most of the iron pins and loosened several of those remaining. Wherever a number of pins were missing, the only way to reach the next one was by lassoing it and pulling ourselves up to it with the rope. Some of the remaining pins had been bent over and were difficult to rope. Often my loop would slip over the ring twenty times before it caught, even though the throws were good. Some of the pins pulled out as soon as I put my weight on the rope.

I discarded my shoes, a poor set of hobnails. When I reached a pin, I would hook my big toe over it and then straighten myself up slowly, always leaning against the stone wall. The only way I could get my toe over the ring was to double up like a jackknife, put my toe on the fingers by which I was holding to the pin, and when I was balanced, all doubled up, pull my fingers out from under my toe.

By noon we had reached the only ledge on the mountainside where we could rest, and there we ate lunch. The ledge was all of six inches wide, and we were able to push a leg down in it and rest without holding on. By the end of the first day we had made about half the distance. Just before sunset we slid down the cable, mounted our horses, and rode to camp. My feet were mighty sore, and to tell the truth I looked at that mountain with a heap of dread, though I didn't let on. Later I found that Sampson was scared, too, but since I showed no fear, neither did he.

Bright and early the next morning we were back at the starting place with all the rope we possessed. The ascent was easy as far as our cable reached, although pulling the spare rope up after us was work. But then our troubles began—everything slipped off the minute we let go of it. We had to lean against the mountain every minute, and it always seemed trying to push us away.

Early in the day my right glove got away from me and went sliding down the mountain. That made changing my weight from fingers to toe much more painful. By then we had reached a place where there were no pins, but fortunately there were a few rough surfaces. It was Sampson's turn to go ahead, since my bare feet would not cling unless I had some support. Using whatever fingerholds he could find, he at last reached a ledge which went up from his level. Clinging to small cracks in the rock, he worked a piece of bail rope from his pocket and tied it to a small shrub just above him. Then, putting just enough weight on the rope to keep from slipping, he inched along until the angle was too great and he had to let go of the rope. Then he worked himself to a little hump, cupped his hand over it, and clung there for several minutes to get his breath. Climbing up several yards more to a safe spot, he fastened the rope, and I pulled up to him.

From there on the surface was deadly smooth. There were few pins, and I had to go ahead with the lasso. About 150 feet above where I took the lead, I clung by my big toe to one pin and lay against the steep granite trying to rope the next one. A wind was blowing, which made roping difficult, but finally the rope caught. I put my weight on it, and it held. Then, just as I was about to let go of my toehold, I gave another yank, and out came the roped pin!

Luck was with me, for the next pin was only five feet above the one that had pulled out. After half an hour of throwing, the loop finally caught on the pin, and I made my way up to it and fastened the cable.

The next pin was the worst of all. It was thirty-five feet above me on a small ledge. It seemed next to impossible to make that rope fly up those extra perpendicular feet. When the loop finally settled over the pin and stayed, Sampson and I both yelled! I crawled up on my knees. Taking hold of the pin with my fingers, I wormed myself over it, got my toe over my fingers, and pulled my fingers free, losing considerable skin in the process. As I rested on the tiny ledge, leaning against the sloping granite, that hellish old mountain seemed more determined than ever to push me off.

The next pin, which was a long way above me, was still wrapped with a bundle of Anderson's broken cable. The wind had come up again, and time and time again my loop dropped over the pin only to slide off.

Finally my leg began to tremble from standing so long in one position. I had to go down or fall off the mountain. Below me the rock face bulged out. To the right it drifted toward Little Yosemite, three thousand feet down. To the left it dropped eight thousand feet into the main valley. If I slipped, there wasn't much doubt which way I'd go. If there had been anything to hang on to, I could have backed off over the ledge. Instead I had to jack-knife my body, reach down below my feet, and grip the cable just under the pin. Then I had to work my toes off the ledge, twist myself out into space, and slide down the cable to a place where I could rest.

By the time we finally reached the top of Half Dome, the sun was low. The valley was spread out below us in all its blue, hazy beauty. We sat for a while enjoying the glow of the setting sun and then built a fire, in view of the whole valley, to let people know that Half Dome had again been conquered. Reluctantly, we left one of the grandest views in the world, slid down the cable, and reached the safety of the ground just at dark.

The next day we learned that our innocent beacon on the peak the night before had disrupted the whole valley. From the valley floor people had watched the fire, which had burned for hours, since we had built it near a dead stump. Apparently they thought it was a distress signal. One watcher, a New

CALIFORNIA AND YOSEMITE

Yorker, offered a hundred dollars to any guide who would hurry up the trail to the bottom of the cliff to assure us of relief early in the morning. There were no takers.

Later in the day we met James M. Hutchings, superintendent of the valley, on his way up to rescue us. Relieved to find us safe, he thanked us for what we had done and promised to put up a permanent cable before taking down our ropes.

After our tour of Yosemite, Sampson and I sold the horses and took a train for San Francisco. Sampson headed south, but I stayed in San Francisco for about a month, visiting with the artist Edwin Deakins and his family, friends of Denver days. Then I set out by train for the trip home.

On the train I began chatting with a young preacher, and during our conversation we discovered that both of us were returning from Yosemite. After I told him about all the regions Sampson and I had visited, he said, "Well, Half Dome is one mountain you didn't climb." When I answered that I had indeed climbed it, I could tell by the expression on his face that he thought I was lying.

"What's your name?" he demanded. When I told him, he grabbed my hand, shook it vigorously, and said enthusiastically, "You *did* climb it, didn't you?" He then told me that he was one of Superintendent Hutchings' party that went up Half Dome to arrange for installing the permanent cable.

Great experiences in a young man's life can produce important changes in the direction he will take. Those two days on Half Dome were for me the division between careless youth and serious manhood. I had decided long before to be an artist; there was no other profession for me. Those hours of anxiety and danger crystallized in my mind the goals toward which I would direct my life.

X'

NEW YORK AT LAST

I can't remember a time when Father didn't have the idea that I should go to Rome or Paris to study art. He never failed to encourage me in my art studies. I never produced a drawing or a bit of modeling too bad for some word of encouragement from him. Father's reading in art literature was mostly about the Greeks and the Italians. His ideal sculptors were Phidias and Michelangelo, and he showed me pictures of their work.

Raphael was the painter he talked of most, though he liked best the works of the English animal painter Edwin Landseer, and our walls were hung with prints of the latter's paintings. They may have stirred my early interest in wild animals.

I became interested in reproductions of paintings of the French school which appeared in magazines and art periodicals. My favorites were the French battle paintings of Alphonse de Neuville; I liked

NEW YORK AT LAST

the dash, freedom, and courage with which he depicted his soldiers. I also admired Edouard Detaille, but his battle scenes had not the freedom of Neuville's.

Both in Des Moines and in Denver the only memorable sculptures I saw were cigar-store Indians, and I'm not sure that their romantic associations didn't stir me more than their artistic qualities.

In Denver, Father constantly looked forward to the time that he could send me to New York or Paris to study. He tried his hand at mining, but none of his claims produced enough income to make it possible. I decided to take up mining myself, in hopes of making a grubstake for the trip east. Assays from the mining claims Father and I sent in ran from a trace to a few dollars' worth of silver or gold, but none of our strikes were worth working.

One day in 1885, while I was visiting my family in Central City, I was induced to join my brother-in-law, John Tregoning, a practicing miner, in leasing and working a mine not far from the fabulous Bobtail Mine. The shaft was already about eighty feet down. The pay streak, galena and copper, was about eighteen inches wide and was melting ore; the crevice matter of free-milling quartz was nine feet wide.

By no stretch of the imagination could I call myself a miner, but I could work hard under the guidance of others. We were so eager for results that we often waited too close to the mine opening while the shots went off and went down into the mine too soon afterward, foolhardiness that knocked us off our feet and then made us nauseated. We soon divided the shaft and cut one side of the tunnel higher than the other, which helped clear smoke out of the mine faster.

After some time we had enough ore for a test, but

the mills gave us nothing. We went back to work for a couple of months, sinking the shaft several feet more. We knew that the crevice material carried gold, for almost any small chink would pan out color. According to all signs and comparisons with paying ore in the neighborhood, we had good prospects. But again and again nothing turned up. It appeared that if my trip east was dependent on my striking it rich at mining I might as well give up the idea for all time.

Then I remembered that my good friend the Reverend Bayard Craig had offered to buy my Grand Lake homestead. That might be the answer; at least it was worth a try. I went back to Central City, told my family of my decision, and began to pack my few belongings. Father believed that it was the right thing to do. Mother didn't want me to go so far from home but also saw the wisdom of the move.

In a few days I was in Denver unfolding my plan to Craig. His offer still stood, and we agreed upon a price. He also gave me a letter of introduction to a friend of his in New York, a Reverend Mr. Tyler. Craig handed me a first payment, and I headed for a pawnshop to buy a big English suitcase I had long admired. I could see myself walking into anybody's house where I might be invited with at least one grand possession. Then I bought a new suit, and I was ready for New York.

I left the Craig house carrying my heavy bag, having shipped ahead a trunkful of oil sketches, painting gear, and such. I had left my rifle with Craig, but my .41-caliber Colt and ammunition were in my fine suitcase.

As the train crossed the Plains, I slept in my blankets, for a tremendous blizzard was on the rampage, and the cold was intense. It took three engines to pull the train through the drifts. The engine windows were boarded up to keep out the snow—at times the leading engine was completely covered.

When the train finally pulled into Hoboken, New Jersey, I tried to look in all directions at once and was off the car almost before it stopped moving. Crossing to Manhattan by ferry, I was all eyes. Finally I set foot in the great city that had been my goal for so long. "At last," I thought, "I am where the best of everything can be had!" The date was November, 1885.

I found the home of J. Harrison Mills, my early art instructor in Denver, who had long since moved to New York. Mills was most cordial and took me in. His family was vacationing in the country, and he invited me to batch with him while I looked for a place of my own. Meanwhile, I began making regular pilgrimages to art galleries and museums. I also got in touch with Irving Hale, one of my best friends from childhood days in Denver. Hale, by then a first lieutenant of engineers, was stationed on Long Island. I also looked up Alden Sampson, whom I hadn't seen since our climbing expedition in Yosemite.

My intention was to enroll at the National Academy of Design, and I wanted to find a room near the school. Finding a suitable room with good light wasn't easy. Coming from the open spaces of the West, where there was light and fresh air every day of the year, I was hard-put getting used to dark, ill-lighted rooms. I finally found a room in a house on the west side of Fifth Avenue, between Fourteenth and Fifteenth streets. It had a small skylight that afforded fairly good light for painting and modeling.

I entered the academy at once and began drawing from casts. An artist named Willmarth was my first teacher, and I quickly found out that my rough-and-ready work did not quite accord with his smooth, painstaking style and refined tastes. I worked very seriously, however, and gradually earned his respect.

While living on Fifth Avenue, I painted a mountain snow scene showing a large bull elk in a startled position, looking back into the picture at a cougar peering through some brush. Sampson bought the painting for one hundred dollars. I never knew whether he really liked it or bought it simply to help me out.

Once I was settled, I thought it time to present Bayard Craig's letter to the Reverend Mr. Tyler, pastor of the Christian Church on Sixty-sixth Street. Mr. Tyler lived in a large house behind the church. When I arrived in front of the building, I hesitated, very much surprised to find Tyler living in such a large place. I thought, "He must be preaching just for the fun of it, or for his health." I passed and repassed the entrance several times before jacking up my courage sufficiently to approach the door and ring the bell. Mr. Tyler greeted me with a friendly smile which immediately put me at ease. I became friendly with the Tyler family and was often invited to dinner. I even joined the church and attended regularly for several years.

In June, 1886, I went to Ontario, Canada, to visit relatives with whom I had been corresponding. I first stayed with Uncle Charley Smith, who, though a Canadian, had fought with the Union troops during the Civil War. Many years before, he had visited us in Clinton, Michigan, and had given me, at the age of three, my first and last chew of tobacco.

From Uncle Charley's I went to stay with Uncle Benjamin Kerr and Aunt Isabelle, Father's sister. Uncle Benjamin was a thrifty old coot who, in addition to owning a good farm, had a fine house in Forest, Ontario. There I spent some time sketching domestic animals in oils and water colors.

Uncle Ben had no use for artists, but he held his tongue for about a month. One day I asked him if I could sketch a certain wild heifer that had never been handled. Then he let out on me. A husky young chap like me fiddling around with paints! Why didn't I get a real job and do some work? Then he remarked scornfully, "Yes, you can paint the heifer —if you can catch her!"

That was a challenge I couldn't pass up. In the barn I found a good rope and made a lariat. When I edged up to the heifer to corner her, she tried to dash by me, whereupon Uncle Ben let out a derisive laugh. But just at the right instant I whirled the loop over her horns and got my right hand, holding the rope, behind my hip, cowboy fashion. At the precise moment that she reached the end of the rope, I threw my weight on it, and the heifer went over on her back. After that Uncle Ben made no more cracks about painters, and we were good friends.

After several months I returned to New York, taking a two-room-and-kitchen apartment on Thirty-sixth Street with a chap named Billy Amsden, whom I had met the previous year. Three things drew Billy and me together: he had recently come from southern Colorado; his best friend, a fellow named Hunt, had also been a friend of mine; and we were both poor.

My second winter in New York I spent drawing at the Art Students' League, then situated on Fourteenth Street. James Carroll Beckwith was our instructor in antique-drawing, and under him I really began to learn how to draw. Beckwith was a competent artist, but he was a hard taskmaster. Whenever he came into the room, everybody sat up and took notice, and there was complete silence. One day he entered in a quick, nervous way, and all of us realized that something was bothering him. The first easel he came to belonged to a student who had ideas of his own and was not backward about expressing them. Beckwith pointed out something radically wrong with the drawing, whereupon the boy answered rather testily that he had been told to do it that way at the last criticism, and that, anyway, he thought the drawing was about right. Well,

NEW YORK AT LAST

every student perked up his ears, and those who could see the drawing were all eyes. The dressing down that fellow got was the worst I ever heard east of Denver.

When the league moved to Twenty-third Street, between Lexington and Third avenues, we had much more room, and many new students joined the classes. It was in my drawing class that I became acquainted with Seymour Thomas, a master draftsman. Seymour later went to Paris, where he lived for many years and secured many honors, among them the Legion of Honor. Not long afterward I met several other students who subsequently made names for themselves, among them C. C. Curran, Granville Smith, and William Whitmore.

With the approach of spring, 1887, it became more difficult for me to keep working in the studio. My thoughts kept wandering to the Rockies—and the deer, elk, sheep, and bears. Just as I was beginning to feel that I couldn't take another year in New York, Providence came to my rescue. Carleton Wiggins, the well-known painter of domestic animals, sent around a man who wanted some small color prints of wild animals for cigarette packages. The job netted me three hundred dollars, which, with some money I had saved from portrait fees, paid my

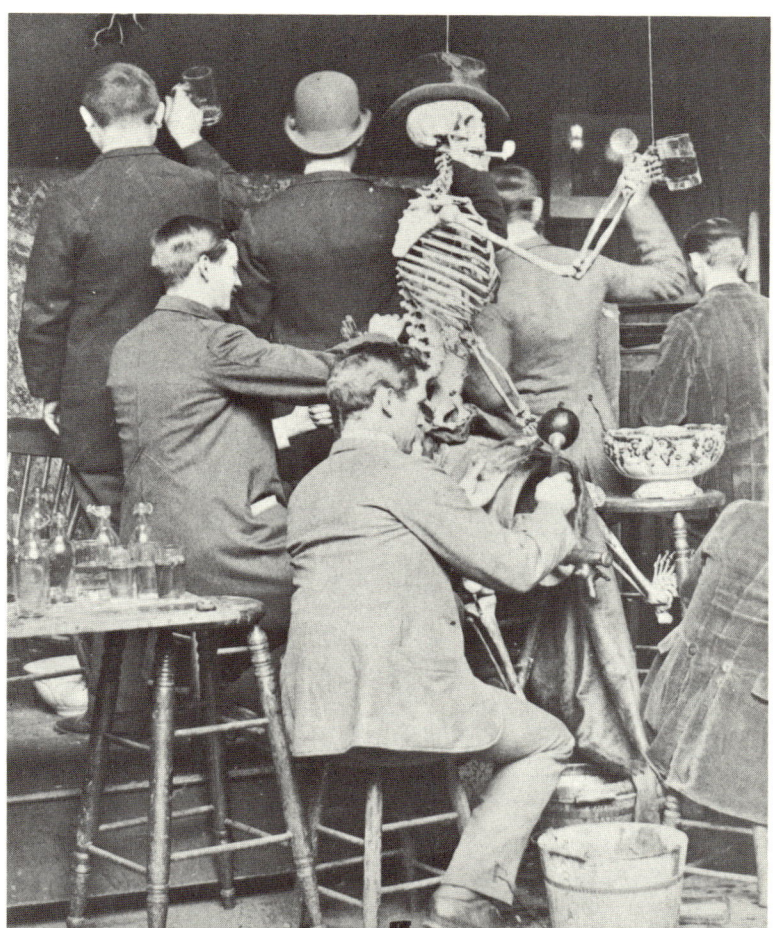

Proctor (bottom, center) attending class at the Art Students' League, New York, 1887

87

way back to Colorado, with enough left over for a sketching trip in the mountains.

XI

LONE CAMP IN THE FLAT TOPS

During the summer of 1887, Bayard Craig and I hunted in the Flat Tops, in western Colorado, for six weeks. Then we learned that Ute Indians had broken out south of us. Craig, a married man with a family, decided to return to Denver, but I was determined to stay. Having returned from New York that spring to enjoy the outdoors, I didn't want to lose any time at it, savages or no savages. Since there was no grub left at camp, I had to ride to Egeria Park, forty miles away.

Just as I had finished packing my pony at the little store, an excited rancher rode up. He had seen seventeen Indians headed for my camping country. The people at the store urged me to stay; they couldn't understand why I wanted to go alone right into country where the Indians were headed.

Striking out on foot and leading my pack pony, I arrived at the ranch of my friend John Elliot just before dark. John was much disturbed by the news, the first he had heard that Indians were so near. His father had been murdered by the Utes nine years before to the day. We decided to say nothing about the Indians to his mother. The mere mention of them made her tremble, and the sight of one made her ill. John kept a couple of cowboys on guard all night, but happily nothing happened.

The next morning I was off to my camp under the Flat Tops rim, keeping a sharp eye out all the way. When I arrived, I took my Winchester and circled camp to see whether there were signs that anyone had been there, but all was in order.

I was on my way back to camp when I saw something moving. Not forty yards away was a big grizzly walking parallel to me. The bear saw the movement as I threw my rifle to my shoulder and started toward me to investigate. Just as he began to bristle, I pulled the trigger. At the crack of the gun old Cuffy let out a roar and fell backward down a bank. I let go again. Another echoing bawl broke loose as he pitched out of sight. I cautiously worked forward, followed by my two dogs. I didn't relish the idea of going up to a wounded grizzly in the gathering dusk, but it was necessary. Suddenly the bear rose up, and I let go another blast. The next shot sent him down for good. The next day I spent sketching the bear propped up in a lifelike pose.

Usually when I shot an animal for study or food, I did so in the evening and left it where it fell for the night. The next day I rode back to the spot, made what sketches I wanted, and then packed the carcass back to camp on my saddle. On the evening of September 24 I shot my fifth deer of the trip and the next morning found that a marauding bear had helped himself, ruining the deer for meat and for sketching. The bear had carried the deer about a quarter of a mile and had then dragged it another quarter of a mile into a willow thicket, where he had eaten a full meal. I made up my mind that Bruin must pay for his sins. That afternoon I hid near the carcass on a small knoll, which commanded quite a range of landscape. At first I sketched the Flat Tops, meanwhile sweeping the mountains with my eyes. As the sun went down, I put the sketch away and, rifle in hand, kept a close lookout. Finally twilight came, but no bear. There was not a sound. Finally I said to myself, "I'll count ten." I strung the last number out to give the bear the benefit of the doubt. Then, "Well, I'll count another ten." Finally I drew a bead on a bush. Yes, I could still see the ivory sight.

Then, swinging the gun a little to the left and uphill, I saw the bear, a beautiful big one, a hundred yards away. A small sapling was just in line with his heart, but I figured that the tree was so close to him it would not deflect the bullet even if I hit it. Bang! went the .44-70 Sharps. The bear, who was side-on when I fired, wheeled around, and, giving a big leap, struck the tree and broke it off where the bullet had gone through it. Then he tore down the mountainside directly toward me. I hastily loaded and ran back ten feet to a spot which would give me a clear space to shoot in, if he came on. The old boy plunged through some willows. Then he was out of sight, but I could tell where he was by the swaying of the brush tops. Suddenly the agitation ceased. Cautiously I walked along the ridge, watching the willows closely. Nothing happened. Presently I saw what looked like his head and fired. The bullet hit the object, which proved to be the bear's hind foot. He was dead. The first bullet had penetrated his heart, and yet he had run seventy-five yards before he died.

In the middle of one pitch-black night there was a terrible commotion as both dogs broke from under the low canvas lean-to in a furious rush. Sitting up, I grabbed my rifle. In a few seconds the dogs began barking furiously some distance away. Then there was a loud yelp, and Blackjack, the pup, came rushing back, bolted into the shelter, and dug right under my blankets, whining and shivering. Shine, the braver of the two, kept barking frantically, and then I heard the crashing and breaking of brush, and a fierce "Woof!" of a bear. Back and forth bear and dog rushed. Then, to my dismay, they came in short dashes to within a few feet of the tent. I felt sure that in an instant both would be on top of my low canvas roof and all over me, but I wasn't happy about getting out and into the battle in the dark.

My heart was beating violently. The dog yelped as the bear connected, then there was a fierce snarl as Shine took a nip at the bear. Then one of them fell against the corner of the canvas, nearly tearing it loose. I brought up my gun, ready to shoot but fearful of hitting the dog. Suddenly, to my immense relief, the battle melted away in the direction of a nearby creek. There was a double splash—both had evidently fallen over the ten-foot bank into a pool. After a while Shine came into the lean-to, trembling and breathing hard. He was dripping wet and had several gashes in his hide, but he didn't seem to be seriously hurt. I built a big fire and washed the wounds on Shine's shoulder and rump. I patted the

old boy. He knew he had done his duty, and that pleased him greatly.

Deciding to move into new sketching and hunting country, I moved five miles nearer the summit of the mountain, making camp in a thick clump of spruce as a protection against the storms that come up quickly at that altitude. I set up my lean-to so that prevailing winds would strike the back and then piled boughs against the sides.

Before long there was a six-inch snowfall, which gave me an opportunity to study forms and color against snow. One morning, as I was tramping up the mountain through a long draw between spruce ridges, something in the distance attracted my attention. While trying to make out what it was, I

raised my rifle into position. Just as the front sight reached the spot, I made out the head of a panther and pulled the trigger. When I got up to the spot, a beauty of a cat was lying in the snow. It took me some time to discover that the bullet had entered the brain through his left eye, leaving not the slightest mark. I brought the pony up and snaked the cat to camp on the snow, and then spent the rest of the day sketching him.

The following day I was doing a color study of the panther when a guide and his tenderfoot hunter came into camp. I was under the lean-to, and neither of them saw me. The sportsman was in the lead. When he rounded the shelter, he found himself face to face with the panther. He gave a frightened snort and took a backward bound that would have done credit to a deer, nearly knocking over his guide.

When they calmed down, I invited them to lunch. Throughout the meal they looked with longing eyes at my bearskins and the panther, as well as my collection of elk and deer antlers.

After many more days of hunting and sketching, I gave up my post as lord of the region and broke camp. Heading out of the high mountains, in two days I made Morrison's summer cattle camp, where I knew the foreman, Charley Moses. With Moses at the camp were two cowboys, Texas Jack and Tony.

Going around the corner of the cabin one day, I saw Tony among the pines. He ducked and made a quick movement as though he were hiding something, but I didn't think much about it. Back in my cabin I looked for my six-shooter. It was gone. Immediately I told Charley. Calling Tony, he said, "Where's that six gun?" Tony said he knew nothing about it. "Get your rope, Jack!" Charley barked. "This coyote stole Mr. Proctor's gun."

"Now, kid," said Charley, "in fifteen minutes you hand over that gun or you go up on a limb. Can't stand stealing in a cattle camp." Tony fidgeted and

LONE CAMP IN THE FLAT TOPS

whined, but Charley just looked at his watch. Five minutes passed. Jack began uncoiling his rope. Another five minutes went by. Tony began to show signs of weakening. Finally he owned up to the theft just as Charley snapped shut his watch and reached for the rope. I don't know whether they would really have strung up Tony, but the threat had the desired effect.

My sketching vacation over, I sold the pony to Charley for thirty dollars. He arranged for a ride for me, with my trophies, to the railroad, where I flagged a freight train and loaded my duffel, horns, and skins into the caboose. I was off for Denver on my way back to New York.

XII

THE FAWN AND THE PANTHER

Whenever autumn came, I was as eager to return to New York as I was to go west in the spring. I had first left Colorado with some misgivings, but now I was gaining self-confidence. I knew that my work was improving, I had made some good friends, and my efforts were not going unnoticed.

On my return to the East in the fall of 1887, I began to do more modeling. I had met John Rogers, the famous sculptor, and I became a frequent visitor at his home and studio. He urged me to take up modeling more seriously. It was through Rogers that I acquired facility in manipulating clay and making the armatures needed in the modeling of wild animals. It was his interest and encouragement that started me on the little fawn that was to become so very important in my life.

One day as I was passing through the deer house at the menagerie in New York, I noticed a new ar-

THE FAWN AND THE PANTHER

rival. She was a pretty whitetail fawn, not many days old. I stopped to get acquainted. Sensing a friendly presence, the trembling little thing came close and tried to reach me. Opening the paddock, I went in and gently patted her. She snuggled close and rubbed me with her dainty muzzle. I sat on my sketching stool and stayed with the baby for some time, studying her young form. Suddenly the idea flashed through my mind that I would make a model of her in wax.

Hurrying back to my studio, I made a small armature. For a support for the body I used a small piece of wood and then securely fastened wires to it for legs and neck. Over all, the model was but seven inches high. Then I made a small stand high enough to work at while sitting down.

So equipped, I went back to the menagerie and set up my equipment. The little fawn watched what I was doing, brushed against me, and sniffed at my ears. I had to be careful to keep her from pushing over and breaking the model. When I wanted her to pose, I'd take the little animal and stand her the way I wanted, either placing her legs in the proper position or turning her head. I had to do most of the work sitting down, both because of the size of the paddock and because my model was so small I

could not see much when I stood up. Since the light was not always right, I often had to do my work after feeling the fawn.

The fawn was most co-operative. The only distraction was curious people who stopped to watch. I soon found out that they would move on if I looked at their feet. Without saying a word, I would stare at their shoes, then look off into the distance, only to stare again at the ground where they were standing. Why it worked, I don't know, but it did.

After days of working on the little figure and days of suffering the jibes of my friends, who thought I was wasting my time, I finished my model and had it cast. An old French plaster molder did the work for me, making the mold in glue so that I was able to save the original wax.

Soon after I finished the tiny fawn, Henry Stimson's grandmother used her influence to persuade *Harper's Weekly* to print a photograph of it. One hunter offered me fifty dollars for the little statue, if I would agree to have but one cast made of it. Luckily I did not accept the offer since the fawn had cost me much more than that to make.

Shortly after I had finished the plaster cast, Frederick Delenbaugh, an old-time Denver friend and by then a well-known painter and writer, saw it and showed it in the yearly exhibit of the Century Club. Only members were supposed to exhibit in the showing, but he thought that there would be no objection. It was a great occasion for me, for I met many well-known artists who became good friends, among them Frank D. Millet, who was later instrumental in obtaining for me my first major commission.

Having begun modeling, I started group after group of both animals and Indians, but many were never finished, and most were later destroyed or lost. Wax, or American plasteline, as it was called, cost about fifty cents a pound. I seldom could afford enough to model all the subjects I wanted to do. Often I had to destroy one model to use the wax for some other figure. Many times I dug wax out of the inside of a figure and filled the space with blocks of wood, leaving only the outside surface. I was also handicapped by not having a regular studio where I could work and store my materials.

About the time I started the statue of the little fawn, I also began a statue of a panther. In the menagerie were two beautiful specimens. Grace and her mate were always on the move, and the only way I could get them was in motion. Some time before, I had struck upon a way of getting a picture of a whole action. Once while I was standing between two buildings, I looked up just in time to see a boy dash from behind one building to the other with arms and legs extended. Applying this experience to the study of animals, I found that I could get an action picture by closing my eyes, opening them for a split second, and then shutting them again. I practiced this exercise until I arrived at the point where I could retain the picture long enough to do a rough sketch. It was in this manner that I made the sketches for my panther.

One day as I was sketching close to the bars of the panthers' cage, I carelessly turned my back on my models to get better light on the drawing. Suddenly I felt needle-sharp pains in my shoulder. Leaping away from the cage, I turned to see the big

male cat's foreleg—at least six feet long, it looked to be—stretched through the cage, *my* blood dripping from his claws. Then and there I learned an important lesson for an artist: never turn your back on a wild four-legged model!

I made the wax model of the panther from my penciled sketches in the studio of the Art Students' League. Although I did modeling both at the league and at the National Academy of Design, no one at either institution knew much about or was much interested in wild animals. I was on my own. My model of the panther, which was subsequently named *Fate*, was three feet long and about a foot high.

While working on the model for *Fate*, I began dissecting cats so that I would be less baffled in trying to reproduce the flexing muscles of felines such as panthers, tigers, and lions. I had taken a workroom with W. W. Deming, the painter of Indians, in the Holbein Studios on Fifty-fifth Street between Sixth and Seventh avenues. The studio was over a stable, up two flights of stairs. George Inness, the painter, occupied two large rooms at the back, and opposite him was his son-in-law, Jonathan Hartley, the sculptor. The painters Frank V. Dumond and Henry Durth were on the same floor. Like many sections of New York, our neighborhood was infested with cats. Two bits was the price I paid to the lads of the streets for a live specimen.

I became acquainted with the clerk in a local drugstore, and he supplied me with poison for the cats. I don't remember the various brands of quick death I tried, but upon the advice of a chemist I switched to cyanide of potassium. I didn't enjoy the execution business but felt that it served a useful purpose.

When the victim was dead, I removed the skin. Before the muscles became rigid, I posed the cat in position and made many drawings; then I made a plaster cast of it.

About this time a cougar died at the menagerie. Charles Knight, the animal and bird painter, bought the carcass and let me dissect it and make a number of plaster casts in a storeroom of the Natural History Museum, where he was then painting.

It also occurred to me to model an elephant. Bill Snyder, the keeper at the menagerie, let me work in the pen with the elephants, which was a satisfactory arrangement as long as he stayed with me. One day, however, Bill had to leave for a short time. I continued to work. When I had finished, I decided that rather than backing out between the bars at the front of the cage and then walking around the building, I would go right through between two of the three elephants in the paddock. Carrying my model and stand, I was passing between the two monsters when one became angered about something. Whirling about, it rushed me, its trunk high in the air.

Although scared stiff, I didn't let on but calmly waited for the elephant to make the next move. The beast let out a steamboat scream right in my face that nearly blew my head off. Though I was deafened, I spoke the animal's name, said a few gentle words, and marched on, expecting every minute to be flattened to the floor. I wasn't molested again, but later Bill told me that I was a damn fool to have moved at all, and I decided he was right. Several years later the model was cast in bronze and named *Trumpeting Elephant* [see page 219].

XIII.

ANOTHER SUMMER IN THE MOUNTAINS

The summer of 1888 found me once more in Colorado. I had talked my preacher friend, Bayard Craig, into inviting me for a nice long hunting trip, during which I expected to spend much time studying and sketching wild animals. With two pack mules and two ponies we went over the Caribou Trail to Grand Lake. We wanted to go to Lost Lake, which was situated in thick spruce timber upon a ridge, not in a valley, where a well-ordered, conventional lake should be. Few people knew how to reach Lost Lake, but everyone had heard about the wonderful fishing there.

About the time we were ready to go, an "outsider" hired old Ike Alden to guide him to the lake, and they set out ahead of us. Since none of us had ever been there, it was a gamble that any of us would find it. Sure enough, Ike and his fellow traveler lost their bearings, and Craig and I overtook

them before we reached the hogback divide between Grand Lake and Lost Lake. The four of us pitched camp together in a beautiful grassy spot close to a rushing stream. While on the ridge, I counted the small creeks between us and the Lost Lake stream and located it well in my mind. Then I followed it to the lake with my eyes. The outsider was terribly keen to lead the party to the lake, but I had my doubts about his abilities.

Early the next morning the four of us started for the lake through the woods. I went along until it was obvious that the outsider was lost, and then I dropped behind. As soon as the others were out of sight, I slipped back, went downstream to the fourth creek, and followed it straight to Lost Lake. After a while I heard shots and answered in kind. When the rest of the party arrived, having followed the sound of my shots, they were quite surprised to find me there.

At the lake we had a fine day's fishing, the trout running from one to two and a half pounds. That evening we were hurrying down the mountain in the dusk when Craig fell, throwing his Winchester ahead of him. It landed with the muzzle pointing back, and the hammer, which was at half cock, struck a rock and broke the trigger dog, discharging

ANOTHER SUMMER IN THE MOUNTAINS

the gun almost in his face and blowing his hat off. Fortunately my friend was not seriously hurt, though it took me an hour to dig the powder out of his face. The little adventure so unnerved him that he decided to abandon the trip. We returned to Grand Lake and parted.

I decided to take the two mules, a horse, and two setters and head out by myself for the old White River Ute Reservation, a couple of hundred miles to the south. The first part of the journey was along the main road to Egeria Park, where I struck off on old Indian trails through Burns Hole country. It was slow going because I had all the work to do myself—packing and unpacking the mules, unsaddling the pony, picketing the animals, cooking my grub, doing the dishes. At night the tent bed had to be pitched and all the duffel stored.

One afternoon I passed over White River, riding along a high, flat-timbered ridge interlaced with open, grassy parks which were joined by partly wooded runways. The sun was getting low, and there was a dreamy loveliness over the landscape. A forest-clad range of mountains with snow-capped peaks made the southern boundary of my view. My pony and the mules were moving along, occasionally nipping off the tops of the high grass. Even the dogs had caught the drowsy spirit of the occasion.

Tarantula, the lead mule, was fastened to my saddle horn by several turns of his lead rope. The other mule was trailing as we wandered along in Indian file. We were all evidently dreaming the same dream when my pony exploded with a frantic buck. I was thrown to one side but managed to hang onto the saddle horn. My mount was not only bucking but kicking out in all directions, biting himself and bawling. Both mules joined the concert with the same racket and antics. My pony milled, and so did the mules. Hoofs flew about everywhere. Then the dogs took up the tune, yelping, rolling, and biting themselves. Then it dawned on me what the trouble was—hornets!

My pony went into the worst bucking gyrations I have ever seen or experienced. He'd jump five feet in the air, sidewheel, and whang at his right ear with his hind foot. If I happened to be falling on that side, I'd get it. Or, while spinning, he'd try to bite between his hind legs. At first I was afraid I'd fall off; then I was afraid I wouldn't. Suddenly I left the pony and landed on Tarantula, just in time to get another trip up in the midst of cans and cooking equipment mixed with the contents of a twenty-five-pound bag of flour that had broken open.

Hornets!

ANOTHER SUMMER IN THE MOUNTAINS

The second time down I landed right in the source of our troubles—a hollow log filled with angry hornets. That log didn't vomit hornets; it volcanoed them. I was up and out in a jiffy, pawing the varmints from my face. Luckily water wasn't far away, and we all made for it—man, pony, mules, dogs—and hornets. After a while the pests gave up, but not until we had plenty to remember them by.

After weeks of solitary travel I reached the old Ute reservation, truly a happy hunting ground. The spruce and aspen covering the mountains were traversed in many directions by narrow grassy parks or meadows, and this meant fine country for game of all kinds. Through every valley and gulch ran a creek. There were game, wood, water, and grass everywhere. In a sheltered spot on the bank of a pretty creek I dumped packs and saddles, and in a few minutes the animals were knee-deep in juicy grass. With my tent up, I was ready for a long stay.

The next morning I shot a nice buck deer within a quarter of a mile of camp and promptly posed him for a model. That set the pattern for days to come. There was no sign of human beings in the daytime or campfires at night; the country was truly "mine." Every evening five buck deer came to feed in a small park about a quarter of a mile away. One of them was a gigantic old boy that made the others look like does.

One day while I was sketching, I saw a man approaching on horseback. So possessive had I begun to feel about my surroundings that I hurriedly pulled down my easel, dragged it into the brush, and hid until he had gone by. The stranger must have been camped a long way off, for I didn't see him again, nor did I see his campfire at night.

One evening I heard elk bugling about a mile away, which meant a fight, since it was mating time for the wapiti. Approaching the racket, I tied my hound to an aspen and climbed the tree. From my perch I could see two fine bulls charging about, but neither appeared ready to tackle the other.

Then, from a heavily timbered mountain close by, came a long bugle call. The two stags answered, and the new challenger came plunging down the mountainside. Scattered about the landscape were a dozen cow elk quietly feeding. Occasionally one of them would gaze at the rampaging bulls for a moment and then resume feeding, with no apparent interest in what was going on.

Another long bugle call floated down the mountain and was answered, and another bull charged

onto my stage. Excitement grew, both on the ground and in the tree. The stags made short rushes, but no attacks. Then two of them squared off, hesitated a moment, and dashed together. The crash was so great that I nearly fell off my perch. I expected that their antlers would cling together and that the animals would try to down each other by main force. But to the wearers those huge antlers were as light as rapiers. Each thrust was parried with as swift a movement by the other, each stag trying for a vulnerable spot in the other's defense.

I named the two combatants Bill and Jack but played no favorites. Suddenly Bill threw his antlers back and smashed them down savagely on Jack's head. Bill tried to repeat the move, but Jack, taking advantage of the opening, dashed at him ferociously, his brow points catching Bill's neck. Then, gathering all his might, Jack dashed forward, hock-deep in the turf, and threw Bill on his side.

"He's a goner!" I gasped. But no. Quick as a flash Bill was up and with a mad rush caught Jack's belly on his brow points and heaved him clear of the ground. Jack landed on his feet, whirled, charged, and caught Bill in the side. Blood covered Bill as the two of them rolled over each other. In a minute they were on their feet, horns locked in deadly struggle.

ANOTHER SUMMER IN THE MOUNTAINS

Meanwhile, the other two bulls charged frantically about but didn't clinch.

Without warning still another bull plunged head down into the two fighters. Staggering, they broke away. Now there were five magnificent stags charging about menacing each other.

Suddenly the field was clear. All the animals had apparently moved through an opening into another park. As soon as I was sure they were gone I went down onto the battlefield looking for broken pieces of antlers. Then I heard a noise, and, looking in the direction the elk had gone, I saw a pair of antlers coming my way. I pulled the dog to me and dropped to one knee, just as the dim shape of another pair of antlers appeared. Soon there were five shadowy forms around us. The dog was trembling but quiet. Two of the wonderful creatures passed, circling, each taking several majestic strides and turning his head as if to study me. Then all of them whirled and crashed through the brush, plunging first to the right and then to the left into darkness.

Shouldering my rifle and calling the dog, I headed back to camp. A full moon came out, and on a barren hilltop I found a set of blanched elk horns, probably the result of an earlier combat such as the one I had just witnessed.

The season was wearing on. Soon snow would be flying, and I didn't want to be caught too far from a wagon road. Denver and New York again began to occupy my thoughts. With my grub running low, I reluctantly decided that the day had arrived to take my tent down and break camp. I placed sketches and paraphernalia in panniers, packed so that their weights were equal, arranged swing ropes and packsaddles, tied cinches to lash ropes, rolled up pelts into convenient rolls, and secured the antlers I had found to one of the skittish mules.

Finally I was ready to start. Since packing and unpacking were so difficult, I made no midday stops. After several days of travel I hit a trail of horse tracks. Following it a couple of miles, I came to a small cabin. As I approached, I saw a man behind a wagon, resting his gun on the bed and pointing it directly at me. I raised one hand, and he came forward to me. "Hell, mister, I damn near shot ye!" he said. "Injuns is about, and I took ye fer one." He was the first settler to locate in that region, and he had come up from White River, just over the range.

After many more days, I came out into rough, rather open country. A cold wind had begun to blow, and my fingers were numb as I fumbled with rope knots in the dark. The sky was perfectly clear, and I decided not to put up my tent. Rolling up in my blankets, I went to sleep without supper. In the middle of the night I awoke, wondering why the blankets were so heavy. As I threw them back, a load of snow fell in my face.

In the morning the snow was fourteen inches deep and still coming down. Dragging myself out of the blankets, I went around kicking the snow off my scattered duds. The campsite was a poor one, but I decided to stay until the storm blew over and put up the tent. By nightfall the storm had let up, leaving twenty inches of snow on the ground.

The next morning all the ropes were as hard as iron, and the animals objected to having frosty saddle blankets put on them. When I'd finally get a pack on a mule, my numb fingers couldn't tie a decent knot. Catching a stiff, frozen rope into the hook of the lash cinch for the diamond hitch was a two-man job under the best of conditions; in the immediate circumstances it was a four-man stunt, with only me to manage it. It made a person think about the wisdom of packing out alone. Finally I got the animals loaded after a fashion.

Little of consequence happened on the slow journey over the main range. Then, within twenty miles of Denver, a fierce blizzard blasted directly

ANOTHER SUMMER IN THE MOUNTAINS

into our faces. By nature animals hate to face into a storm, and it was difficult to keep mine pointed in the right direction. We had to break trail through constantly increasing drifts, and we bucked snow belly-deep on the animals for three days before we finally stumbled into Denver.

XIV

WASHINGTON AND THE CASCADES

Back in New York, I spent the winter months of 1888–89 studying and working. My usual practice was to go to the menagerie very early, work at the league later in the morning, and model in the afternoon. I also went to the Metropolitan Museum of Art as often as I could. My visits led me to realize that the best of the ancient Greek sculptors had eliminated all tool marks and evidence of method, especially in the Parthenon sculptures, and I strove to emulate them.

Throughout my life, through the study of nature and other sculptors' works, I have been fortunate in discovering technical methods which I could use to advantage. One day at the Metropolitan Museum I drifted into the Egyptian section. There I came upon some small birds and other objects carved in soft stone. I was simply amazed at the beauty of design and modeling. After I had studied them for a long time, it suddenly dawned on me that, in addition to great skill, the sculptor must have had wonderfully fine and delicate tools. I decided then and there that I was going to remodel and reshape all my tools so that I could gain a much finer control. I did so and immediately began to see an improvement in my work.

I also worked with water colors. A painting I entered in a contest held by the Water Color Society came within four votes of winning the prize. The painting, of a cougar, received a bronze medal at the Pan-American Exposition in Buffalo, New York, in 1901. It was later bought by Cottier and Company and later still by George D. Pratt, of the Pratt Institute.

During my years in New York I spent many pleasant hours in the home of Henry Stimson's father, and there I met a number of influential people, among them Gifford Pinchot. Pinchot and I became the best of friends. In his later life I made a bronze bas-relief for him [see page 250]. I also met the artist Abbott Thayer, whose work I much admired. Thayer had heard that I was a hunter and wanted to discuss with me the protective coloration of wildlife. He had seen a small oil painting I had done of a cougar, in which the white under part of the animal's belly appeared not to be in shadow. I explained that this was nature's trick to make the killer less easily visible to his prey. In my outdooring I had learned many of nature's less-well-known devices, and I portrayed them in my art.

During this time I sold a picture of a bull elk in the high mountains. An art critic commented that the hind legs of the elk were too long. He didn't know that elk and deer are provided by nature with longer hind legs than they seem to need and that the legs are somewhat bent. I had concluded that the hind legs are so constructed that, when surprised, the animal does not have to crouch to make a leap; one movement starts him forward instantly.

Many years later, in 1935, while hunting brown bear in Alaska, I saw a demonstration of my theory. My guide and I had ascended a swift river, and, coming to a small stream that flowed into the larger one, we found bear tracks with the water still roily in them. While inspecting the tracks, we saw a beautiful buck deer walking up the river to hide his scent. We stood perfectly still, and the animal came within three paces of us and then stopped to look around. We were in full view and so close that we could see the animal's every eyelash. The wind was blowing from him to us so that he could not scent us, and, though keenly alert, he evidently felt no danger in our presence. Suddenly the guide threw his hands into the air and jumped forward. Without the least sign of a downward preparatory movement, the buck leaped sideways from the water, cleared a six-foot bank, and was gone. His naturally bent hind legs acted like a bow, shooting him up and away like an arrow.

In the late 1880's young artists considered it a great honor to have their works handled by N. E. Montross, the noted art dealer. The first time he invited me into his sanctum at the back of his gallery was quite an event. He had not yet offered any of my paintings or sculptures for sale, although he seemed interested in my work. He was a good friend to me on more than one occasion, and he always gave me sound advice. When I was to be in the West for a summer, he insisted that I place the models of my fawn and panther in a storage vault for safe-keeping. In 1890 he sold one of my pictures to the brother of Vice-President Levi Parsons Morton (later governor of New York). It was a small oil painting of two panthers lying in the grass, with low blue mountains in the distance. One of the cats was on his back asleep, the other was on the lookout.

In the spring of 1890 through Montross I met Sir

William Van Horne, president of the Canadian Pacific Railway, who gave me a station-to-station pass over his railroad from Quebec to Vancouver. The pass was good for six months' continuous travel back and forth on engines, passenger trains, or hand cars. Since my family had moved from Denver to the state of Washington, I decided that I would head there for the summer.

When I arrived at Snohomish, Washington, in the early summer of 1890, I found my brother George about to start on a prospecting trip. The Great Northern Railway was just approaching the townsite of Everett, and there was great activity in real estate, lumbering, and mining. George and a friend, Alex McCartney, were interested in mining claims both in Monte Cristo Park and in the Skykomish River country. I caught the fever, too, and when a young friend of the family named Ed begged to go along, I remembered my early desires and consented. The four of us set out on foot for the mountains, carrying packs on our backs.

It was my first back-pack mountain trip, and when I started, my pack weighed about seventy-five pounds. George kept hinting that I had better leave some articles behind, but I was sure my pack was the smallest I could get along with. However, the morning after our first camp, I left several articles on a log, and for some mornings after, I left a few things behind, until my outfit, except for sketching materials, was about as light as George's. I quickly learned what was absolutely necessary and what was not. When you must carry everything on your back through ferns, briars, and brush as thick as the hair on a bear, through forests so heavy that the branches constantly grab at you, over logs piled every which way, and up mountainsides so steep that you can climb them only by using your feet and hands at once, then "necessary" becomes a very flexible word.

After several days we arrived at the spot on the Skykomish River where we planned to set up camp. From this spot George and his partner intended to prospect, and I to prospect and sketch. In spite of the popular idea that prospecting is more exciting than sketching, it was on this trip that I nearly lost my life, a few days after we made camp.

On the other side of a steep mountain close by was a deep valley. From a distance I had seen mountain goats there, and I was determined to sketch them. I set out with Ed, taking my long-barreled revolver. The going was rough. At the top of the mountain I shot a young billy goat and added his

WASHINGTON AND THE CASCADES

carcass to all the gear I was already lugging.

Finally, below us appeared my sketching ground. I rested the dead goat on a rock level with my head and for many minutes stood looking down. I was standing at the top of a steep, rooflike ridge, which sloped down seventy-five or eighty feet to the edge of a sheer, thousand-foot canyon wall. About six feet above the brink a stunted shrub was growing from a crevice in the rocks. In the depths of the valley the treetops merged in a bluish haze. Down the main canyon I could see a glacier. Half a mile above us was another ice field, and there I saw a fine flock of fourteen mountain goats. Two little billies were having what I supposed was a fight. They stood side by side, the head of one at the tail of the other, and then one hauled off and whanged the other in the flank with his nubbin of a horn.

Higher up I spotted a bear moseying along. Twenty yards above him was a big billy goat, rambling in the same direction at the same pace. Neither animal paid any attention to the other. After a while Bruin stopped at an old snag of a tree and ripped off the bark in search of grubs. Finally, both disappeared over the summit.

I was enjoying the beauty spread out before me when suddenly I was in the air, pitching headlong

Short Cut to Kingdom Come

into the abyss. The dead goat had fallen from the rock and knocked my feet from under me. My first thought was to grab a bush as I plummeted down. My second was to protect my head when I struck the rocks below. I didn't succeed, and when I hit, colors flitted before my eyes. Sprawled out to retard my speed, once more I smashed against the rocks. Then a bush was under me and I grabbed for it with both hands and hung on tight. When my speed checked, my feet flew into the air, and my body whirled around, coming to a jarring halt.

After a few seconds I managed to take a deep breath and look around. I must have come near fainting, for Ed's yelling seemed to waken me. I couldn't see him, and my position was so precarious that even to yell was dangerous, but I called out, "Safe!" though I didn't really think I was. I lay quietly on my back, trying to collect my thoughts and regain my strength. Nothing was visible between my feet but the misty valley. If I closed my eyes to shut out the sight, I wanted to go to sleep.

Gingerly I pulled my foot onto the rock. It skidded, and the jolt nearly tore my grip loose from the shrub. I noticed a crack running from the bush to the edge of the cliff. Into this crevice I pushed my right heel and, holding my breath, put on pressure. My heel slipped, but I tried again, and the second time my foot held. I couldn't make a quick move for fear the branches would break or my heel would slip. I pushed myself up one inch, and then one more. Then, by twisting my neck, I was able to see my hands. The smallness of those two fists full of twigs almost threw me into a panic, but again I pushed and gained an inch. My heel slipped a little, and I thought everything was over.

I had to get a higher hold on the bush. Would the branches in one hand alone hold me? Clinging tightly with my left hand, I slowly opened my right one. Those branches, freed, snapped into place with such force that I thought everything had let loose. Swiftly but carefully I grasped the stem nearer the roots with my right hand. Slowly I worked myself up. At long last, after what seemed eternal hours, I was on the upper side of the bush. Fate was with me again, for Ed had been carrying our rope, and he snaked the end of it down to me. I got hold of the rope with one hand, then the other, and finally made my way up the smooth rock.

After a long rest on safe ground away from the cliff edge, I felt like continuing our quest for mountain goats. They were still where we had spotted them, and we climbed steadily to the ice field.

WASHINGTON AND THE CASCADES

Sneaking through a cedar thicket, we saw a tawny cougar stalking our quarry. The instant he saw us, he vanished—one second he was there, the next he was gone. Luckily the goats hadn't been aware of the cat, or they would have scattered. I watched them with my glasses and made small pencil sketches. Occasionally loose rocks would roar down the canyon, but the goats paid little attention except to look up now and then.

After six weeks in the mountains we returned to Snohomish and Seattle to enjoy a visit with the family. Three of my sisters who had been attending the University of Washington were at home, and it was a real reunion. Only William, my youngest brother, was absent, away at school. When summer was over, I returned to New York via the Canadian Pacific Railway.

The summer of 1891 found me again in Washington, and again George and I set out for the Cascades. There were just as many bushes, briars, and crags on that trip as on the previous summer, but, perhaps knowing by then what to expect from the country, I found the trip less exhausting. We camped for a while in a cabin near the Apex Mine up the Skykomish River.

One morning after several days of rain I asked Ed, who had again come with us, to take my gun outside and shoot it once to dry it out. Ed went out and looked around for a target. Seeing a knot in a tree next to the cabin, he blazed away, firing across the cabin door just as I stepped out. Luckily the knot was a couple of inches higher than my head. As it was, the explosion blew my hat off and deafened my left ear for a week. I doubt that Ed ever shot across a door again.

I spent another happy summer sketching and hunting in the Cascades. When autumn came, we broke camp and headed back to Snohomish. I had planned to return to New York, but on the way to Snohomish I received a telegram from an official of the Columbian Exposition inviting me to Chicago to do some work for the exposition, which was to be held in 1893. It was my first big commission!

XV.

THE WORLD'S COLUMBIAN EXPOSITION

I arrived in Chicago on September 27, 1891, my thirty-first birthday. Frank Millet, director of external exhibits for the exposition, met me and as soon as possible took me to the fairgrounds so that I could see what I was to do and look over possible sites for a studio. After several conferences it was decided that I would sculpture life-size animals to decorate the bridges crossing the fairgrounds lagoons. They were to include, among others, polar bears, elks, cougars, and moose, mountain lions, a cowboy, and a western Indian. In addition, the art authorities intended to make duplicates of the sculptures, and I was also to oversee that work. Eventually, thirty-seven models were completed [see pages 210 and 211].

After securing clay and other materials, I hired two associates, Lee Lowrie and John Jack. Lowrie was young and very talented, though inexperienced.

THE WORLD'S COLUMBIAN EXPOSITION

Jack knew little about methods but helped put up armatures and throw the masses of clay.

The first animal I started was a polar bear with head down. At the Chicago Zoo I made a small model, about ten inches high [see page 210]. I brought it to the studio, where my assistants and I began copying it full size. Again and again I returned to the zoo with the little model to improve on details. By the time the small model was finished, the men had carried work on the big one as far as they could. Meanwhile, I began work on the jaguar so that the men would have something to do while I finished the big model of the bear.

Since I knew little about the technique of modeling large figures, I also had that to learn as I worked. In the West I had cut up wild animals and studied their anatomy and had made drawings of many animals dead and alive. Now the important thing was to learn how best to put up and construct armatures for such large figures. Most of the other artists doing work for the exhibition had studied in New York or Paris and were familiar with the methods. So I would make the rounds of the studios, studying the techniques and examining the results. Then I would go back to my studio and apply what I had learned.

Now and then a sculptor would visit the studio and offer constructive criticism. There is a very warm place in my heart for Olin Warner, who to my mind was one of the very best American sculptors. He often dropped by and gave good advice, which I was quick to take. He had no special criticism of my construction and lines but thought that surface treatment was my difficulty. According to him, however, that was of minor importance, especially since the work for the fair was for decoration and of a temporary nature.

Another acquaintance was Edward Kemeys, the self-taught wild-animal sculptor. He was engaged in modeling grizzly bears, buffaloes, and pumas. Both he and his young wife, who was working with him, were cordial and quite helpful. Kemeys had hunted buffaloes on the plains and was full of interesting stories. He had a pleasant voice and enjoyed singing cowboy songs, accompanying himself on the guitar.

Life at the fairgrounds was fast and furious, and

all of us worked hard. Painters, sculptors, department heads, and army officers ate at a restaurant in the fairgrounds set aside for us. At the lunch hour the place was always full, and jibing and joshing were the order of the day. The painters made cartoons of everyone who dined there. John Boyle, another sculptor, was a nice chap but a big talker. A painter named Simmons made a crayon drawing of Boyle showing him with both feet in his mouth. Simmons made one of me sitting on a grizzly, smoking gun in hand, hair straight up, and looking fearfully cross-eyed. There were many clever artists, and they produced some first-rate cartoons. Kenyon Cox, Carroll Beckwith, Alden Weir, Robert Reed, William Dodge, Daniel French, E. C. Potter, Herman McNeill, Lorado Taft, Philip Mariny, and Charles Reinhart were but a few who made the time gay.

Most of the joking was good-natured, but occasionally someone got a "wee drap too much." One day Bobby Reed said something that annoyed Reinhart, who rose and angrily stalked over to Reed with the intention of knocking his block off. Bobby stood up to his six-foot-five height, which was topped with long hair and fierce bushy whiskers, and looked down at his irate antagonist. Reinhart decided on the wise course of action and went back to his seat.

The architect Charles McKim, the sculptor Augustus Saint-Gaudens, and the architect Daniel H. Burnham, chief of construction for the fair, also came to my studio. Saint-Gaudens encouraged me a great deal, as did Alden Weir and George Maynard. It was a wonderful experience for me to be associated with such leaders in American art and to have the benefit of their criticism. One day Ignace Jan Paderewski, the great Polish pianist, on tour in the United States, paid a call. He was struck by my stalking panther and also appreciated my little fawn. He said that he could not understand how the same man could model so fierce a beast as a puma and such a delicate, timid little fawn. I said that I couldn't understand how he, Paderewski, could play a crashing thunderstorm and then play a dainty little sonata to a water lily. His far too generous answer was, "I interpret; you create."

Late one afternoon I was working alone on my first large model of the polar bear. In Lorado Taft's studio next to mine one of his assistants, a girl, was working on a small model. The canvas covering of the doorway between the studios was open. I happened to be facing the open door when a figure passed, and I looked up to see a pretty girl about seventeen years old walk across the other studio. For a moment her profile was sharply defined against a large white cast like a cameo. My hand, raised for a stroke on the model, stopped in midair. I heard the assistant say, "Well, Daisy, you're late!" I quickly washed my hands and dusted off my white flannels. I had to meet that girl.

I casually sauntered into the other studio. Bessie Potter, the assistant, didn't know my name and didn't introduce me to the girl. Not to be put off, I began talking about the model Miss Potter was working on. Then I invited them to my studio. While they were looking at the bear, I stole several glances at Daisy. I suppose she noticed, but she didn't seem to mind. Then I showed them my small models, taking them out one at a time and lingering over each one as long as possible.

Miss Potter finally said that they had to go, but it seemed to me that Daisy was not eager to leave. I wanted to accompany them, but I was not dressed to go out, and that huge bear had to be bedded down with wet cloth. I gazed after them until they moved out of sight. Once it seemed to me that Daisy turned to look back, but it may only have been wishful thinking.

I returned to my work, knowing full well that I must see that girl again. I tried to tell myself that I was a fool. She would not care for me. She was much younger than I, and I was busy and was not looking for a wife. Still, her hazel eyes haunted me. I did not leave the studio until very late that evening. The memory of her kept me there until it was too dark to work.

Days passed. I wandered often into Taft's studio to get better acquainted with him and his assistants. One day a luncheon party was held for the studio workers. Dressed in our working clothes, we sat down together at a long table. *She* was there, and I managed to sit near her. I learned that her name was Margaret Daisy Gerow and that she preferred to be called by her first name. I also learned that she was a talented artist in her own right and was also working on the exposition exhibits.

One evening a gathering was held in Machinery Hall at which several artists and architects were to receive the Designer's Medal. Thousands of people filled the gigantic building. The artists met in an anteroom and marched down a long aisle to the platform where we were to sit until the awards had been presented. The moment the procession entered the hall, I began to search for Margaret Gerow. Halfway down the hall we halted, and I turned to look over the sea of faces. There she was, not five feet away, smiling at me.

She came to another studio luncheon, and once she invited me, along with a few others, to her home. That evening she showed us many photographs she had brought back from a trip to Europe. She also showed me several pictures of herself, one of which I slipped into my pocket. From then on, the last thing I looked at before I turned off my light was her picture. Then I would turn the light on again for another look. Needless to say, it wasn't long before Margaret and I were on a first-name basis.

The year before the exhibition opened, the Boone and Crockett Club built a log-cabin meeting place on a tiny wooded island in the lagoon. The island, reached only by narrow footbridge, was given over exclusively to the club. Its membership included big-game hunters of the United States, as well as a number of English sportsmen. Colonel Theodore Roosevelt, the founder and president of the club at the time, often went to the cabin. Elihu Root, Austin Wadsworth, George Bird Grinnell, Daniel Burnham, General William D. Whipple, Winthrop Chandler, Charles Deering, and other well-known sportsmen also frequented the cabin. One day I was honored by an invitation from Deering to have lunch at the club, at which time I met Colonel Roosevelt.

Later, when the club held its annual dinner and meeting in the cabin, Colonel Roosevelt asked me to attend. The place was dimly lighted with lamps and candles. On the walls hung skins of wild animals and old firearms, as well as horns of elk, bison, deer, and mountain sheep. Everybody was animated and full of good humor, and since all the members were good friends, banter and jokes were the rule. Before the meeting began, I was asked to step outside for a moment. When I was called back, they notified me that I had been elected a member of the club.

I was deeply honored by the election. More than fifteen years later I had an opportunity to repay the members by making the club's "mascot," a bronze bear's head [see page 233].

Roosevelt was tremendously interested in the club. He took an enthusiastic part in all its activities and was responsible for most of them. While he was police commissioner of New York City and governor of New York State, we always held our club meetings in New York City. When he became president of the United States, we held our meetings in Washington, D.C. Later, through Roosevelt, I was com-

THE WORLD'S COLUMBIAN EXPOSITION

missioned to do two models of buffalo heads for the State Dining Room in the White House, and after his death I did a large statue of him, *The Rough Rider*, for Portland, Oregon.

At the last meeting of the club which I attended, held in New York in 1941, Senator Jesse P. Walcott, the president, asked me to stand, saying, "There is a man here tonight who has been a member of this club longer than any other living man. Proctor's name was put up by Theodore Roosevelt at our cabin at the World's Fair in Chicago before the fair opened." Several of my friends, Henry Stimson, John Rogers, and Gifford Pinchot, had been members almost as long as I had.

One day in Chicago I had a date to lunch with Roosevelt and one or two other men at a Chicago hotel. A little before time to leave, Margaret Gerow came to the studio and invited me to lunch with her. Fearful of missing an opportunity to see her, I accepted her invitation and telephoned Roosevelt that I would not be able to meet him. In later years when he was president I often thought of that canceled luncheon date. I never told him the reason, but I am sure that under the circumstances he would have forgiven me.

By this time I had finished work on my original assignment, and I was given another commission: two statues, a mounted cowboy and an Indian scout. William Cody's "Wild West Show" was performing at the fair, and Buffalo Bill gave me a pass that admitted me to the show or behind the scenes at any time. Cowboys and Indians posed for me whenever I needed them. All Cody's Indians were genuine products of the Plains, and the cowboys were right off the western ranges.

Some of the Indians were too superstitious to pose for me. There was one fellow, named Kills-Him-Twice, whom I wanted for a model above all others. He was tall, wiry, and eagle-eyed—a warrior of the first rank. I made a six-inch study of his head from memory with pretty good results, but I wanted the final touches from life. A cowboy friend of mine helped, through an interpreter, to arrange for him to sit for me in a large tipi.

I went to the tipi early and arranged a box to work on and another for a seat. Pretty soon in marched Kills-Him-Twice, his stone war club in his hand, accompanied by six or seven braves. All the Indians sat down opposite me in a row, with Kills-Him-Twice in the middle. The model was still in the box before me, and the Indians had not yet seen it. They

scowled at me as though I were about to throw down on them.

I then took out the portrait model and placed it on the box facing the Indians. Amazement showed on every face. There in front of them was the head of Kills-Him-Twice, true to life. Hot words broke from the Indians. They had thought that I was merely going to take a photograph, which was bad enough, but to make a "real" head was going too far. Kills-Him-Twice glared furiously at me and jumped to his feet, making a move as though to demolish the model with his club.

All the Indians spoke furiously, if incomprehensibly. Then the interpreter, who really spoke very little English, said something, whereupon one of the braves dashed out of the tipi. Presently another interpreter came in, and the Indians told him what had happened. He turned to me and said that I had offended them. It was very bad medicine for me to sit there for a couple of minutes looking at Kills-Him-Twice and then take a likeness of him out of a box. According to the Indians, I had removed a part of his soul, and if I carried it away, evil spirits would harm him when he wasn't there to defend himself. It was indeed a serious matter to the Indians.

THE WORLD'S COLUMBIAN EXPOSITION

The interpreter talked to them for a while and then suggested that I pay Kills-Him-Twice two dollars. I did so, and that settled it, but he would pose no more and avoided me from then on. I had to use Jack Red Cloud, a Sioux, for my mounted Indian, instead of the fierce, majestic Kills-Him-Twice.

In Buffalo Bill's show it was the habit of the performers, who were of many nationalities, to congregate after supper in the space in front of their quarters. Clad in their native costumes for the evening performance, they wandered about or engaged in some form of amusement that suited their mood. One evening I stayed to watch this picturesque gathering. Several of the men were throwing a baseball high in the air. The person standing nearest to where it fell was supposed to catch it. Once the ball descended near me, and a cowboy and a burly, bewhiskered Cossack in full uniform dashed toward it from opposite directions. They crashed together just under the ball. As they bounced back from the impact, the ball fell on the Russian's head. Angered, the Cossack shoved the cowboy, who took it as a joke and smiled. But when the Russian shoved again, the puncher handed him a crack on the jaw that sent the Russian spinning. In an instant the pair had locked horns in the midst of the crowd. Two other Cossacks, seeing their countryman getting the worst of it, jumped to his assistance. Three against one was not according to western ethics, so two more cowboys joined in.

One of the cowboys, Johnny Miller, was tussling with Prince Somebody-or-Other, leader of the Cossacks. Johnny was getting the better of the fight when a knife flashed into view. Wheeling on his boots like a cow pony, Johnny took off for his tent. The Russian followed in hot pursuit, his red-topped boots shining and his long coattails flapping straight out behind. Dashing into his tent, Johnny seized a blanket and threw it over his adversary. Before the irate Cossack could disentangle himself, Johnny cracked him over the head with his heavy Colt.

Meanwhile, the fight raged on—a real free-for-all. Suddenly a tall, powerful figure dressed in fringed and beaded buckskin appeared. Heedless of drawn revolvers and knives, Buffalo Bill strode through the melee, knocking fighters right and left. As if by magic, quiet was restored.

The mounted Indian, my last piece of work for the exhibition, was put in place at the side of the water gate of the Transportation Building, opposite the big broncobuster. Newspapers all over the country carried pictures of my work, and I was receiving attention in all parts of the United States. Above all, my work seemed to be liked by the artistic fraternity as well. Things seemed to be coming my way. I had made some good friends and had met many important people. I was making what looked like a lot of money.

Nevertheless, I felt the need of more extensive and intensive art education. The painter Gari Melchers was one of my friends who understood what I felt and the ideals I cherished. He also knew wherein I fell short. In a kindly way Gari pointed out my failures in technique and said that, although technique wasn't the most important quality in art, it was indispensable in realizing the fullest expression of one's strivings. One day we were discussing the matter when another friend joined us. The latter became effusive about my work and said enough to fill a young man's head with inflated ideas of his own merit. Melchers said, "Yes, yes," and, looking at me, added significantly, "We know, don't we, Proctor?" I did know, and I decided to go to Paris as soon as I could.

I had seen Margaret all too infrequently, and my spirits were in constant agitation—first up, then down. One night I was invited to dinner at her house, and later we were going to a dance. The dinner passed pleasantly, but then Grace, Margaret's older sister, who was to accompany us, developed a severe headache. At first Mrs. Gerow was averse to allowing her youngest to go to a dance with a man the family did not know very well. Grace finally persuaded her that I was trustworthy, however, and off Margaret and I went.

Dancing was not one of my accomplishments, but I managed to worry through most of the evening. We decided to leave before the affair was over. Rain was falling, and we were several miles from Margaret's home. I had bribed the carriage driver to miss the road and wander about town. Margaret wondered why it took so long to reach her home, but I explained that some of the streets were undoubtedly torn up (as was usually the case in Chicago) and that the driver had to make several detours.

It was still raining when we reached Margaret's home. I left her in the cab and, taking her key, went into the house to get an umbrella. Mrs. Gerow was lying awake, waiting, as she usually did when her daughters were out in the evening. This time, hearing the door open and close and no voices, she decided that I had gone and promptly went to sleep.

THE WORLD'S COLUMBIAN EXPOSITION

Left to ourselves, Margaret and I went into the dining room, where we found strawberries and cake. I had intended to make known my feelings toward her, while we were in the carriage, but I hadn't had the courage. Here was my chance. How I blessed the strawberries and cake! Margaret could see in my eyes what was going on in my brain, and her own beautiful eyes told me that she felt the same. To my great joy I found that she was mine.

After leaving the Gerow house, I spent the rest of the night in a daze. I went back to the studio, but not a wink of sleep came to me. I was afraid I would wake and find the evening a dream. Now and then during that fateful night I heard the roar of Karl Hagenbeck's African lions, whose cages were near the studio. Suddenly it came to me that a proposed hunting trip to Africa with Carl Akeley, which I had been considering for some days, was off. The next day Frank Millet, the artist and illustrator, asked me when I expected to start for Africa. When I told him that I had given it up and was engaged to be married, he remarked, "Well, you were bound to get into *some* kind of danger, weren't you?"

Since I had finished my final sculpture for the exhibition, I was now free to enjoy its wonders with Margaret. Her mother was rather upset that I wanted to carry away her youngest and at first insisted that we wait three years to be married. The more I talked of my proposed trip to Paris, however, the less Mrs. Gerow wanted me to go alone, and finally she agreed that we could be married on September 27, 1893, my thirty-third birthday.

XVI

THE FIRST TRIP TO PARIS

The day after our wedding my bride and I left Chicago for a week's vacation in Oregon City, Illinois. We returned to Chicago for another week and then went to New York. On October 27 we sailed for France on the *City of Paris*.

Before settling down to work in Paris, we visited all the museums, beginning with the Louvre. The Cluny Museum, which was in an old Roman bath, interested me immensely, not only for its exhibits but also because it was the oldest building that I had ever seen. To a new arrival from the American West, Paris was indeed a wonder and a marvel. It was autumn, and though the fall colors were not as gorgeous as those of Colorado, there was a soft, dreamy haze over all, an atmosphere that the Rockies did not possess. The beautiful gardens and buildings filled me with delight. I spoke no French, but Margaret was quite fluent in the language and did most of the communicating.

THE FIRST TRIP TO PARIS

One of the first things that we did was to take a letter that Billy Amsden, my New York artist friend, had given us to Charles Lasar, a good friend of his. The Lasars were charmed by Margaret, and we rented a small adjoining studio in the same building. Under their tutelage we bought simple furniture for our new home. Margaret concentrated on the household supplies, while I gathered modeling stands, easels, wax, and tools. I also started a series of French lessons, to enable me to get by when my wife wasn't around.

Eager to learn French methods of sculpture, I started morning classes at the Académie Julien, making studies from life. I spent most afternoons studying wild animals at the Jardin des Plantes. On some evenings I attended a drawing class; on others I worked at home. Denys Puech was the sculpture teacher, and his ability in modeling, as revealed in his criticisms of our figures, was amazing. Most of the young students were serious, but some cut capers and fooled about, which annoyed the more serious-minded among us.

We had brought from Chicago the three-foot plaster model of the stalking panther, as well as a wax model of the little fawn, both packed with Margaret's trousseau for protection. I now worked on the panther in plaster. For a model we procured a Parisian alley cat we named Tiger.

One day I decided that Tige had too much hair for me to see his muscles properly, and Margaret agreed that he should be clipped. Coaxing Tige into her lap, Margaret amused him while I made passes at him with my clippers. Tige didn't stay amused very long but flailed about so wildly that Margaret had to put on a pair of heavy gloves to protect herself from scratches. I succeeded in trimming away a little hair, in spite of the animal's gyrations, but the fine fur next to the skin kept getting caught in the clippers. The cat became more and more agitated, and so did I. The harder I worked the more fiercely Tige fought back. Finally the clippers jammed firmly in his tail. Frantically he wound himself around my arm, biting, clawing, and hissing.

When I shook loose, the cat tore about the room yowling and screeching, the clippers sticking to his tail like a bur. Jumping over tables and chairs, rolling over and over, he fought a losing battle with them. Finally he dashed between a bureau and the wall and stuck, kicking and clawing. My patience gone, I yanked the clippers away from him, taking with them all the hair that was stuck in the teeth. We had succeeded in exposing nearly a quarter of one muscle on the cat, but he got more of our skin—a whole lot more—than we got hair.

At last the panther was ready to be cast in bronze. When it came from the foundry, we couldn't leave it alone but rubbed it with loving hands to bring out the patina. It was our first real bronze, and we gloated over it [see page 209]. Finally I put the panther on the floor; it appeared to be charging out from under the table.

Just then who should stroll into the studio but Tige, whose hair was only beginning to fill out again. Coming face to face with the panther, Tige's back humped up and the fur on his tail spread to three times its normal diameter. He tore out of the room and up the stairs, taking four at a leap, snarling and hissing at every jump.

After finishing the second fawn in clay, we cast it in plaster in the waste-mold process. Margaret, who knew as much about casting as I did, worked with me. First we carefully studied the contours and cut very thin brass sheeting into narrow strips, which we set into the clay, thus forming the mold into sections that could be removed easily. When the mold was finished, we removed the sections one by one, thoroughly cleaned the inside of the mold, and soaped it.

Then we placed wires in the hollow places where arms, legs, neck, and other projecting parts might connect and wired the mold tightly together. Turning the mold upside down, we poured liquid plaster into it, turning it this way and that and shaking it so that the soft plaster would adhere to all sides. Once the plaster was sufficiently set and hardened, we used a small mallet and light chisel to chip off the mold. When the fawn was finally denuded of its plaster garment, we stood back and admired the little casting [see page 207].

One evening, just as we were about to sit down to dinner, I happened to look out of the window and saw in the adjoining courtyard a hungry dog gnawing a bone. Seizing pad and pencil, I made a hasty sketch. The next day I persuaded the owner of the dog to let me use his pet for a model. I bought a piece of horse neck from a nearby butcher and set the dog to work on it, using a flat-topped trunk as a platform. When the model was finished, Margaret and I cast it in plaster and also had it cast in bronze [see page 212].

At the end of our first winter in Paris the annual competition, or "concourse," for prizes took place. The model was a "pug," a boxer who worked the

THE FIRST TRIP TO PARIS

fairs and shows, challenging all comers. He had a fine set of cauliflower ears and a handsome broken nose. At the beginning there were artists representing many different countries: Spain, Portugal, Armenia, Bulgaria, Germany, the United States, Great Britain, and Scotland. The competition lasted a month, and as time went on, more and more artists dropped out.

To my great surprise, my figure won first prize. Though there were figures better executed than mine, I was told that mine had won because of its vigor and force. Margaret was delighted when I brought home the model and a golden one-hundred-franc piece.

In the spring of 1894 we closed our Paris apartment and studio and left for Brittany and a Continental holiday. At Illier we stayed in a charming peasant house and took our meals at a picturesque hotel. Several other American artists were vacationing there, and we settled down for a pleasant vacation.

While in Illier, I decided to do a statuette of a horse and arranged with a farmer to supply a model. I found that to seal the bargain I was supposed to drink about a quart of the hardest cider man ever produced. I took one taste, which nearly choked me to death. Four drops of that cider, as we used to say in the Rockies, "would make a canary whip a turkey buzzard." When the farmer wasn't looking, I poured it out.

We were hardly into the summer when a cablegram arrived from Augustus Saint-Gaudens. It started us packing at once. It said: "Will you come to New York to do the model of the horse for my equestrian statue of General Logan, for Chicago?"

XVII·

HORSES FOR SAINT·GAUDENS

Returning to New York in the autumn of 1894, I immediately got in touch with Saint-Gaudens, who was working in his studio on Thirty-sixth Street. He had already begun the statue of General John A. Logan. Several sculptors had tried to do the horse, but none had succeeded in satisfying him. General Logan's son had a stallion that he thought would be suitable for a model, and since he was indeed a beautiful animal, I decided to use him.

Saint-Gaudens had a studio near Windsor, Vermont, which he agreed to lend me, while he remained in New York to work. The stallion was shipped there, and Margaret and I arranged to stay at a farmhouse a mile from the studio. The farm was situated on a hill overlooking a wide expanse of country. Several artists were in residence in the area, among them Thomas Deming, Charles Platt, George de Forest Brush, Herbert Adams, and Henry

Prellwitz. Robert Payne, the sculptor who had invented the pointing-up machine for enlarging statues, came to do some enlarging. Architects Stanford White and Charles McKim visited the studio. The adjoining farm belonged to William M. Evarts, former secretary of state from 1877 to 1881.

Although Saint-Gaudens worked in New York, his wife and their son, Homer, stayed in Windsor. Homer was about thirteen years old, and a more mischievous youngster never tormented a neighborhood. One day while he was flying a gigantic kite in the Evartses' pasture, the kite started a long, gliding dive directly toward a fine herd of twenty blooded milch cows. Frightened, the cows started off on a run. When the kite fell on them, the animals panicked and stampeded down the hill and across the meadow, shattering the closed corral gate as they went through it.

Every few weeks Saint-Gaudens came up from New York to check on my progress. In the original sketch of the statue he had drawn the angle of the horse's head similar to that of the head in the General Sherman equestrian statue, on which he was also working. I suggested modeling Logan's horse with the head down and the neck curved, and he agreed. I made the original model two feet high, and in New York we pointed it up. Saint-Gaudens often criticized my work, and I learned a good deal during that period. When the large working model of the horse was finished, I did the saddle and saddle covering, and then he modeled the figure of Logan astride the horse [see page 214].

About the time I finished the second model of the Logan horse, Saint-Gaudens asked me to do the horse for his equestrian statue of General William Sherman. Margaret and I took an apartment and found a studio on West Fifty-first Street.

As soon as I was settled in the studio, Saint-Gaudens began to look for an animal that would answer for the model. General Logan had been a flamboyant figure, and his statue had required a picturesque horse. Sherman, on the other hand, was a campaigner, and he required a plain, more serviceable mount. A horse show was being held in New York at the time, and we haunted the place looking for a suitable model. Though there were plenty of beautiful horses, none was quite right. One that I particularly liked we finally eliminated because he was a bit too showy. Moreover, the owner said that he would be delighted to let us use the animal as a model—for a fee of fifteen hundred dollars!

About that time we heard of a famous jumper on

Long Island named Ontario. The horse suited Saint-Gaudens, and his owner graciously offered him as a model. We boarded him at Dorlan's Riding Academy at Fifty-ninth Street and Central Park and hired a handler to bring him to the studio. One day as John rode Ontario out of the stable, a hurdle was standing just outside the door, placed flat against a brick wall. Ontario saw it out of the corner of his eye and, knowing that hurdles were meant to be jumped over, made a dash for it. John turned him just in time and swung him around. Ontario evidently thought that his rider considered the first start unsatisfactory, for he wheeled and made another start for the hurdle. John was hard put to keep the horse from taking the hurdle in spite of the wall behind it.

When modeling from fidgety animals, I always tied my wax model to the top of the stand, which, being on wheels, was easily removed from danger in case the animal got excited. Though at first nervous and touchy, Ontario soon became used to the ways of artists and studios, with one notable exception. One cold day we had stoked the pot-bellied stove in the studio, and Ontario was tied near the stove. I was working on the hock joint of the right hind leg, and John was humped at the back of the leg, holding it in place so that I could see the contours. John was singing softly in a low bass a ditty entitled "Just Because She Didn't Know the Way."

All of a sudden Ontario exploded, hoofs, tail, and head going in every direction. My first thought was for the model, and I shoved it out of danger. When I turned back to John, I was horrified to see him spread-eagled against the wall, his eyes popping out of his face like marbles. The horse was at the other end of the studio, stamping his feet, shaking his head, and licking his mouth. John wilted to the floor and then, to my relief, stood up shakily. It seemed that Ontario, becoming bored, had put out his tongue to lick the hot stove.

The weeks I spent modeling passed quickly and pleasantly for Margaret and me. In the same apartment hotel where we were staying lived Horatio Walker, the distinguished Canadian painter of cattle and rural landscapes. Walker was reputed to be very critical of his friends' wives, which gave Margaret some concern, and she cried when she learned that we were to share a dining table with him. As it turned out, however, though seemingly brusque and fierce, Horatio Walker had a good sense of humor and proved to be a delightful companion.

One day while I was working on the Sherman

HORSES FOR SAINT-GAUDENS

horse, a friend brought a lawyer named Dixon to my studio. Dixon, a lover of good horses, owned a fine Arab stallion, which had been bred in the stables of the czar of Russia and had on his neck the czar's brand, a crown. Dixon commissioned me to do a portrait model of the horse and was so pleased with the small statuette that he gave me permission to have bronze casts made for sale, besides paying me a fee of five hundred dollars. Dixon also gave me permission to make a model of another horse of his, not a thoroughbred. This model I used for my eighteen-inch statuette *Indian Warrior*. Later, in Paris, I enlarged it to three feet and sold a good many statuettes of both sizes.

By that time I had made several small animal bronzes, and they began to sell, providing a more or less steady, though not large, income. I also found that other artists wanted to exchange work with me, and that was gratifying. Several years before, I had been elected to the American Water Color Society, as well as to the National Sculpture Society (1893), and while in Paris I had been elected to the Century Association. While working on the Sherman horse, I became an associate member of the National Academy of Design, and in 1895 I was made a full academician.

About this time William Astor Chandler returned from one of his African hunting trips, and I met him several times at the Boone and Crockett Club, where he gave talks about his adventures. He was very enthusiastic about the seven-millimeter Mannlicher rifle, which he had used successfully on rhinoceros, elephants, and other big game. I was interested in the rifle and went to a gunshop to look one over. Though I was very eager to possess it, it was much too expensive for our budget. On one of the last days I worked with Saint-Gaudens, a messenger from the gunshop delivered to the studio a box containing a Mannlicher rifle and five hundred rounds of ammunition. Saint-Gaudens mysteriously disappeared when the messenger said that the rifle was for me. I told him that I had looked at the gun in the store but had not bought it. He insisted that it was for me, and I insisted that it was a mistake. Finally Lewis Saint-Gaudens, Augustus's brother, said, "That's a present from Gus to you." Saint-Gaudens came back then to hear my expressions of gratitude.

By August 1, 1895, I had finished the Sherman horse [see page 215]. For some time Theodore Roosevelt and other members of the Boone and

Crockett Club had been discussing a project to make a national park of the beautiful mountain section of the Blackfoot Indian Reservation in Montana. George Bird Grinnell, who for years had been a good friend of the Blackfoot Indians, was already in the mountains studying the proposal. Henry Stimson, a law partner of Elihu Root, had planned a fall hunting trip in the region, and I was invited to join the group. Eager to study the Indians from a sculptural standpoint (as well as to try out my new rifle on big game in the area), I headed west about a month before the Stimson party, leaving Margaret in Chicago to make a long overdue visit with her family.

At Browning, Montana, where the headquarters of the Blackfoot Agency were located, the excitement of a gold strike was in the air. Gathered at the agency were several friends of the reservation superintendent, who opposed allowing "outsiders" to enter the reservation. If there were to be any pickings, the local people wanted them all. They were suspicious of my avowed intentions to sketch and hunt, but finally one of them said, "Hell, he doesn't know quartz from a grindstone," and I received permission to enter the Blackfoot country.

When the Stimson party arrived, we started on horseback for Hank Morris's cabin, at the foot of Lake St. Mary. Since Henry Stimson knew the way, he decided not to follow the wagon road but to cut across country. Then, unexpectedly—for it was early September—we ran into a fierce blizzard just as we were entering timber. In no time at all the snow was a foot deep, falling so thick and fast that we could see but a few yards. Finally Henry stopped and pointed ahead. "From now on," he said, "there won't be any landmarks to guide me. We must keep the horses in a straight line and not let them vary an inch."

As was to be expected, the horses insisted on turning tail to the storm, and it was a constant struggle to hold them in line. At last, just before dark, we emerged from the timber, and there, across the St. Mary River, was the Morris cabin.

Camped near the cabin were Dr. William Draper and his wife and a man named Billings. After spending a week at the cabin, our party, which now included Hank Morris, moved over to Swift Current River, where we camped. Beyond Lower St. Mary's Lake there were only Indian trails to follow, and in those magnificent mountains there were no houses of any kind.

At Swift Current River, Hank and I shared a tipi. An Indian policeman came up to keep tab on our actions, but when he decided that we were not going to steal the mountains, he returned to Browning, accidentally leaving his bedroll behind. That night I was sitting in the tipi cleaning my gun by the fire when Hank brought in the Indian's blankets. Hank was standing with his back to me on the other side of the fire. I heard something dropping to the ground. Looking up, I saw rifle cartridges slithering out of the end of the blanket roll into the fire. With a wild yell I was on my feet and dived through the tipi door just ahead of Hank.

At that instant an explosion ripped the air, and a red-hot shell casing caught Hank's rear elevation. I was just scrambling to my feet when his two hundred pounds landed on top of me. Bawling like a bull, he frantically grabbed at his posterior with his hands, trying to extinguish the blaze.

When we realized that our belongings in the tipi were likely to catch fire, we reached under the canvas and fished out whatever we could reach. Whenever a cartridge exploded, the bullet shot one way and the shell the other. We had to lie flat so as not to present a good target, and it was some time before we rescued our bedding and clothing.

When the trip was over, we headed back toward

Browning. Henry and Mabel Stimson, who were in a hurry to return to New York, rode ahead in a wagon, while Hank and I stayed at the agency so that I could make more Indian studies. Finally the two of us started out with riding ponies and a wagon pulled by a pair of horses. Not long after leaving, we reached a long hill that was too steep for the team. To help out, I fastened my lasso to the wagon and to my saddle horn. We had nearly reached the top of the grade when the wagon got the better of the horses and started dragging them back downhill. I had no spurs and couldn't keep my pony's head uphill. He whirled, wrapping the rope about my body and crushing me against the pommel of the saddle.

The horses had given up trying to hold the wagon and were taking my pony and me downhill with them. Then one fell and tangled in the harness.

Hank leaped to the ground, grabbed the team's heads, and with all his weight jerked them to the left, cramping the front wheels of the wagon. Luckily the wagon stopped and didn't turn turtle. If it had, we would all have rolled down the hill together.

Altogether it was a fine trip. We got no mountain sheep, but I shot one buck deer for meat and a coyote for fur. I saw a few elk, but since in past years I had killed a number of them for food, I didn't molest them.

While staying with the Blackfoot Indians, I began a small model of an Indian warrior, which I later finished in New York and Paris. That was the first of several pleasant summers I spent modeling Indians on the Blackfoot Reservation.

XVIII

THE RINEHART SCHOLARSHIP

At the suggestion of Stanford White, the noted architect, the city of Brooklyn gave me a commission to do some standing pumas for two of White's pedestals in Prospect Park. Soon after signing the contract, I received the Rinehart Scholarship for three years of study in Paris. Since I had already agreed to do the pumas, the Rinehart Committee was kind enough to allow me to do them in Paris, along with the scholarship work. Also, since I was primarily interested in Indians, animals, and western subjects, I was not required to work along the classical lines usually required. With much work ahead, Margaret and I made our plans to sail for Paris in the fall of 1896.

In our early married life my tendency to keep my own counsel was a puzzle to my wife. For instance, whenever we changed our address, which we often did, I was reluctant to let it be known where we were going. My idea was that we could notify interested people by letter after we were settled. That habit, I am sure, was formed during my Rocky Mountain days, when I hunted alone in the wilds. When I had good luck, I usually brought in my game surreptitiously so that no one would know from what direction I had come. Otherwise game wouldn't have lasted long at my favorite hunting grounds; other chaps would have killed it all or scared it away because they didn't want to take the trouble to scout new regions. In prospecting also, it was well to keep one's movements secret.

Before leaving for Paris, we lived at a boarding house in New York. On sailing day I ate breakfast at the big table as always with the usual group of boarders. As I was leaving the dining room Margaret entered, dressed for the voyage. I went on, having some business to attend to before returning for her. Just as Margaret was finishing breakfast, she remarked that she was glad it was a nice day for sailing.

"Sailing?" someone asked. "Going up the Hudson? Sailing to Boston?"

"For Paris," said Margaret.

Our friends were dumfounded. "Returning immediately?" they wanted to know.

"Three years," said Margaret.

When we arrived in Paris, we took temporary rooms in a small hotel near Place de la Madeleine. The Dreyfus trial had just begun, and on the evening of our arrival the square was filled with a mob yelling, "À bas Dreyfus!" People carrying wood swarmed into the square, built a huge fire not far from our hotel, and cast an effigy of Dreyfus into the raging inferno. Then another mob poured into the square, bearing on their shoulders Major Esterhazy, Dreyfus's accuser. Our landlord slammed and bolted all the doors and riot shutters on the lower floors. The tumult finally subsided at midnight, much to our relief.

During subsequent weeks while studying at the Académie Julien, I frequently passed by the military prison where Dreyfus was held before his conviction and imprisonment on Devil's Island. Quite often I saw Dreyfus on horseback approaching the prison or waiting for the ponderous gates to open, always guarded by three grim-visaged cavalry officers, one riding on each side while the third brought up the rear. Several times, as the gates swung open to allow the group to enter, I saw the square where later Dreyfus's commanding general tore off his badge and broke his sword.

The French sculptor Alfred Bouché owned a group of studios on the Impasse Ronsin, off the Avenue du Maine. I rented one of them just opposite a studio occupied by my old friend Seymour Thomas and immediately began work on the two pumas for Prospect Park, as well as a three-foot equestrian Indian figure for the Rinehart Scholarship Committee.

Margaret and I moved out of the hotel and rented a picturesque old house. One evening, just after Margaret had finished cooking supper and we were sitting in the dining room, a fearful crash came from the kitchen. The foot-thick plaster ceiling, which had held for a couple of hundred years, had suddenly let go, reducing tables and chairs to splinters and shattering dishes. As soon as possible we moved to a less romantic but newer building at Eighty-eight Boulevard de Montparnasse.

THE RINEHART SCHOLARSHIP

Often on pleasant evenings we boarded a bus and went to what the French called "le pays à six sous," "the country that costs six sous to reach,"—though sometimes we went to country that cost more. We would wander happily until rather late and then eat outdoors at some pleasant restaurant and go home after dark. Those were wonderful days.

During this second stay in Paris, I met many French sculptors. Georges Gardet was the leading *animalier* in France. His work was always beautifully modeled and technically perfect, but French sculptors thought that it lacked force. Many times we worked side by side at the menagerie of the Jardin des Plantes. Gardet's life-sized leopards in the Luxembourg Museum were wonderfully done. Another *animalier* named Peter did fine technical work, but his work also lacked force. Peter always had in his studio a number of Rodin's sketchy groups in plaster, which he was copying in marble. He finished details in Rodin's figures and groups, such as faces, hands, and feet, very nicely. In other words, Peter would take a Rodin plaster sketch and make a finished marble statuette of it. Hundreds of the statuettes were purchased by American visitors to Paris.

Bela Pratt, a Boston sculptor, and his bride moved into a house near us, and we became fast friends. His first son, Dudley, and our daughter, Hester, were born about the same time in the winter of 1897. In the spring of 1898 we rented a duplex at Meudon, across the Bois de Boulogne. On Sundays our two families picnicked together in the woods, and on weekdays Bela and I bicycled into Paris.

My working time was divided into three periods. Early in the morning I studied pumas at the Jardin des Plantes. At nine o'clock I hurried to the Académie Julien to model from the human figure. In the afternoons I worked at the studio on the full-size pumas or the *Indian Warrior* for the Rinehart Committee.

When my first full-sized puma for Stanford White was finished and sent to the foundry, I began on the second one. The *Indian Warrior* was also progressing. I was glad that I had modeled my Indian from a real one, since the Indian's anatomy is somewhat different from that of the white man. Along with these larger works, I also modeled several smaller pieces, which I turned over for casting to a man who had learned the art of chiseling bronzes in the studio of the sculptor Antoine Barye.

Finally the second puma was cast in bronze and shipped to the United States [see page 216]. The

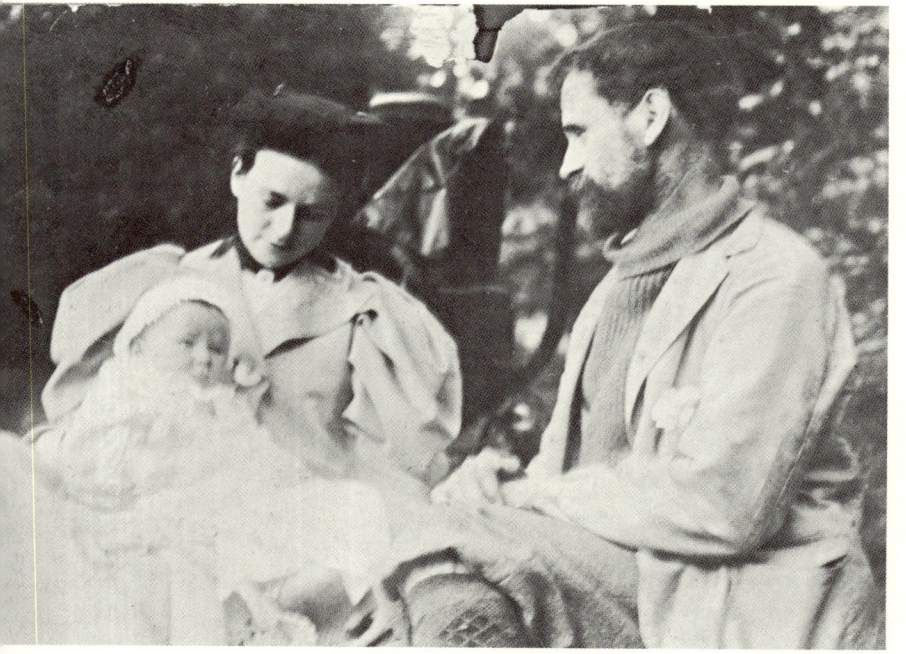
Proctor, his wife, Margaret, and their daughter Hester, 1897

Indian Warrior was eventually finished and shipped to the Baltimore Museum as my contribution to the Rinehart Prix de Paris Collection. (Unfortunately that cast was lost, and I never recovered it. Later, in America, I made a duplicate cast for the mu-

seum.) About that time we moved to a pretty house in Hameau Boileau in Auteuil, at the edge of the Bois de Boulogne. It was close to the country and to the race tracks, where we often went to study horses.

By the end of the summer of 1898, I had finished my work and the end of my scholarship was at hand. The Rinehart Committee had kindly offered me the Prix de Rome, but that meant that I would have had to do classical statuettes. Since I was not interested in such work, Margaret and I decided not to accept it. We were to return to the United States on the S.S. *Scala*, which was to sail from Antwerp, and a week before sailing time with our little Hester we took rooms in a hotel in Antwerp.

Fortunately for us, the Belgian Congo Fair was taking place at the time. The procession through Antwerp was led by King Leopold and the royal family riding in a gorgeous carriage drawn by four huge white horses. The part I remember best was a long line of Negroes in native costume, carrying enormous elephant tusks, two men to a tusk.

Just before we sailed, another ship, the S.S. *Bourgogne*, went down with a terrible loss of life. Some of the passengers on our ship told of passing

THE RINEHART SCHOLARSHIP

the spot soon after the disaster and seeing bodies floating in the ocean. One night, when we were passing through those same waters, our ship stopped, much to our alarm. The conditions were nearly identical with those of the *Bourgogne* sinking—there was a heavy fog and another ship following us. We could hear the foghorn blowing in answer to ours. Dressing hastily, Margaret and I put chocolate bars in our pockets and tied a bunch of them to Hester.

Remembering how the crew of the other ship had beaten and thrown passengers from the lifeboat, I put my revolver in my pocket. I didn't intend to have that happen to my wife and baby if I could prevent it. After several anxious hours of lying quietly we continued on our way with no further trouble.

We arrived in New York early in the autumn of 1898 for what turned out to be a brief stay. Within a few months I received a commission to do the *Quadriga* for the American Pavilion at the International Exposition of 1900, and once more we returned to Paris. We again rented a house in Hameau Boileau in Auteuil, and I took a huge studio that belonged to the house next door. As helpers I hired Fin Froelich, Henry Herring, and a French modeler named Peuffle.

One day as the work was getting under way, a meeting of the painters and sculptors was held at the commission offices. I went to the building in my ordinary clothes, probably with a little plaster on my shoes. As I started up the main stairway, the concierge told me to go through another door on the side street. In the course of the meeting I noticed that several of the men who were in their "store" clothes came up the main stairs, while others dressed as I was entered from the side. That was too much for my Highland Scots and Rocky Mountain background. I decided that it was the front door for me from then on.

At the next meeting the concierge again tried to head me off. I pushed him aside and went up the main stairs. He followed right behind me, protesting at every step. At the door of the commission offices he grabbed the knob before I could open it. I don't remember exactly what happened, but I sent that concierge, with his big wooden shoes, rattling down the steps, where he crashed on the landing below. The next day, Commissioner Peck, director-general of American interests at the exposition, came to the pavilion to tell me that he would back me up with the United States Army and Navy, if need be; however, nothing ever came of the matter.

That was not my only brush with the French. Our son Alden was born in March, 1900, and while Margaret was still confined our Breton maid began drinking and raising a fuss. She insisted on taking the big one-pound doorkey with her and then coming home late, drunk. One night as she was leaving to meet her soldier-brother who was waiting for her in the yard, I yanked the key from her and in so doing scratched her hand. Her brother rushed at me, and I scurried upstairs to get my revolver. Halfway up, I realized that if I shot a French soldier I'd never get out of jail. Racing to the door, I managed to keep the fellow out, while our English nurse ran to the police station. Before long two husky officers appeared and yanked the soldier and his sister out of there. I heard nothing more about that episode either.

The *Quadriga* consisted of Victory riding in a chariot, drawn by four horses abreast, with an outrunner on each side [see page 218]. It was to be executed in plaster. Since time was pressing, I also hired a couple of American helpers, both of whom specialized in horses, and all of us worked madly. Later I employed Helen Meyers to work on the large figure of Victory. As soon as a figure or horse was finished, it was delivered to the pavilion.

Our frantic efforts amused visitors and reporters who came to the studio. The following account of some of our periodic crises was sent from Paris to the United States in March, 1900:

THE NARROW ESCAPE OF THE CLAY HORSES
Vance Thompson
for the
Saturday Evening Post

RUE BOILEAU: a large studio—large enough to wheel a coach-and-six in; a glass roof and a glass north wall through which the winter wanders in at will: in the center of the studio a huge plaster chariot; near by, mounted on their scaffoldings, four ramping plaster horses—five times larger than life. Two French stoves of the biggest sort—and they are not very big—are blazing their best, while a heart-broken boy (think, then, coal is sixteen dollars the ton here!) is shoveling in unlimited coal. Still it is cold—freezing cold. The plaster hide of the ramping horses is crinkling into all kinds of queer patterns. And it is midnight.

Even as the bells of Notre Dame of Auteuil tell the hour the door opens, and a bearded sculptor and his assistants come rushing in with armfuls of blankets and quilts, overcoats and furs, and they wrap up the ramping horses as though they were croupy babies. All the while the chariot is freezing on its wheels. The sculptor sees cracks running up the carved front. He dashes to his house, reappears with the drawing-room rugs and the baby's pelisse. He takes off his coat and wraps it around the chilled tail of the rearing charger. Always the little French stoves are blazing away and the heartbroken boy shovels in coal. Out of doors the weather grows colder and all the cold night sifts into the glass-roofed studio.

It was one o'clock—by the bell of Notre Dame—when the man who writes these true words was startled out of his bed by a mighty clanging at his door-bell. He opened: "A note from Monsieur Proctor, sir—it's a matter of life and death." And the man who writes these true words read:

"For Heaven's sake send me all your blankets and coats and rugs and furs—the horses are freezing to death —Proctor"

And the man who writes these true words sent them, and for the rest of the night he slept on the kitchen stove and dreamed fitfully of art. Rome was saved by geese: I like to think that I saved the quadriga—chariot, horses and all—that is to look riverward from the United States building during the Exposition of 1900.

As time for the opening of the exposition drew near, the jury of selection for sculpture was appointed. Saint-Gaudens, Frederick MacMonnies, W. H. Bartlett, and I were chosen. I was represented by some small animals, a standing puma [see page 216], and the *Indian Warrior* I had done for the Rinehart Scholarship. My exhibit received a gold medal.

In the fall of 1900 Margaret and I went back to New York. Very soon I received a commission to do some works to be exhibited at the Pan-American Exposition, to be held in Buffalo, New York, in 1901. Karl Bitter, the director of external decorations for the exposition, had seen my *Quadriga* in Paris and wanted to exhibit it. He was successful in making arrangements, and the exposition authorities reproduced the work for the four corners of the Anthropological Building. In addition to overseeing their work, I was commissioned to do two original pieces: a horse and bull plowing and a group of horses. I finished only the former group, which I executed in plaster in heroic size.

While I was busy on the work for the exposition, Mary Lawrence, a close friend of Margaret's, found us a nice house at Sneden's Landing, opposite Dobbs Ferry, on the Hudson River. The rental was nominal, and our relations with the Lawrence family

THE RINEHART SCHOLARSHIP

were very pleasant indeed; there was nothing they wouldn't do for our comfort and happiness. When we arrived at the house, it was fully furnished: the icebox was filled with food, and the shelves were stocked with canned goods. Mary's mother built a large studio on a hill behind the house, and there I made a number of models for the House of Primates for the Zoological Park.

I had to spend a good deal of time at the exposition grounds, where my groups were being enlarged. Since I was on the Jury of Awards, my exhibit was *hors concours* (out of competition), but a small water color received a bronze medal. At Buffalo I met Henry Smith Pritchett, then president of Massachusetts Institute of Technology and later president of the Carnegie Foundation. He had hunted in Middle Park, Colorado, and knew my friend Billy Cousins, and we had many pleasant get-togethers.

After the Pan-American Exposition closed, plans were made to hold the Louisiana Purchase Exposition in St. Louis in 1904. Early in 1903 I was given a commission to sculpture a copper griffin for the exposition and also an equestrian statue of Louis Jolliet [see pages 221 and 222]. I made the sketch model for the Jolliet statue at Sneden's Landing. Then I learned that Austin Corbin, a horse fancier and sportsman, had, at his huge game preserve near Croydon, New Hampshire, a fine Morgan stallion which he said I could use as a model. To make the trip a vacation as well as a work session, I took Margaret and the children. Corbin also gave me permission to study buffalo and elk in the preserve.

After a pleasant summer in Croydon, we returned to New York, where I finished the five-foot model of Jolliet and sent it to St. Louis to be enlarged to heroic size.

XIX.

A TRY AT COUNTRY LIFE

Late in 1903 I was commissioned by the architectural firm of Carrère and Hastings to do four sleeping lions twelve feet tall, to be placed at the base of the McKinley Monument in Niagara Square, Buffalo, New York. In order to have access to the Bronx Zoological Gardens, where I could study lions, we moved to Tremont, in the Bronx. By the following year, however, the region was building up so fast that we decided to move farther out into the country. Our babies were arriving pretty fast, and New York City was no place for growing children.

My wife's mother sent us a newspaper clipping describing a farm for sale in northern Westchester County, New York, which seemed to be just the place to work, raise animals, and let the youngsters run. I boarded a Harlem River train for Bedford, where I was met by real-estate agents. But as one of the agents drove me farther and farther from

A TRY AT COUNTRY LIFE

civilization, I began to get nervous and asked whether he didn't have something a little closer to the railroad. Yes, he had a sixty-acre farm on top of Indian Hill, a mile from Bedford Village, with about the best view in Westchester. There was a large old barn with a smaller one adjoining that would do for a studio. The house was small but had possibilities. Also, there was a fine bit of woods with some wonderful rocks and cliffs on one side. It was the ideal location for a growing family weary of city life.

Shortly after we bought Indian Hill, Seth Low, mayor of New York City, appointed me a member of the New York Art Commission. The law required that the commissioners must be chosen from men recommended by the National Academy and two other recognized art societies in the city. The membership included the presidents of the Metropolitan Museum, the New York City Library, and the Brooklyn Institute, together with one painter, one sculptor, one architect, one landscape architect, and one citizen. Although the appointment involved a good deal of work, there was no remuneration. It did carry the title of "honorable," which isn't very valuable to anybody but a politician.

The commission was really formed to stop Tammany Hall from filling the city with architectural horrors and to help prevent graft. A little story I heard in those days illustrates Tammany methods. During the time Boss Charles Murphy was ruler of Tammany and New York City, it became necessary to appoint the artist member of the commission. After the mayor had procrastinated for more than a year, Harry Watrus, president of the National Academy of Design, went to see Boss Murphy.

"Now, why can't one of our boys get in on that job?" Murphy wanted to know. "How much salary goes with it, anyhow?"

"Not a cent," answered Watrus.

"Aw, hell!" said the boss. "Why didn't you tell me that before? Take the job and be damned to it!"

Of all the works I did while living at Indian Hill, probably the most important were the lions for the McKinley Monument. Although I had worked in granite during the time I was modeling animals at the zoo, these figures were my first important work in Vermont marble. Before we moved to the farm from the Bronx, I had finished sketches of lions in the Bronx Zoological Gardens, which served as a basis for the modeling of the figures at Indian Hill. Working in clay, I made first two-foot and then four-foot models which were cast in plaster. Because of the size and weight of the finished marble figures—

each was twelve feet long and weighed about twelve tons—the final work had to be completed near the site where they were to be permanently installed.

After several months of work in Buffalo, the lions were ready to be placed on their pedestals. Heavy ropes were wound around the huge figures, in preparation for hoisting them into position with a derrick. The man in charge of the moving was afraid that the plinths—the bases of the pedestals—might crack if the figures were not settled perfectly evenly. Consequently, the pedestals were covered with finely crushed ice, and the lions were lowered onto it. As the ice melted, the figures slowly settled into place. To prevent the ice from melting more rapidly in one spot than in another, a man with a hose stood

by to turn a stream of water on the ice. As soon as the lions were safely in place, I returned to my family on Indian Hill.

The next piece of work I set out to do was a small group that I called *Panther with Kill*, portraying a panther crouching over a dead deer. Models for the group presented no problem, for we had a caged panther at the farm, and I was permitted to make sketches of a deer that had died at the menagerie. I had to prod the panther with a pole to get her into the position I wanted. After a period of poking she seemed to grasp the situation and kept a pose pretty well. I spent some months on this little group (finished, it was only about a foot long and five inches high) and sent it to the foundry for casting in bronze.

My working habits would have made family life a problem if my wife and children had been less understanding. One Christmas Eve a composition of an Indian pursuing a buffalo popped into my head. On Christmas morning I was up at daylight and had a fire going in the studio. Quickly I made an armature and settled down to work. At noon Margaret brought Christmas dinner to the studio and left it on the steps. By five o'clock the sketch was

The Kill

finished. It was a lost day as far as festivities were concerned, but a valuable one to me.

Late one winter afternoon we were surprised to see someone hoofing up our steep hill through deep snow, carrying a suitcase. Since there was no place for him to be bound for except our house, I started down the hill and to my joy met George de Forest Brush. He had come to do some sketches of our two handsome boys, Alden and Phim (born January 17,

A TRY AT COUNTRY LIFE

1902). He could stay for only three days, he said. He was on his way to Italy, where his family awaited him. As we entered the house, our curly-haired Ona Mary (born January 25, 1905) met us at the door. Grabbing her up in his arms, George exclaimed, "My God, I must do you first!"

The three days stretched to three months, while George worked steadily on heads of Ona and the boys. One day while he was staying with us, Jeanne Clemens, one of Mark Twain's daughters, rode over on her horse from Redding, Connecticut, to see him. That was our first meeting with her, and in the succeeding months she occasionally returned to have lunch with us. We were surprised when she told us that she was only then reading her father's books.

Finally the day came when George said that he must go. I took him to the local railroad station to catch a train for New York. Sitting down to wait, we started to talk about art. After a while we asked the station master whether the nine o'clock train was ever coming. He grinned and said, "That train? Mister, that one went by two hours ago, and two others have passed since." Perhaps it was a good thing that George was going to Italy without me.

We loved life at Indian Hill, but after a time we began to realize that we would have to leave. The responsibility of looking after such a large place took time that I felt I should devote to my work. I had completed the decorations for the elephant house in the Bronx Zoo [see page 223] and the McKinley lions, but they had been started before we moved to Indian Hill. Commissions were not coming in, and I was definitely not satisfied doing only water colors and small pieces. Furthermore, I had a family to support. With Jean's birth (on August 8, 1907) we had five children.

Accordingly, we made plans to move to Stamford, Connecticut, which would be within commuting distance of New York City.

XX.

TIGERS, DUCKS, AND RAMS

In my first week in the New York City studio I received a commission to do two tigers for the entrance to Nassau Hall at Princeton University. The next week I received a commission to do four colossal tigers for the Sixteenth Street Bridge in Washington, D.C. In no time at all I needed more space to work and had to move to a larger studio, on Sixth Avenue near Thirteenth Street.

Woodrow Wilson was then president of Princeton, and the tigers were being presented to the university by his class, the class of 1879. One important specification was made concerning these pieces: the bronze had to be thick enough to withstand the treatment undergraduates would give the statues. While I was working on the tigers, Wilson often came to the studio, and Margaret and I visited him at his home in Princeton.

The Princeton tigers were dedicated on Com-

TIGERS, DUCKS, AND RAMS

mencement Day, 1909. Standing on the platform in front of Nassau Hall, flanked by the statues, Margaret and I were introduced by President Wilson and honored with the Princeton yell. Several years later at a dinner in New York the two-foot cast of the working model was presented to Wilson—then president of the United States [see pages 227 to 229].

The tigers for the Sixteenth Street Bridge were soon finished and in place. Although the specifications for the work had called for cement figures, I decided that they should be bronze and they were so finishd [see page 226]. One of the commissioners of the District of Columbia was very much surprised that I had the animals cast in bronze, a much more expensive process than cement casting. "No accounting for these artists," he said.

While waiting for my Princeton tigers to be cast, I decided that I needed a change from the studio. Dr. William T. Hornaday, director of the New York Zoological Park, had told me of some wonderful sheep country in Canada between Banff and Waterton lakes. It took only a few days for me to decide on the trip, and soon I was camped on the prairie east of the northern Rockies with a guide. We hunted two weeks without luck; however, I did

make a good many water-color sketches of the mountains.

Looking through my glasses the evening before the last day of my vacation, I saw four rams cross a high mountain into a grand amphitheater that we hadn't visited. Bright and early next morning we were off, and at noon we stopped for lunch. As I was eating, the guide was scanning the basin. "There are the four rams up there a mile away," he said, "but it's damned dangerous country between here and there."

With my glasses I saw that the animals were of a dark color, which meant that they were big ones. I also studied the mountainside. About halfway up, just under an overhanging cliff, was a gorge that we would have to jump since there was no way around it. I had promised Margaret that I would take no unnecessary risks. Was this one necessary? I decided that it was.

When we got past the gorge—or over it—we could see the rams just beyond a rocky knoll, a hundred yards away. The guide branched off to one side, while I crept straight forward. Picking out the biggest animal, I fired. He ran for about twenty yards and then fell. The next in size dashed up and around the cliff, and I shot again. The bullet struck him in the top of the shoulder and went through his neck. He fell over the cliff but caught on a ledge. Another ram ran to the left, and the guide got him.

Since it was then late afternoon and we had a dangerous two-hour descent to make before dark, we dressed the sheep and left them where they had dropped. Next morning at daybreak we climbed back and skinned the animals, cutting off the heads for mounting.

Again we started for camp, the guide carrying the head of the biggest ram. We were crossing a steep ditch, and I had just stopped to suggest that we tie a rope around the guide when he slipped, landed heavily on his back, and began to slide. Frantically spreading out his legs and arms, he stopped at last. The head bounced past him down the mountain. Helping him to his feet, I gazed down the mountain where the head had disappeared. It was beginning to snow, and I was sure that if that head was left out all night we would never find it. Determined not to lose it, I crawled down and around until I found where the horns had struck the soft slide at the bottom of the cliff. I went farther down, keeping the first landing place in sight, until I saw another landing place a hundred feet below. Taking a sight on the two points, I found the head undamaged in a dense cedar thicket fifteen hundred feet from where it had first struck the slide.

The next morning the guide made a lone climb up the mountain, this time in six inches of snow, to get the meat and skins. He simply turned them loose downhill, while I watched from the bottom of the cliff. The first hide slid out over space, and about a hundred feet from the starting place opened out. Then, like a huge butterfly, it fluttered down.

The following day I sketched the big head. Its horns measured eighteen inches around the base. The other head had a set of horns that measured seventeen and a half inches. When I got to New York, William Hornaday, director of the Bronx Zoological Gardens, said that the big head was the record for a ram killed by an American sportsman and scientifically measured.

TIGERS, DUCKS, AND RAMS

Shortly after my return to the city George D. Pratt, secretary of the Pratt Institute, came to my studio. Hornaday had told him about the ram's head, and he asked to see it. Noticing some of the work that I had in progress at the time, he became interested in a four-foot buffalo, which he thought his brother would like. A few days later his brother, Herbert L. Pratt, purchased the buffalo for the garden of his Glen Cove, Long Island, estate. He also ordered two large statues of reclining tigers [see page 231].

Before I began work on my third tiger job, Alden Sampson and I bought a lot at 168 East Fifty-first Street in New York and contracted for a building that was to serve as a double studio for both of us. Perhaps the new studio helped me in selling my work; at any rate, the things that I sold helped to pay for it. About this time George Pratt presented the Museum of the Brooklyn Institute of Arts and Sciences with a collection of my small bronzes. At one of the luncheons at the Century Club, the trustees of the Pratt Institute told me that they were looking for something in marble for their gallery.

"I have just what you want," I said jokingly. They took me at my word and bought a marble sleeping lion that I had been working on for some time [see page 230]. It was also at the Century Club that I met H. C. Frick, who asked me to do two lions for the entrance to the Frick Building in Pittsburgh, Pennsylvania. The plans for the building were changed later, and the lions were placed inside the entrance [see page 220].

Either chance or arrangement permitted an annual hunting trip during this period. It always seemed that a statue was ready for the foundry, or a bit of modeling was at the stage where an assistant could point up or enlarge it without my assistance. Since I worked hard, the trips to the wilds offered a welcome break.

In September, 1910, George Pratt and I met at Edmonton, British Columbia, for an antelope hunt on the prairies. Close to camp, which we set up on the side of a low mountain, was a spring. Deep buffalo trails, which were then being used by cattle, led to the spring from every direction. The water gushed from the ground twenty feet below its original outlet, which showed what centuries of buffalo traffic had done. It was a fascinating spot. From the effects of buffalo travel it was apparent that many of the gulches leading to the river about two miles below had been formed in the same way. The sharp hooves

of millions of animals tramping to water had cut up the soil, fierce winds had blown away the dust, and the rains had gradually eroded canyons.

In the autumn of 1911 I set out for British Columbia with my long-time sculptor friend John Rogers. By that time the railroad had reached Mile 17 in British Columbia, and we went by freight train to the Athabasca River, where we met our guides with horses. Though we had permits to hunt in Jasper Park, our luck was rather poor. The first day out an Indian boy scared off a fine ram only a few hundred yards away.

Lake Maligne was the most beautiful lake I had ever seen. We were camped at the south end, which put the sun at our backs, excellent lighting for either a landscape or a statue, since it gives a nice proportion of sunlight and shadow at any time of day.

While sketching at the lake one day, I saw above me on a mountain a combat between mountain goats and an eagle. The goats, nine in number, were huddled in a circle, with the kids inside. When the eagle dived to grab a kid, all the old ones reared up on their hind legs and struck at it with their horns. I watched the battle until the group passed from view.

When Rogers and I headed back to New York, I went down to Edmonton to meet my wife. On an impulse, however, I decided to go on to Wainwright to look over the herd of buffaloes on the 200,000-acre game preserve there. I had received a commission to sculpture four large bronze buffaloes for the Q Street Bridge in Washington [see page 233]. I wired Margaret to leave the train at Wainwright instead of Edmonton. I had a double purpose in going to Wainwright: on the train I had met an official of the railroad who had wired ahead to make arrangements for us to go duck hunting.

Margaret received my message and got off at Wainwright, but she had brought no camping clothes; her baggage had gone to Edmonton. The man who met us rustled up a raincoat and a hat, and for footwear she used a pair of my overshoes over her high heels. Our new friend and I enjoyed a successful shoot, while Margaret sat in an old flatbottomed boat hidden in the tules.

In August, 1912, George Pratt and I decided to hunt in the Peace River country of Canada. Our guide met us at Jasper, Alberta, where we were to obtain horses.

From Jasper we traveled north past majestic Mount Robson and Mount Bess and up the Moose and Smoky rivers. Over the pass on Jack Pines River we made our hunting camp, and there, on the first day, George shot a grizzly. We were so close to the Alberta–British Columbia line that we didn't really know in which province we were camped and we were in doubt about what we could shoot. Our guide knew the answer: "In British Columbia it's open season on moose but closed on caribou. In Alberta it's just the reverse. If you shoot a moose, you know you're in British Columbia. If you shoot a caribou, you know you're in Alberta." Since I shot a moose while we were in that camp, we must have been in British Columbia.

Bear trails were everywhere. In that north country they were not smooth paths as they were farther south; they consisted of a pair of parallel rows about two feet apart, each row eight or ten inches deep and almost as wide.

August of 1913 found me, as always, longing for a big-game hunt in the wilds, and George Pratt was haunted by similar yearnings. We decided to start from Fort Steele, British Columbia, and hunt mainly mountain sheep. When S. Hart Merriam, of the Smithsonian Museum, heard about our plans, he

asked me to bring back a ram and a ewe for the museum, and procured permits for both George and me to shoot the extra specimens.

At Fort Steele, Arthur Fenning, a former guide of George's, met us with an auto and drove us to Sinclair Pass. There Nicol, our head guide, met us with his outfit and crew: Nick, a French cook; Bill and Happy, packers; Francis, a full-blood Kutenai Indian guide; and Lum, a Chinese-Indian mail carrier and horse wrangler. From Sinclair we pulled out for Cross River, fording the Kootenay and White rivers several times on the way. At Cross River we pitched camp. George and I were quartered in an Indian tipi, a warm place for dressing on cold mornings and a comfortable place for eating when it rained.

It was new country to all of us. One day Francis, Happy, and I entered a dry amphitheater, where game trails were scarce, and we saw nothing until early evening, when a billy goat appeared. I took one shot, but the goat didn't move. Happy thought that the bullet had gone too high. I fired again, and the billy went down. We later found that the first shot had pierced his lungs.

Between the brush and snow and the steepness of the canyon, we had no end of trouble trying to get out. Happy began to swear like a Missouri muleskinner. Francis said, "Well, it's against my religion to swear, but blankety-blankety-blank anyway!"

George and his party returned to camp that evening with three fine pairs of ram horns. We gathered around a big campfire for a pleasant evening of stories and songs. Nick gave us some *voyageur* and *habitant* ditties, and Lum sang a Chinese refrain or two.

One day when George and I were riding together up Cross River before separating to go to different hunting grounds, I saw a band of nineteen ewes and

TIGERS, DUCKS, AND RAMS

lambs about two hundred yards away. I wanted George to shoot the ewe for the museum, but he insisted on my taking the shot. While we were arguing, the sheep disappeared. One evening after a full day's hunting Nicol and I saw a ewe standing on a steep hillside, head on in the bushes. I thought that I had a bead on her, but the shot went wild, and so did the ewe.

A few days later Francis and I made a long climb in the snow. We spotted several ewes. Picking one that didn't have a lamb, I fired and had my museum specimen. A few days later we spotted four rams lying down. My first shot hit the biggest one. The others jumped to their feet, but two shots downed a second animal.

On the last day, while we were breaking camp, I made a water-color sketch of a nearby snow-covered mountain. It was so cold that the colors congealed and brushes froze to the paper, necessitating many trips to the fire to thaw them out. On the way back downriver we had to follow the sandbars, fording the river forty times. Fenning did not meet us with the automobile where we expected him, and we had to ride another six weary miles to Sinclair Pass, where George and I said good-by to the boys and headed back to New York.

XXI

A SUMMER WITH THE CHEYENNES

In the spring of 1914, Margaret and I planned a trip to the Cheyenne Indian Reservation in southern Montana. Besides giving me an opportunity to study the Cheyennes and do some work, the weeks away from New York would be a real change for Margaret, who all too often had to remain at home. We made arrangements for our children to be well cared for and were off to "our West" together.

The terminus of our rail trip was Crow, Montana, a picturesque Indian village on the Little Bighorn River, a short distance from the battlefield where Custer met his end. After paying our respects to J. R. Eddy, the Indian agent, we visited the site. The ground was littered with relics of the battle. Margaret picked up a flint arrowhead and also found a matchbox which had been made by fitting two Springfield cartridges together. I picked up an unfired cartridge, as well as several pieces of the original grave markers.

After camping at the reservation for a few days, we were adopted by Chief Little Wolf, who gave Margaret his wife's name—Minoahmahho, Willow Woman. I was honored with his own name, Okomahkahchitah, meaning Large Coyote.

Little Wolf had a "civilized" name, Robert, given him by the church. Since I could never see the sense of ruining a perfectly good Indian name, we called him Wolf.

I decided that Little Wolf would make a good model for a statue I wanted to do of an Indian on horseback being pursued by an unseen enemy.

When I was ready, Wolf came out of his tipi wearing only a breechcloth and mounted his pony. My idea was to depict the Indian riding downhill and at the same time making a wheeling motion. To capture the motion and the realism, I had Wolf ride uphill on the walk, turn, and then gallop down, sometimes on one side of me, sometimes on the other. This arduous work—for both model and sculptor—went on for several days while the eighteen-inch statuette, *Indian Pursued*, took shape.

One day Margaret and I decided to attend an Indian dance at Rosebud, Montana. Eddy took us in

Little Wolf (Okomahkahchitah), chief of the Cheyennes, Proctor's "foster father"

his car, and as evening approached, drums began to sound through the camp, which consisted of about twenty lodges.

The dance tipi was about forty feet long and twenty feet wide, with a smoke hole in the center. Near the center was a straw-covered platform for the chief and other notables. When it began to get dark, the braves started coming into the tent. A fire was built in the center, and a pot of meat and some canned foods were prepared.

After the meal two dancers gave a marvelous exhibition. Then the older men took the floor, and the regular business of the evening began. A fierce-looking fellow named Crazy Head got up to give a dance and relate his experiences in the Fetterman massacre. He had donned a war shirt that was very much the worse for wear. As he pointed at it and narrated his tale, our interpreter explained that he was telling about being knocked down and ridden over by several horsemen. Crazy Head then pointed out several bullet holes in the shirt and, lifting it, displayed the scars on his body. With dramatic gestures he told how he had dashed up and killed a soldier with his coup stick and escaped from the breastworks. He also gave a description of the Custer fight. He had worn that war shirt for fifty years.

Meanwhile, work was progressing on *Indian Pursued*. We were visited by Little Wolf's father, Laban, one of the most dignified gentlemen I have ever known and, according to Grinnell, one of the handsomest Indians he had ever seen. Sitting around the campfire in the evening, Laban would tell of the days of the buffalo hunts and fights with white men and other Indian tribes. He was very proud of the little English that he knew, which consisted mostly of the word *buppano* ("buffalo"). He had killed at least five Indians, but he would never tell how many whites he had put away. Few Indians would confess to having killed white people, evidently fearful of punishment.

At last, to our regret, the time came for Margaret to return to the children, who were staying in New Rochelle, New York. After her train left, camp seemed terribly lonely to me, and I decided to move to a new site by the Rosebud River, not far from Little Wolf's ranch. On the way we passed the battleground where the Cheyennes had defeated General George Crook's soldiers. Old Laban showed me where he and his band had pursued and killed some of the troopers. The camp I chose was part way up the mountain near a little spring in a clump

of twisted trees. I placed some poles around the camp for a barrier to keep out the Indians' livestock.

The barrier worked fine for animals, but it did not deter the Indians. As soon as they learned my whereabouts, I found myself running the most popular free-lunch counter in America. Red Fox was a regular patron, as were Grasshopper and Woman's Leggings. Old Wounded Eye was the most ancient relic in the shape of a man ever to visit me. A medicine man, he tried to fool me with childish tricks, which I usually pretended to believe. When my visitors found that I was interested in Indian artifacts, they swarmed in with all the castoffs they could carry, from worn-out moccasins to war bonnets and baby carriers. One woman brought me a buffalo robe which she insisted was "ten hunnert" years old. I didn't believe her until she unrolled the relic, and then I decided that she had underestimated its age.

For about a month Little Wolf and I worked together quite peacefully. One day, however, I happened to be working on the underside of the horse in a ticklish position both for myself and for my model. Just then old Laban and a nephew of his named Duster rode up, and Wolf turned to talk with them. Suddenly his horse jumped, sending me rolling and knocking over the model. I was unharmed, but the model was damaged, and I let loose a flood of Rocky Mountain fancy language. Not realizing what all the work meant to me, the old chief blazed up, and so did Wolf. The fierce look in the Indians' eyes scared me for a few seconds; we were a long way from anyone who might come to my defense. I realized that there was still a lot of fire in the Indians, and the thought flashed through my mind that they must have caused terror to captives in the early days. I finally made them understand how important the model was, and we all cooled down. Then began the tedious work of repairing the damage.

One of the Indians on the reservation, a fellow named Little-Black-White-Man, reluctantly promised to take me to a spot where Cheyennes had killed several whites just before the Custer battle. His pay for guiding me there was to be three dollars, and if I took any of the skulls, cooking utensils, or other articles at the site, I was to pay him six dollars. Little-Black-White-Man kept emphasizing that all the braves who had participated in the killings were dead. He kept putting me off for so long that I finally decided to try to find the place alone. One day after a vain search I was riding through a deep gulch when I came on a pile of partly buried bones. I thought I had found the site, and my disappointment was keen when I discovered that they were only cattle bones. I later learned that the Indians were slaughtering their cattle on the sly. The government allowed them only half enough to live on, telling them to conserve their cattle and let the herds increase. Once in a while when they got hungry enough, they stole away and had a good feed.

Before long Little Wolf had to return to his job of riding fence, and I moved into the school building. Rolling Bull, my next model, had a good figure, and he was willing to pose in a G string and braids, despite the onset of cold weather.

At last the little model was finished and ready for casting. Plaster of Paris was not available in that region, of course, and I sent to Salt Lake City for a supply. Dental plaster was what I got back, and it set so fast that I couldn't keep ahead of it. When I finally finished casting, I said good-by to the Cheyennes and headed for Portland, Oregon.

XXII

COWBOYS AND INDIANS

After shipping the model of *Indian Pursued* to New York late in 1914, I went from Portland to Seaside, Oregon, where I made a fourteen-inch statuette of Martin Biddle and his pony, Martinet. Returning to Portland, I did a couple of bas-relief heads for my good friend Colonel Charles Erskine Scott Wood. Then, since it was nearly time for the Pendleton, Oregon, roundup, I headed east.

Armed with letters from Wood, I was received with cordiality by the officials of the Roundup Association and was given a pass to the grounds. The *East Oregon Journal* gave out the information that I was in Pendleton to carry on my studies of western life, especially of cowboys, Indians, and wild horses, with the idea of using them in my sculptures. Since sculptors were then quite a novelty in eastern Oregon, I was almost considered an exhibit myself.

Though I had access to the roundup grounds, the

officials were worried about letting me go into the arena, because they didn't consider an "easterner" able to take care of himself. When they learned that I had grown up in the West and had hunted big game all over the United States and Canada, they felt somewhat less anxious and gave me a riding pony; they considered that having a mount somehow lessened the danger of having me around. I couldn't sketch too easily on horseback, however, and continued to go about on foot with pad and pencil in hand.

One day the association scheduled a grand dash by all the mounted performers across the arena, right up to the front of the grandstand, where they would be greeted by the 25,000 spectators clapping, shouting, and stamping with excitement. I wanted to join the stampede, but so that I would miss the pile-up I anticipated when the cavalcade hit the fence, I decided that the place for me to ride was near the tail end of the procession. I hadn't counted on one thing, however. When the riders reached the fence, they whirled in an about-face and dashed back the way they had come. I was caught between the leaders and those behind me, and I got the worst knocking about of my life.

Once during a bucking contest I was making quick action sketches when one of the old-time cowboys, a fellow named Johnny, was called. The instant Johnny hit the saddle, his bronc dashed straight for me. I was off like a scared rabbit, but no matter how I dodged, the horse kept right on my tail. Just as he was descending from a high buck almost over me, I made a frantic leap to the side, and Johnny's stirrup whacked me as horse and rider plunged by. Charles Furlong, who was at the time writing his book *Let 'Er Buck*, told me, "If you had lost your head for a split second, you'd have been a goner."

To me, bulldogging was the most daring and dangerous event of all. To see a cowpuncher on a swift horse dashing neck and neck alongside a longhorn steer is pure excitement. Then to see him drop the reins, lean way over, seize the steer by the horns, and throw himself from his horse is breathtaking. Bulldogging requires all the skill the best horseman can summon. The speed of the horse must be timed exactly with that of the steer. If the horse is too slow, the cowboy's feet will hit the ground when he grabs the horns. Then he can't throw the animal, and he will be dragged, and maybe even trampled, until he lets go. If the horse is going too fast when the man's weight falls on the steer's head, the steer is

The Artist Goes into High

"hoolihaned"—thrown into a somersault—and lands on his back, and both steer and cowboy may be injured. In the early roundup days, when a bulldogger threw his steer, he was supposed to grab the steer's upper lip between his teeth, hold the animal down, and put both hands in the air. Later they began simply holding the animal down by lying or sitting on his head.

The last act of each day of the roundup was the wild-horse race. In those days top-notch buckaroos usually competed only for fun. Beginners and hangers-on—anyone who could rustle a saddle—were the usual contestants, but they made the event exciting. They lined up about fifteen feet apart on both sides of the track in front of the grandstand. Each had a saddle and a helper. Then other cowboys galloped in, each leading a wild bronco by lead rope and halter. When each contestant had a bronco, the signal was given: "Saddle up!" Then each rider tried to throw his saddle onto the rearing, plunging bronc, mount if he could, and ride around the track. The first rider home was the winner.

At one wild-horse race I witnessed, a contestant at the end of the line kept refusing mounts, though the entrants were supposed to take mounts in the order of their arrival in the ring. The man next to him made a remark, and like two wildcats they tore at each other, no holds or punches barred. Later I learned that the end man was waiting for a gentled horse that he knew was in the wild bunch. The fight set the stage for the whole race. When "Saddle up!" sounded, all hell broke loose, and the place turned into a mass of plunging horses, yelling buckaroos, tangled ropes, and empty saddles. One man and his helper had managed to get the saddle on the horse and were ready to cinch up when another horse circled them with his rope and dragged pony and men all over the lot. Another horse dashed into a bunch of cowboys, unseated his rider, and then loped all around the arena, winning the race, though not the money. One horse even tried to climb into the box next to me.

There were plenty of subjects of interest at Pendleton: cowboys and Indians, buffaloes owned by the Roundup Association, frontiersmen, and a western atmosphere similar to what I had known in Colorado. I was so pleased that I sent a long telegram to Margaret asking whether she and the family would join me. Within two weeks she had given up the big house in New Rochelle, stored the furniture, and sublet my New York studio.

When Margaret and our seven children arrived,

COWBOYS AND INDIANS

people outdid themselves to help us. I had bought two horses, one to ride and one for a model, and Sheriff Til Taylor and the Roundup Association allowed us to keep them on the grounds. They also let me borrow one of their buildings for a studio and cut a skylight in the roof. Although the roundup had not been all play for me (I had made dozens of sketches that I expected to use later), I was eager to get to work on my buckaroo. I had made one in plaster for the Columbian Exposition in Chicago about twenty years before, but the statue I now had in mind was to be in bronze.

There were plenty of possible models, and I struck a bargain with a six-foot-three cowboy named Red. Red was one of the most colorful characters around Pendleton. If anyone gave him five dollars and a drink of whisky, he would ride one of the buffaloes.

The cayuse I was using for a model was a wall-eyed brute, a direct offspring of the devil. One day when Red brought him into the studio to pose, he nearly kicked my hat off my head with his left hind foot without seeming to move a muscle. Then began a scene that can be imagined better than described. The studio was only fourteen by sixteen, just large enough for a horse and two men if everyone was quiet. With a kicking and bucking horse, there was

only room for the horse and one man, and that wasn't me. I had sometimes had trouble in close quarters with wild animals but had always managed to save myself and my model. That time all I wanted to save was my hide. Stovepipe, splinters, boxes, table, and high profanity flew around for a time until Red finally got the beast settled down. Red insisted that I would be able to climb all over the critter in a week, but I had no intention of trying it.

I was sketching on the edge of town one day when

167

Washday at the Ranch

a friend came by to talk about a projected hunting trip. Afterward he turned his horse to go back to his cabin just as a wild gust of wind flapped the sheets and clothes on a nearby line. The next second all hell broke loose. His cayuse side-jumped, sunfished, swapped ends, and landed right in the middle of sheets, red longies, and unmentionables, which wrapped all around the rider and his mount. The last I saw of them, the horse was bucking over the brow of a hill with a streamer of clothes behind him. The temptation to sketch the scene was too great to resist. Incidentally, there wasn't much left of that wash.

It has usually been my practice to keep more than one piece of statuary in progress at a time, and although *The Buckaroo* claimed most of my attention, I found time to complete the model for a small bronze Indian head later called *Jackson Sundown* [see page 237]. I also worked on a little two-foot statue called *Indian Pursuing Buffalo*, which I had started years before, using for a model one of the buffaloes belonging to the Roundup Association.

By the spring of 1916 I had finished the buffalo for the group and was ready for a suitable Indian model to complete it. Jackson Sundown, who was a nephew of the famous Chief Joseph of the Nez Percé tribe, was exactly the model I needed.

Sundown agreed to pose if I would go to Lapwai on the Nez Percé Reservation near Lewiston, Idaho, and arrangements were made for me and the family to camp on his ranch. With my plasteline model, my wife, our seven children, and our camp outfit all loaded into a big Cadillac, we made it to Lapwai in no time. Sundown and his wife, Cecilia, had pitched

COWBOYS AND INDIANS

a big tipi for us among magnificent trees by a pretty trout stream.

Serious work began as soon as we were settled. Every day Sundown rode back and forth in front of me or posed quietly while I modeled details. Sundown worked patiently all summer. Occasionally his wife would entice him away to visit relatives, and I would take the day off to go fishing.

One day the older boys and I had to make a trip to town for supplies. We had to walk about five miles from camp to the end of the road to get the car. After collecting the groceries, we started back to camp up the twisty, one-lane trail. Suddenly a team appeared pulling a wagonload of lumber. There we were, a cliff above and one below. The team couldn't back up, and I wouldn't. The air was blue. Just a few feet behind the car was a "wide" place in the road—all of three feet across. I backed that far and surveyed the situation. If the car could perch right at the very edge of the cliff, I thought the team could get by. One of the wagon drivers and I took a tree trunk from the wagon and slipped it under the car as it hung over the cliff, with us underneath. The boys stood on the upper running board to try to keep the weight of the car on the road. All of us held our breath while the lumber wagon eased up the bank

and scraped by. When it was all over, I could hardly crawl up the bank and into the car. I shook for an hour.

Just before snowfall we rented a house in Lewiston. Cecilia and Sundown set up their tipi in our back yard, and the model was finally finished [see page 235]. As we were looking at the work one day,

Margaret asked Sundown how he liked it. Sundown made the sign for "fast." "We go like hell," he said. "But if me know how goddamn long he take, me no do!"

One day while I was in Pendleton, I heard about a roundup on McKay Creek. We set out with Alden, our oldest son, and three of the younger children. We camped a short distance from the corrals near a cow outfit that we knew. The boys hailed us as they passed, and I noticed that one of them, Charley Runyan, who was on horseback leading an outlaw bronc, had been drinking. All the boys knew I was studying buckers, and the roundup boss called out, "Who's goin' to ride that buckskin SOB for Proctor?"

George, one of the best riders in the outfit, offered to do the honors, but Runyan broke in with, "There ain't nobody kin ride this hoss but me."

"I guess I kin ride any hoss a sheepherder kin ride," George said.

"You callin' me a sheepherder?" demanded Runyan.

"I sure am," said George, grinning.

I looked up just in time to see Runyan pull a six-shooter and send a .44 bullet into George's stomach. George dropped to the ground. Runyan yanked his horse to a stand, leaned over, fired another shot, and then sank the rowels into his horse's flanks and galloped into the timber.

I rushed over to George, who was rolling about with his hands on his stomach. "Shoot me, shoot me —for God's sake, kill me!" he cried.

Cowboys and Indians were dashing about on horseback and afoot, and the camp was in an uproar. The nearest doctor was in Pendleton, twenty-five miles away. I dreaded leaving Margaret and the children in that wild place, but mine was the only car at the roundup. Giving my revolver to Margaret and a rifle to Alden, I yanked the duffel out of the car, and Jim Thompson, the roundup boss, and I loaded George.

Just as we were passing a tumble-down ranch house a few miles down the road, Runyan dashed out to intercept us. He had taken a short cut and beat us there. Thompson yelled, "For God's sake, keep going!" I crowded on the gas. About five miles from Pendleton we met the doctor and a deputy sheriff, summoned by an Indian who had ridden ahead and telephoned. We left George at the hospital, and I streaked back to my family. The next day the doctor told me that five minutes more and George would have cashed in his chips.

During our first year in Pendleton we heard a good deal about William Hanley, the cattle king of eastern Oregon (and later United States senator). At last I met Hanley in Portland, and was delighted when he invited us to one of his ranches.

When I finished the working model of *The Buckaroo*, we boarded a train for Crane, in southeastern Oregon. In addition to Margaret and me there were the seven youngsters, ranging in age from Hester, eighteen, to Wee MacGregor, four; Mary, the cook; and our dog. I had come a long way from my Rocky Mountain days, when there was only myself to look after.

That summer of camping at Hanley's was one of the most pleasant times the family ever had. Old Borax Sam, the gardener, brought us vegetables every morning, and we found other groceries at the ranch store; the ranch provided us with beef and mutton. There were ponies for all of us to ride, and we had a stream full of fish right at our tent door. Sage hens and pheasants were but a step away waiting to be shot. We found that young sage hens that had fed on dandelions made the juiciest, tenderest fowl imaginable. Jackrabbits were pests, and the county paid a bounty of five cents for every pair of ears turned in. We had good sport and practice for pistols, rifles, and shotguns. In season there was deer hunting in the Steens Mountain range. Alden and Phim had wonderful times riding with the cowboys after the cattle scattered over the 200,000-acre ranch.

When it came time to leave in the fall, I went to the ranch office to pay for the food we had bought during the summer. Tom Allen, the cowboy in charge, looked through the book and remarked, "I can't find any bill against you."

I told him about the groceries, vegetables, and meat.

"Mr. Proctor," he said, "There's no record of anything against you. You don't owe the outfit a damn cent."

There wasn't a thing I could do about it but be glad that I had done a relief of Bill Hanley's face [see page 234] and another of Allen.

Back in Portland, I received a letter from Red, my cowboy model. He was in jail awaiting trial for stealing horses, and wanted eight hundred dollars for bail money so that he could get out of prison and clear himself. His letter read, ". . . them damn fools that stolt them hosses used a hot frypan to wipe out the brand instead of acid. You don't think I'd mix up with a damn outfit like that."

Bill Hanley believed that Red was innocent and put up his bail. Red was convicted, but Hanley, who attended his trial, thought that it was Red's past record that did him in rather than the evidence in the case. It seemed that a number of the stolen horses were found in his hideaway corral.

"Them fellers left them hosses in my corral," Red claimed. "How in hell'd I know they'd been stolt? I jes' cain't pick up a rope nowheres but they's a goddamn hoss on the other end."

XXIII.

BACK TO DENVER

During the last few months I was working on *Indian Pursuing Buffalo,* I found that when I leaned over the model I had difficulty regaining my balance. A local doctor found that I was bleeding internally from stomach ulcers and advised me to go to the Mayo Clinic at Rochester, Minnesota, for an examination.

On the way to Rochester, Margaret and I stopped in Portland to see Joseph N. Teal, a well-known lumberman, who commissioned me to do *Pioneer,* a statue which he intended to give to the University of Oregon. Also about that time George Pratt asked me to do a statue of a Mohawk Indian which he proposed to give to the state of New York. I had not had any large commissions recently, and the two new ones brightened my financial prospects. All I had to do was get well.

At the Mayo Clinic, I had surgery and apparently recovered. But after standing around one day in a snowstorm waiting for a taxi, I had a relapse and came within a hair's breadth of passing in my chips. While I was delirious, I had hallucinations about an equestrian statue of Buffalo Bill that I had finished. It was in a park in Russia, and I was lying on the base exposed to a terrific blizzard and in the firing line of two factions of battling Russians.

The doctors weren't very optimistic when Margaret talked with them. They recommended another operation but said that I probably wouldn't live through it. "What do you want us to do?" they asked.

"Exactly the opposite of what you *are* doing," Margaret said. "Give him a cheerful nurse, and let *me* take his mind off his stomach." They turned me over to her.

Margaret came to me with a radiant face, assuring me that "the doctors say you are all right now. All you need is a little sleep." She watched by my side for several hours. The moment my eyes opened, she didn't give me time to think of myself but started talking about a fishing trip. Every time my hand went to my stomach, she talked enthusiastically about some pleasant camp that we had had, or some wonderful fishing spot, or some well-remembered trip to the mountains. By the spring of 1917, I was well on my way to recovery.

As soon as I was able to travel, Margaret and I went to New York, where details were arranged about my commission for the Mohawk Indian. On our way back west, we decided to stop in Denver. For some years there had been talk of a statue of Buffalo Bill, and Theodore Roosevelt, who had been president of the Buffalo Bill Association, had strongly recommended me as the sculptor. Bill died just before we arrived in Denver, and we attended his funeral services. The movement for a memorial took on new life, and the association decided to place a monument at Buffalo Bill's grave on Lookout Mountain.

I had been in Denver several times since the early days, but had not really toured the city. One day Mayor Robert Speer offered to show us around town in his car. We stopped in a residential section, and while we were admiring a charming lake surrounded by homes, Speer asked whether there was any particular spot I would like to visit. "Yes," I said, "old Smith's Lake, several miles out on the prairie, where we boys used to go duck shooting and where we sometimes camped all night."

"You're looking at Smith's Lake at this moment," Speer answered.

On another occasion he drove us through the mountains near the city and again asked whether there was any special place I'd like to see. I thought a moment and then told him, "The place we used to stop the third night when traveling to Grand Lake in our covered wagon. But that's too far away. It was called Idaho Springs."

"We passed it two hours ago," Speer laughed.

I gave up. Denver's phenomenal growth was beyond my comprehension.

Speer told me that he had wanted me to do two statues to replace my *Equestrian Indian* and *Broncho Buster* that had once decorated Denver's Civic Center. They were the two statues I had done in plaster for the Columbian Exposition in Chicago in 1892, and over the years they had disintegrated. Luckily I had with me the small model of the *Broncho Buster*. Losing no time, Speer called J. K. Mullens and Stephen Knight, two local millowners. Mullens said that he would donate the cowboy, and Knight agreed to donate the Indian.

Now with commissions for five statues in hand, Margaret and I returned to Portland and the children. Since I already had a small model of *Broncho Buster*, I decided to do the pioneer for Teal first. And I knew just the model I wanted—Jess Cravens, a trapper I had met at Bill Hanley's ranch two summers before. He was six feet tall, had long hair and whiskers, and even wore buckskins.

Excitedly I asked Hanley whether he thought Cravens would pose for me. "Sure he will," Hanley said. "He's out trapping varmints somewhere up the Salmon River. Why don't you go out and find him?"

When I tracked down Cravens, he agreed to model, and with the family we set up a camp on the bank of the Clearwater River and started to work. Occasionally pack trains passed on the trail near us, led by prospectors, hunters, fire fighters, and the like, going into the mountains. We decided there was too much traffic and moved upriver ten miles or so.

Often while I was working that summer I was seized by hunting or fishing fever. Once Cravens's dogs were needing exercise—at least that was our excuse—and we decided to go after a bear. He and young Phim and I followed a tributary of the Clearwater to its head and camped on top of a high, wide plateau. We had heard that this was good Indian hunting country, and all about the springs and creeks we found rotting tipi poles. Everywhere we saw caribou and deer antlers and even an occasional bear skull.

I was not yet completely recovered from my operation and could carry nothing heavier than a six-shooter. One morning the dogs raised a big tumult, indicating that they had jumped Bruin. Cravens and Phim dashed after them down the mountain through the thick brush, leaving me behind. I discovered bear signs and began to investigate.

All through the tangled mass of underbrush were tunnels leading in every direction. Keeping my revolver pointed ahead, I crawled into one of them. I could still hear the dogs barking furiously down in the valley. In the gloom of the dense tunnel I couldn't see far, and my nerves were as taut as piano wires.

Suddenly a hell-roaring noise broke loose behind me. Twisting around frantically, I got a glimpse of Cravens's big hound in a buzz-saw clinch with a bear. The dog had grabbed the bear just as he was starting into my tunnel, and in the confusion of battle the bear came up pointing out instead of in. While I was congratulating myself on my good luck, both bear and dog disappeared over the crest of the hill a few yards away.

I dashed after the pair, forgetting that I wasn't supposed to be strong. At the top of the hill I got a glimpse of the two pinwheeling downward. Then in my excitement I slipped and went tobogganing after them. I was trying to ease off the seat of my pants and onto my hip, when I struck something and catapulted into the air. When I struck the ground again, the six-shooter flew out of my hand in one direction and I went in another.

At the bottom of the slide was a pool in the creek. The fighters plunged over the bank, splashing water in all directions. Then the bear broke loose and clambered up the bank on the other side with the hound right on his tail. Fortune was still with me, because by the time I landed in the pool, water had filled it again, which saved me from cracking every bone in my body. Pulling myself together, I scrambled to shore and sat down. Feeling a pain in my stomach, a horrible thought struck me. Had I torn out the partly healed incision in my belly? I ripped open my shirt. No, Dr. Mayo's hemstitching still held. I'd had enough though, and made my way back to camp, not caring much one way or the other whether the bear got away.

With winter coming on, we headed back to Lewis-

BACK TO DENVER

ton. I had planned to go to New York to reclaim my fine studio. The sculptor Frederick MacMonnies was renting it, and his lease was soon to expire. He wired that if he had to move it would cost him twenty thousand dollars to dismantle the colossal monument he was working on, and so I let him stay on, despite my disappointment. Then we decided to go to California for the winter. My brother William, a professor at Stanford University, was living in Los Altos, a few miles from Stanford, and found us a house there. Margaret took the younger children on the train to enroll them in school, while I drove with Hester and Alden Sampson, who had joined us.

XXIV

BETWEEN CALIFORNIA AND NEW YORK

When we arrived in California in October, 1917, Hester decided not to return to Smith College, where she had been enrolled, but to register at Stanford. I found a barn in Los Altos to use for a studio and kept it for a while, even after we moved to Palo Alto in 1918.

About that time Jess Cravens, who had posed for the working model of *Pioneer* in Idaho, came to Palo Alto and settled down in a cottage near my studio. Before long he decided to get married, and we had the wedding at our house.

When *Pioneer* and *Broncho Buster* were ready to be pointed up, Robert Paine, an old sculptor friend of New York days who was living in Berkeley, agreed to help me. While the full-size statue of *Pioneer* was being pointed up, I worked on the small model of *On the War Trail*. Then while I was finishing *Pioneer*, Payne and an assistant enlarged *Bron-

cho Buster from the small plaster cast I had made in Pendleton. The plaster cast of *Pioneer* was sent to Providence, Rhode Island, for casting in bronze [see page 239] and in due time was placed on the campus of the University of Oregon. Before long *Broncho Buster* was also sent east for casting, and final preparations were made to place it before the Civic Center in Denver [see page 240].

Then I began serious work on *On the War Trail*. Louis O'Neil, a San Jose lawyer, owned a horse ranch in the hills not far from Los Altos, and he let me keep one of his ponies at our home. The superintendent of the Nez Percé Indian Reservation in Idaho gave Sundown permission to come to work as a model, and Cecilia, Jackson's wife, insisted on coming too and bringing their son, Willie. We fixed up a cottage for them, and I began work on the sculpture.

With the onset of spring we got caught up in one roundup after another. Though a good time was had by all, we accomplished little work until the season was over. When the roundups finally ended, I decided that the Indians had had enough good times and that we could get back to work. But by then, Sundown and Cecilia wanted to go back to Idaho. Pancho Villa's depredations had frightened Cecilia, who got the idea fixed in her head that Mexican bandits were going to come up and murder her.

Then something else happened to sour her on California. At that time trains from the north were ferried across the Sacramento River between Vallejo and Benicia. When we were at the ferry one day, the brakeman thought the Indians would be interested in seeing the long train run onto the gigantic ferry. Yes, Cecilia was interested, so much so that she wouldn't get on the boat herself. "Me know boats," she said. "Me see 'em Snake River. If boat carry train, me no go." When persuasion failed, the trainman grabbed her arm and rushed her aboard. She sulked for several days after.

Then Sundown began to get restive. "Me leave'm harness on ground back home," he explained. "Must go hang up."

I argued that fifteen hundred miles was a long way to travel to hang up a harness.

Then he said, "Calf in wrong pasture. Me go change'm."

I wired the Nez Percé superintendent, who telegraphed Sundown that he would personally hang up the harness and put the calf in new pasture. But the Indians went anyway, leaving me without a model.

I had started a four-foot plasteline model of the Indian for *On the War Trail*. I took it with me in the car and drove alone to the Blackfoot Reservation adjoining Glacier Park in Montana. When I arrived, some kind of celebration was going on. In the crowd was a brave named Gray Eagle, who was absolutely the ideal Indian. He was tall, sinuous, and dignified; his every movement was masculine grace itself. When I asked him to pose, he responded in a reserved but friendly way, saying that he would have to discuss the matter with his wife. She believed that making likenesses was bad medicine and refused to let Gray Eagle co-operate. After a little adjustment in modeling fees, however, they finally agreed.

Since I wanted to stay in the mountains, I rented a cottage at a hotel in Glacier Park. But by the time I was ready to go to work, another baby was due, and I returned to Palo Alto by train to be on hand for the occasion. As soon as Margaret was sufficiently recovered, I started back for Glacier Park, but at Seattle I received a wire that she and the baby were very ill. So back I went and stayed until they were out of danger.

When I got back to Glacier, Gray Eagle backed out of the bargain and refused to go to work. He said he was afraid of the bears in the mountains. I learned that most Blackfoot Indians were afraid of mountains. Finally I gave up with Gray Eagle and drove to Browning, Montana, with my still-unfinished model.

In Browning I hired another Indian named Big Beaver. He was about thirty years old, tall and handsome. He spoke English quite well, and I looked forward to working with him. The Indians around Browning were so curious that they kept disrupting the work, and I accomplished little until the superintendent gave me permission to work at the hospital six miles from town.

The move seemed a simple enough matter. Beaver was to collect his wife, his tipi, and his cooking outfit and camp close by the hospital. But it took two days to pry him away from town. Finally I thought we were on our way. Beaver was harnessing up his horses in preparation for leaving when suddenly he dropped everything and fled. I followed, cussing and fuming, and corralled him behind a barn.

"My mother-in-law was coming," he said. It seemed that an Indian male must not meet his mother-in-law face to face, and under no circumstances was he allowed to speak to her. When con-

BETWEEN CALIFORNIA AND NEW YORK

frontation was unavoidable, he must talk to her through some other party. If Beaver had looked into his mother-in-law's face, he would have had to give her a pony. It seemed a terrible burden for a man to carry. The wise Indian donated the pony and got the business over with at once.

Big Beaver and his pretty wife finally arrived at the work area. At last, I thought. The next day I had to go to town to have some work done on the car. I took Beaver along. When we returned, he couldn't find his wife. He looked all around and finally said, "Well, she's flew the coop. Let her go if she wants to."

When winter came, I arranged for Big Beaver to go to California with me so that I could finish both Indian statues—the equestrian for Denver and the Mohawk for George Pratt. Beaver was a great one for the women. When we stopped in Pocatello, Idaho, two Indian girls passed, and Beaver immediately "made coup" for them: he tapped them on their shoulders, meaning, "You my squaws now." They were not offended but to my surprise asked me what he had meant by the gesture. I explained, and they laughed and went on. Undaunted, Beaver wanted to stay and press his claim.

While we were crossing the desert, seemingly a million miles from anywhere, a tire blew out. Beaver immediately began a death chant and, going back up the road a way, piled up some rocks. Standing by the mound, he muttered and gestured in several directions. He thought that we were going to die right there.

"The evil spirits not to come beyond that pile of stones," he said.

Close by were several old graves that helped increase Beaver's jitters. He was convinced that they held the bones of others who had blown out tires at that very spot.

When we finally got to Palo Alto, *On the War Trail* was my first project. By the time the four-foot model was finished, the full-size horse was cast in plaster, ready to be shipped east. A few months' work cleared the docket in Palo Alto, and then I left for New York, sending Beaver on ahead.

It was pleasant to be back in my New York studio, which had the big stands, chain hoists, and other implements necessary for carrying on big projects. I resumed old friendships, particularly among members of the Century Club.

Work on the big statue dragged on into the spring of 1920. Getting restless, I wrote Margaret to join me. After she arrived, things were more cheerful.

At last I finished *On the War Trail* [see page 241] and the Mohawk Indian. My contract with Big Beaver was now ended, and we saw him off on the train ride back to his home on the reservation.

While we were in New York, I received a commission from Dr. Waldo Coe, of Portland, Oregon, to do an equestrian statue of Theodore Roosevelt as a Rough Rider see pages [242 to 243]. The commission brought back memories of my associations with Roosevelt. I recalled the pangs I had felt when he organized the Rough Riders. If I had not been in Paris on a scholarship, and if I had not had a young wife and newborn baby, I would certainly have joined him.

Just before President Roosevelt left the White House, he commissioned me to do two models of buffalo heads for the State Dining Room, which was being redecorated by McKim, Mead, and White. I made two small models and took them to the President. As I passed a door, Roosevelt looked up, saw that I had the models, waved his hand, and said, "Bully for you, Proctor! I'll see you in a minute."

I stood in the waiting room with several senators and representatives. When the President came in, he walked directly to me, shook my hand, and said he was delighted I had come. He wanted me to meet him at an appointed hour to show the models to the National Art Commission that he had just appointed.

William Mitchell Kendall, of McKim, Mead, and White, and I went in together at the appointed time, to find the President addressing the commission. Kendall and I hesitated, each waiting for the other to move. When the President saw us, he laughed and said, "Well, come on in, Alphonse and Gaston."

After the meeting, as Roosevelt was leaving, he said, "Now I must go to the Senate and fight with the wild beasts of Ephesus."

It was at about this time that I received a commission to sculpture a bronze buffalo head for the cornerstone of the Arlington Cemetery Bridge in Washington [see page 238]. Back in Palo Alto, I was eager to begin work; however, my studio was suddenly too small. Perhaps it only seemed cramped after the size and convenience of the New York studio, but it definitely was not large enough for a big project. Dr. Ray Lyman Wilbur, president of Stanford University, turned over to me a large room in the engineering building, and before long I was established with all the necessary trappings, ready for work.

BETWEEN CALIFORNIA AND NEW YORK

Soon the statue had reached the stage where it had to go to New York. There I turned it over to an old friend, Gozo Kawamura, to be pointed up. I had met Gozo in Paris in the 1890's, and he had worked for me at different times over a period of years. While he was working on the big pieces, I modeled on a new project, *Indian Maiden and Fawn*.

Before the Roosevelt statue was finished, A. C. Dixon, a good friend from Oregon, came to the studio to tell me that R. A. Booth, of Eugene, Oregon, wanted me to do an equestrian statue of a Methodist circuit rider, to be erected in Salem, Oregon. Back I went to Palo Alto to work on it. By the fall of 1921, *The Circuit Rider* had been finished and shipped to Long Island for casting in bronze [see page 244].

XXV.

The Pioneer Mother

I have often been asked how sculptors get their ideas for statues. Most of my inspirations for statues or compositions came without apparent effort on my part. Sometimes a filmy image would flicker in my brain for months or years and then suddenly appear clearly in my mind's eye when I least expected it. *The Pioneer Mother* came to me in this way.

For many years the desire to do a statue of a pioneer woman had been strong and insistent, but the image was vague. I thought about it off and on for a long time without being able to form a clear picture. It seemed to me that most people, in thinking of pioneers, thought solely of the men. I considered the heroism of the women equal to, and perhaps greater than, the men's. As Mark Twain said, "The women had to endure everything the pioneers did, and then they also had to endure the pioneers!"

Whenever I speculated on a statue of a pioneer woman, I decided that I didn't want to show her doing ordinary tasks, plodding westward in a calico dress or driving cattle before her. I wanted to be true to life, but I also wanted to show another, no less heroic, side.

One night in 1922, in Palo Alto, I saw the statue at last. Why the complete picture came on that particular night, at that particular place, I do not know. I hadn't thought of the subject for some time, and yet there it was, suddenly clear and distinct in my mind.

My vision of the statue was a group of weary pioneers traveling westward over the prairie. The young mother, the principal figure, rode horseback, carrying a baby in her arms—the hope for the future of the West. My pioneers were not beginners. Their equipment and attitudes showed that they had already had much experience. I wanted to convey the sense of travel across the dreary expanse of plains under burning sun, rain, and storms, braving hunger and thirst, fording rivers, beset by many dangers on the way.

Such was my conception. Once the composition was settled in my mind, the next problem was to find someone who would put up the money to have a working model enlarged and cast in bronze—no

The Pioneer Mother

easy task, for the cost of pieces of this size was considerable. I tucked the idea back into my mind and went on about my business.

In 1923, Margaret and I loaded our car with small plaster casts and bronzes and drove to Los Angeles to give a one-man show. In itself the show was not unduly profitable, but it had one important result. Among the pieces exhibited was a charging panther, which was purchased by Howard Vanderslice, of Kansas City, Missouri.

Vanderslice proved to have a keen interest in sculpture, and in the course of several conversations with him I learned that he had come from a pioneer family and had long cherished a deep desire to erect some sort of memorial to the pioneer women. I hesitated to mention my own ideas for such a work, feeling certain that the project would be far too expensive for one person to sponsor. But Vanderslice returned to the subject so often that I finally told him that I had something that might interest him. His first reaction was one of caution, and he asked what it would cost to make a small model. When he found that there would be no charge for the model, he asked me to go ahead with a sketch.

I didn't let Vanderslice see the clay model until it was finished, and when I pulled the covering off and he looked at it for the first time, he grew tremendously excited and trembled like a leaf. It was exactly what he had dreamed of, but when he learned the cost of finishing such a piece and erecting it in bronze, he was staggered. He hesitated to discuss the proposed work with his wife, fearing that she would be against it. Though reluctant to commit himself, Vanderslice did express a desire to see a larger model. For my own part, I really couldn't afford the expense, but I was so fired with the desire to do the work that I threw caution to the winds and decided to make a five-foot model.

Certain that western characters would be easier to find in Hollywood than anywhere else, we sold our Palo Alto home and moved to southern California. On our first day in Hollywood we saw a rickety Ford driven by an old bewhiskered gentleman—just the man we needed for the trapper. "Sure, I'll pose," he said. "Done that in the movies—doubled for Ernest Torrence in *The Covered Wagon*."

Then I found just the horse we needed, bought her for $110, and kept her in a barn nearby. Margaret made the woman's costume. George Cole, an artist friend, loaned me the packsaddles. A woman in Eugene gave us a sidesaddle on which she had ridden across the Plains as a bride in 1852.

Since I had started the project without a definite commission, money began to get scarce. Though he sympathized with my problems and wanted the statue, Vanderslice still had not made up his mind to undertake so great an expense. With all our expenses we didn't know whether we would be able to make the current payment on our new house. Then Gifford Pinchot, governor of Pennsylvania and an old friend, loaned us enough money—without interest, note, or time limit—to make the house payment, and the property was saved. And finally Vanderslice advanced two thousand dollars on the fee.

At that time I had to go to New York on another matter, and Vanderslice invited me to stop over in Kansas City. I arrived just in time to learn that Mrs. Vanderslice had died that day. When Howard Vanderslice saw me at the hotel, he told me that after months of hesitation—partly because his wife was suffering from a bad heart—he had finally told her of the project. To his astonishment and delight she had shown an enthusiasm equal to his own.

After I returned to Hollywood, Vanderslice arrived with his lawyer to see the model and draw up the contract. In my eagerness to do all I could to allay Vanderslice's uncertainty, I figured the costs much too low. Fortunately, his lawyer proved to be a brother of the late Bela Pratt, a sculptor friend from Paris days. He had negotiated all of Bela's contracts and knew the economics of sculpture. He not only dispelled Vanderslice's fears but also told him that he was not paying me nearly enough. Consequently, Vanderslice paid me ten thousand dollars more than the sum originally discussed.

Ready now to begin work in earnest, my first problem was modeling the horses. With an equestrian statue I have always found it best, after the general plan of the composition has been settled, to model the horse very carefully before beginning the rider. If the horse is not right and changes have to be made after the rider has been added, the rider's figure as well as the horse may have to be changed, which entails much extra work. As a foundation for the work, I made armatures of jointed gas pipes. I made a wooden platform for each horse and secured the armatures to them and then wired strips of wood to the crossbars of the armature and added other wires for further foundation.

Since there were to be two horses and four figures, I decided to cast the first horse in plaster as soon as the plasteline model was finished. In moving the horse about as I worked on the other figures, there

The Pioneer Mother

would be less likelihood of damage to a plaster model than to one in plasteline. Plaster can be readily patched, but if clay is bashed out of shape so that armatures are bent and surfaces damaged, repairs are difficult.

I found a young woman who answered for the pioneer mother. I prepared a dummy horse and mounted the saddle on it. She sat on the dummy while actually posing but in between times rode about the yard on the real horse, both to give her the feeling of being mounted and to give me a sense of action.

One day as I started to work, I realized that the folds of her long dress were hanging perfectly. I worked feverishly, and she held the pose for a couple of hours without rest, while Margaret stood watch to detect any indication that the model was about to faint. When I finished the drapery, the woman had to be helped to the floor.

To keep from going stale, I changed from one figure to another, and the work progressed rapidly. Finally the working model was finished. It was four feet eight inches high by six feet long. Next I had to cast the entire group in plaster, a formidable task for there were no plaster molders in Los Angeles. With the assistance of fellow sculptor Robert Paine, the casting was finally finished. The next step was to enlarge the group, making a full-size plaster model which would be an exact reproduction of the small working model. This work could not be done in Los Angeles, and we decided to go to New York.

Except for brief visits we had been away from New York for several years, and when I went east to investigate conditions and costs, I had an unpleasant shock. It was the middle of the twenties, and New York had become a very expensive city. When I wrote Margaret about the situation, she wired back, "Why not consider Rome, Italy?"

I consulted with several sculptors who had worked in Italy and also spoke to William Mitchell Kendall, who was then chairman of the American Academy in Rome. When Kendall offered me the use of a studio at the academy, I decided that Rome was the place to enlarge the statue and have it cast in bronze.

The company that undertook to ship the working model to New York claimed to be experienced in shipping plaster casts. But instead of separating all the pieces and packing them properly, they sent the work off as a unit. I had just arrived back in Los Angeles to prepare for the cross-country motor trip with the family when news reached me that the statue had arrived in New York broken in several places. I wired our sculptor friend Victor Salvatore, who, with the assistance of Attilio Contini, a most competent and skilled plaster molder, fitted all the broken pieces together and restored the work.

We decided to take with us to Rome the five children who were still living at home. Our oldest son, Alden, had just been married and had decided to move east with his bride. Hester was working in San Francisco, and Phim in Palo Alto. We had a new Nash car, and our son Alden had a Hudson. We decided to form a two-car expedition and camp all the way to New York. It was a fascinating two-month trip. We zigzagged from one place to another but in general held to the old Oregon Trail, following the track of the early pioneers.

Early in October, 1925, we arrived in New York and immediately began preparations for Italy. While were were getting ready, Kermit Roosevelt called to say that a friend of his wanted to buy my *Stalking Panther*, the same model that the "tennis cabinet" had given his father when Theodore Roosevelt was president. When Kermit and a friend came to the studio, the working model of *The Pioneer Mother* was on view, and Roosevelt's friend ordered a bronze cast of it as well as of the panther and another sculpture.

This time I supervised the packing of the plaster working model and sent it ahead. After a pleasant voyage on the *Conte Verde* we docked in Naples and then went on to Rome.

I began enlarging the working model of *The Pioneer Mother*, engaging several Italian sculptors as helpers. I soon discovered that the best workers I could get were indifferent copiers. They seemed to think that it wasn't really artistic to copy figures faithfully. Each one wanted to add his own individuality to the work. One man modeled the shoulder of the young pioneer four inches too large and was very much surprised when I objected.

The one year we had planned to spend in Rome stretched to two, 1926 and 1927, during which time I worked early and late, day after day. Finally the group was finished, and the plaster molder took charge. Italians excel at plaster molding, and the cast was soon complete. Then the full-sized *Pioneer Mother* group, in plaster, was mounted on a big truck, and off it went to the bronze foundry. The sight of plaster casts on trucks was not an uncommon one in Rome, but it was rather unusual to see a pioneer woman of heroic size mounted on a horse and followed by a pack horse, all on an open truck bed.

The Pioneer Mother

The final bronze casting was made by the lost-wax process. First, a model for each figure in the group was cast in wax. I spent many days retouching the figures, giving them their final work. Then the molds were put on. After that, each piece was covered with a mixture of brick dust, plaster, and molding sand. The pieces were placed in a deep pit, bricked up, and packed carefully in sand. Then a fire was built, and the molds were slowly baked until all the wax had melted and run out, leaving them empty and dry, ready for filling with molten bronze.

At last the day arrived for casting the first large pieces in bronze, and we went to see the process, which hadn't changed since the days of Benvenuto Cellini. The mold was surrounded by a brick wall, and the space between mold and wall was filled with molding sand. Air vents had been left in the top of the mold so that the molten metal would flow through all the vacant places, driving the air up and out of the vents. If air formed a pocket, the hot bronze could not enter, which would mean an open space in the cast, or at best a cast that was porous and full of holes.

A twenty-foot trough made of the same material as the mold led from a spot quite a bit higher than the mold. Why the trough was so long I never learned. Under its full length a fire was kept red-hot so that the molten bronze would not cool before it reached the mold. My family watched as the glowing metal ran down the trough into the mold. When molten bronze spurted out through the vent holes, we knew that the cast was finished.

It cooled for two days. Then the brick wall around the cast was pulled down and the sand dug out. The outer mold was chopped away with pickaxes. Air vents and conduits filled with bronze had to be chiseled away, and fins caused by the fine cracks in the mold had to be smoothed down. Then the mass of bronze was dipped in a vat of acid, which removed all stains and left it gleaming like a new penny. Finally each part of the statue was chiseled, to make every detail exactly like the original plaster model. When all the pieces had been cast, they were fitted and welded together, and the job was done.

But Kansas City was far from Rome, and the huge statue had to be transported across the ocean and halfway across the United States. The only Italian railroad cars that would carry such a group and still have clearance under bridges and through tunnels were gondola cars. When the mother of the group was cut apart at the waist, the packing case had just enough clearance.

After the finished statue had been shipped, we turned to other things and made a motor trip across the Alps to Brussels. At last the time came for me to leave for Kansas City for the unveiling of the monument, which took place on November 11, 1927, five years after the first clear conception of the work had come to me [see pages 246 and 247].

XXVI

GENERAL LEE AND THE MUSTANGS

After the unveiling ceremonies for *The Pioneer Mother* I hurried back to my family in Rome. Months before, I had received a commission to do a statue of Til Taylor for Pendleton, Oregon, and I was eager to complete work on it. Til had probably been the best-known sheriff in the Pacific Northwest. He was proud that he had never killed a man; he had a certain way of persuading outlaws to go with him without having to use his gun. After I left Pendleton in 1916, Til was killed by several prisoners who broke jail while he and his deputy were out for lunch and shot them with their own guns when they returned. Taylor was much loved by the people of the area, and they decided to erect an equestrian statue of him as a memorial. The money was raised through donations ranging from fifty cents to several hundred dollars. Many of the Indians whom Taylor had defended and befriended gave small sums.

I had started work on the statue shortly before I finished *The Pioneer Mother*, and shortly after I got back to Rome I was able to ship the five-foot model to Brussels [see page 245]. The work, confined to two figures, seemed to go rapidly in comparison with the previous group, which had four figures and two animals. The model took only about a year to complete. After it was cast in bronze, the statue was ready to be shipped to Pendleton, and we were ready to go back to the United States.

On our return we decided to settle in the East, although I preferred living in the western part of the country. Since I disliked commuting long distances to and from New York, we settled in Wilton, Connecticut.

The first commission I received was another *Pioneer Mother*, this one for the campus of the University of Oregon [see page 251]. The donor, Burt Brown Barker, originally from New York, had moved to Oregon and become very much interested in the university.

Barker wanted his pioneer woman to be somewhat different from other such sculptures. He said that whereas most statues of pioneers depicted some aspect of the westward movement he wanted this one to seem to look back at the past, as his own mother was then doing. His conception was of an elderly woman sitting in repose with her hands in her lap. In her hands would be a half-closed book, her fingers marking a place. Her head would be tilted slightly forward in contemplation.

After the first details had been worked out and I understood what Barker wanted, he left everything to me. I didn't realize how successful I had been in executing the work until one evening George Fraser, the architect of the American Academy in Rome, suddenly came face to face with the finished figure in my studio. "My God," he said, "that woman is looking a thousand miles from here!"

One day I received a letter from Mrs. R. V. Rogers, of Dallas, Texas, regarding a commission for an equestrian statue of Robert E. Lee, which the Southern Women's Memorial Association was considering for Dallas. According to the letter the association would like a group showing two mounted figures, the general and a young soldier representing the youth of the period who had admired Lee for his superb leadership and looked to him for guidance.

I had always had high regard for Lee as a man and as a general. I pictured Lee as a leader fighting a fierce struggle against fate and insurmountable difficulties. With this picture in mind I made a little model showing the general and the young man wearing capes. They were in a storm. Their garments were blown by the wind, the brims of their hats bending, the horses' manes and tails flying. The horses' heads were lowered as they faced the storm. That was the model I showed to Mrs. Rogers and her sister when they visited my Connecticut studio.

The ladies liked the composition, calling it dramatic and forceful—but it was not their idea of Lee. We discussed the matter for a time, and I made other sketches. Mrs. Rogers decided that I could capture the spirit of Lee and asked me to go on. I promised to make more sketches. I realized that her Lee was a many-sided man and that he might be represented in several ways. I began to make other studies of him. The more I reviewed his character and his campaigns, the more I accepted the southern view that Lee himself had not been defeated. As far as I, with my limited understanding of military tactics, could judge, his strategy was usually right. He hadn't the resources of his enemies; the forces against him were overpowering.

GENERAL LEE AND THE MUSTANGS

Even Lee could not accomplish the impossible. That is why I believed that Lee himself was not defeated, and I tried to create a statue showing the hero marching on. I presented a small working model which I thought embodied these ideas. It was accepted and a contract was drawn up. I decided to decline the commission, however, because the terms of the contract were unacceptable, and turned to other things, among them a large bronze statue, *Indian and Trapper*, for the McKnight Memorial Fountain in Wichita, Kansas [see page 249], and a memorial tablet to my old friend Irving Hale, for West Point Military Academy [see page 250].

In August, 1933, Margaret and I were returning from a trip west. As we were crossing Arizona, it occurred to me that Dallas was only a few hundred miles away and that I might see whether I could pick up the threads of the negotiations for the Lee monument. In Dallas I made another sketch model, which was accepted, and I signed a new contract. The statue would require two years to model, and there was no time to be wasted. When I had the composition fairly well established in New York, I shipped the plasteline model to my Connecticut studio, because there I could work on the horses out of doors.

I easily found a mare for the general's aide, but when it came to Traveller, the general's horse, that was a different matter. I had little information about that famous horse that was of real help to me. I found a retouched photograph taken after the war, but by then both the general and his horse were old and showed little of the spirit of their active years. At first I worked mostly from Lee's own description, which gave Traveller's general characteristics and height. Then I learned that a neighbor had a horse that might resemble the great one. Margaret and I went to see him in the stable of a riding club, and to our delight he proved to be as nearly a duplicate of Traveller as we could find.

Within two years the working model was ready to be shown to the committee [see page 252]. It was a time that every sculptor looks forward to with some trepidation. A selection committee—especially one made up of women who know what they want—is a formidable group. The model was cast in plaster and sent to my studio in New York. Mrs. Rogers's brother-in-law and sister, Mr. and Mrs. Rhodes Baker, also of Dallas, approved the model, and prospects looked fairly bright. Finally the committee as a whole approved photographs of the working model, and preparations were made to start

on the full-sized model. I invited Dr. Bowling Lee, grandson of the general, to inspect the model, and much to my satisfaction and the committee's, he also approved it.

I decided to go directly into plaster for the enlargement to full size, a rather unorthodox procedure. Although it did away with modeling the group in plasteline, which would cost about two thousand dollars for materials alone, I knew that that saving would be absorbed in the extra labor of doing the model directly in plaster. For the pointing up from the working model to full size, I engaged my old friend Gozo Kawamura.

The heads of Lee and the young soldier were pointed up in plasteline, because it is easier to do small details in the softer material, which is easily changed and corrected. While Gozo was enlarging the figure of Lee and his horse, I devoted my time to reproducing the likeness of Lee. The available photographs of the general were not very satisfactory; there was no full-face view and but one side of his profile had been taken. It was interesting to learn that a good many of the pictures of Lee in books had been printed from the wrong side of the negative plate. I could identify some of the reversed pictures by the way the coat was buttoned

GENERAL LEE AND THE MUSTANGS

or by the part of the hair. One problem in doing a portrait head for an equestrian statue is that the committee members usually want to judge the work on the ground at eye level, not realizing that when it is in place high up it looks very different.

When the larger parts of the statue had been pointed up in Gozo's shop, they were moved to my studio in Connecticut. The completed plaster model weighed about six tons, which required a heavy turntable and platforms, as well as strengthening of the studio floor. I had nearly the whole north end of the studio cut out and installed two large, steel-framed glass doors. Then I built a platform even with the floor, extending into the field about forty feet. When I wanted to see the statue out of doors, we hooked pulleys to the platform and dragged it out on rollers.

Building up and finishing the large model required another full year of my time, plus the efforts of several assistants, including those of my son Gifford. When it was completed, the committee approved it, and then the plaster group was removed for casting into bronze.

As soon as the large model had gone to the foundry, Margaret and I went to Sarasota, Florida, for the winter. We had hoped that the sunshine and swim-

*Gozo Kawamura
pointing up the statue of Robert E. Lee on Traveller*

ming would be beneficial to both of us, but it rained most of the winter and we had very little sun.

The committee was constantly requesting me to come to Dallas and help decide where the statue should be placed, but since the roads were bad, we remained in Sarasota until late April, 1936. When we arrived in Dallas, the ground had already been broken for the site of the statue. It was a corner site, facing south—a very good choice. If at all possible every statue should face south, because as the sun moves from east to west there is a good light on the statue all day long. When a statue faces north, the front, which is the important view, is usually in shadow.

The Texas Centennial Exposition was to open on June 6, 1936, and since Franklin D. Roosevelt was expected to attend the opening, the committee invited him to dedicate the statue. Though we hurried up the construction of the pedestal, it was not yet finished when the bronze cast of the statue arrived. Then Congress delayed adjournment, and the President sent word that he would arrive in Dallas on June 12, which gave us a little more time.

Finally, on June 9, the hour arrived for placing the statue on its pedestal. Seven tons of bronze had to be hoisted about twenty-five feet into the air, swung over the granite work of the wide-stepped exedra, and placed upon the pedestal. The bronze caster adjusted the cable in the right places and told the foreman of the hoisting gang to go ahead. With raised hands the foreman gave the signal. There was a rumbling of gears, wheels began to turn, the cable stiffened, and the bronze group began to tremble and quiver.

Then the big crane began to move up. General Lee sat impassively upon his horse, as he had often done in life with shot and shell flying about him. Slowly the crane raised the group a few inches from the ground and moved it forward to the side of the granite structure. When the statue reached the spot where it was to be hoisted higher into the air, the huge bronze swung slightly to the left. My heart went into my throat.

A young onlooker standing nearby asked me, "D'you think he can make it in one jump?" His companion asked the identity of the younger figure. "Oh, that's Gen'l Lee when he was a young feller," answered the first.

The tackle was carefully examined and then the group began to rise slowly. Up, up it went until it was hanging twenty feet in the air. Then it moved over the central die. Still there was danger. If any-

GENERAL LEE AND THE MUSTANGS

thing was to give way the base of the bronze would hit the pedestal on the side and the statue would topple over on its head onto the hard floor of the exedra. It seemed like ages before the group was at last firmly and safely in place.

Three days later, on June 12, 1936, a large crowd gathered about the statue. Bands were playing, and the militia was out in numbers. The statue was enshrouded in a mass of drapery; greenery and flowers were arranged about the base. In front of the base was the speaker's stand, where I stood with my family and the ladies of the committee.

The screaming of police sirens and the cheering of the crowd announced the arrival of the President of the United States. The autos following the presidential car were halted outside the ropes, but the big black car in which President and Mrs. Roosevelt were riding moved on behind the statue, where it came to a halt. The President and his party sat in the car, and the dedication ceremonies began.

At the proper moment, Robert E. Lee IV, the general's great-grandson, handed the President the cord he was to pull to release the curtain that enveloped the monument. At the sound of a bugle the President pulled the cord and the draperies fell away.

"Magnificent!" he said, as the statue came into view. I felt well rewarded for four years of work [see page 253].

Shortly after the Lee monument was in place, I decided to take time out from sculpture to do some dry points of wild animals. I had a lot of fun for a couple of years, but it was just as well that I hadn't counted on selling the dry points, because I was obviously the only one who got real pleasure out of them. I can truthfully say that I have the biggest collection of A. Phimister Proctor dry points in the world.

Sometime in 1938, when we were living in Seattle, I received a letter from J. Frank Dobie, the western historian. Though I had heard a great deal about Dobie, I had never met him. The letter stated that a friend of his, Ralph Ogden, wanted to donate a sculptured group of mustangs to the University of Texas at Austin. I immediately started a small model, about fifteen inches high, of six mustangs in a compact group. As soon as it was completed, I packed the plaster model in the car and, with Margaret and our youngest daughter, Joanne, left for Texas.

We exhibited the model to Ogden and his wife, to Mr. and Mrs. Dobie, and to a few of their friends. During the discussion of the group that evening, we decided that a colt should be added to the group. The contract was drawn up, and as we shook hands all around, Dobie said, "Well, we're going to like trading with you."

Dobie, who was Ogden's art "confessor," wanted the group to represent real mustangs, and above all they were not to be modernistic caricatures. I heartily agreed to that. With those matters settled the next question was where to obtain the models. Dobie had the answer: on the million-acre King Ranch in South Texas. Dobie made arrangements for me to use any of the horses I wanted.

We drove to the ranch, and Dobie introduced us to Tom East, the son-in-law of the principal owners. East asked me how many days I would need to make my studies.

"Days?" I answered. "It will take months!" Then, noting the surprise on his face, I added, "Probably."

Dobie showed surprise, too, but there was also a look of pleasure in his expression as he realized that I really wanted to study mustangs carefully.

East drove us to Agua Dulce, where the ponies had been rounded up, and we went to the corrals to pick out fifteen mares from which I would select my models.

East then took Margaret, Joanne, and me to Rancho Los Palos, where we were to live while I worked on the group. When I asked the size of Los Palos, he said, "Only nine thousand acres. Your mustangs will be in that pasture."

"How many acres in it?" I asked.

"Oh, just nine hundred," was the answer.

Our cabin, just a hundred yards from the ranch headquarters, was a one-room-and-kitchen structure with a porch. We had brought with us a two-wheel trailer bedroom, which we rolled up to face the porch. Margaret and I slept in the trailer, while Joanne slept in the cabin.

With the help of one of the Mexican ranch hands I built a studio twelve feet long and seven wide with a roof and floor. Three sides were boarded up, but the fourth, the north side, was left open. The structure protected me and my model from the hot summer sun, but it did leave us exposed to the torrential rains and northers in the fall and winter. Next we built a strong modeling stand on wheels, which could be easily rolled about the studio. Then I made iron-and-wire armatures for each horse so that I could work on them separately and put them together to study the entire composition. The group was composed of one colt, one stallion, and five mares, which represented a small family unit of mustangs in the wild state. In the early days a stallion would round up as many mares as he could control and hold by fighting off other stallions. The more fierce and powerful the stallion the bigger his harem. None of the fifteen mares I used as models had ever been handled, and they were as wild as the outdoors in which they lived. At first the horses wouldn't allow me near them, and I had to keep constant watch for their teeth, forefeet, and heels.

In order to show up each animal of the group as much as possible, I planned to place the group on a mound, with the stallion at the top dominating the composition. The working model was three and a half feet high, making each horse about twenty-two inches high at the withers. I modeled the stallion first and then worked on the others to make the group into a harmonious whole [see page 254].

Because I wanted my mustangs to look like mustangs, not just horses, I made measurements and recorded them both for the working model and for the full-size model. In enlarging a group from three feet to fifteen feet there is a great chance for error, and when the time came for pointing up, I wanted to be sure of accuracy. When a model three feet high, with width and length in proportion, is thrown up to fifteen feet, it becomes more than twelve feet wide and eighteen feet long. That meant that my finished statue would be many, many times the size of the small one. I did twice as much work as was necessary on this group, but I couldn't bear to slight any part of it. I modeled every horse on all sides as though it were to stand alone.

I had thought that the model for the little colt would be easy to handle, and the little fillies were fairly docile. Not so the young stallions. They just kept cavorting and jumping, and what I had thought would be the easiest unit of the composition took as much time as any other part.

The spring of 1939 passed, and the Texas summer burst upon us. The thermometer in our cabin sometimes stood as high as 114 degrees, and in my open studio it was occasionally 119. I had to sprinkle the plasteline model with ice water to prevent it from melting. By hanging two layers of burlap loosely on all sides of the cabin and then soaking the burlap with water, we made a "Texas cooler" out of the place. Some days we had dust storms that nearly obliterated the landscape, and I had to cover my group to keep the surface from becoming caked with dust and dirt.

The fall of 1939 found me still working on the group. Northers blew into the studio so violently that I often had to stop work. Finally, however, the group was finished and my son Gifford came out to help me get it ready for shipment east. Gozo Kawamura pointed up the group and sent me the last piece of plaster on the day that he left to return to Japan.

For several war years the mustangs reposed in the Gorham Bronze Foundry at Providence, Rhode Island, waiting for release of critical metals. I had paid for ten tons of bronze and had reserved it for casting, but it seemed that Uncle Sam needed the metal more than I did. Finally, in 1948, the mustangs were cast and installed at the University of Texas [see page 255]. My heart was sad, for Margaret was not there to share my triumph. J. Frank Dobie delivered the dedicatory address and also wrote the words engraved on the base of the statue:

These horses bore Spanish explorers across two continents. They brought to the Plains Indians the age of horse culture. Texas cowboys rode them to extend the ranching occupation clear to the plains of Alberta. Spanish horse, Texas cow pony and mustang were all one in those times when, as sayings went, a man was no better than his horse and a man on foot was no man at all. Like the Longhorn, the mustang has been virtually bred out of existence. But mustang horses will always symbolize western frontiers, long trails of Longhorn herds, seas of pristine grass, and men riding free in a free land.
—J. Frank Dobie

XXVII

EPILOGUE

My friends used to say that until I married in 1893 I rarely slept in the same bed twice. Even with marriage few of my habits changed much. Smoke from my tent has curled into the sky in many places. When I was off on a hunt, toting about forty pounds of guns and ammunition, I'd wish—though I'm not sure the wish was genuine—that I could settle down like most other humans and not be eternally chasing about.

Before I married I never argued with my guns. When they said it was hunting time, off I'd go. After the children began arriving my old shooting irons would often give me the message, and sometimes, with an aching heart, I would have to say: "Can't go this time, boys. Got a wife and babies to feed." Margaret used to tell me that she always knew when hunting season was approaching. In my sleep I'd shout, "I got him! I got him!" When the urge was more than I could bear, Margaret would smile, and I'd be off.

Eventually some of the hunting urge rubbed off on Margaret. One night at Wilton, Connecticut, we wired our daughter and her husband that we couldn't accept their invitation to join them on a bear hunt in British Columbia. Sorrowfully we wandered into the garden to walk off our disappointment. It was September. Suddenly we heard wild geese honking. Looking up, we saw between us and the bright hunter's moon a flock of Canada honkers winging southward. Without a word we hurried into the house and wired: "Disregard first telegram. We're coming."

I was born during the frontier period of the United States and grew up in Colorado in the best of it. It colored my life and influenced me greatly. I would not change my life for any other, but my love has always been divided. I am eternally obsessed with two deep desires—one, to spend as much time as possible in the wilderness, and the other, to accomplish something worthwhile in art. With a fine wife as inspiration in my work and as companion in the wilderness, with a fine family of children, and with good friends, my cup has been full to overflowing.

It is now September, and the hunter's moon is up. I must put my tools away and get ready for another hunt. After that I'll get back to work.

End of the Flight

A GALLERY OF SCULPTURES
BY ALEXANDER PHIMISTER PROCTOR

Fate

Small bronze fawn begun in New York and completed in Paris, 1894

Cub and Rabbit

Bronze statuette, 1885–88

Stalking Panther

Small bronze begun in New York and completed in Paris, 1894. Presented to President Theodore Roosevelt by the members of his cabinet in 1908.

Polar Bear

Small bronze of life-size sculpture for World's Columbian Exposition, Chicago, 1893

Moose

Small bronze of life-size sculpture for World's Columbian Exposition, Chicago, 1893

Dog with Bone

Small bronze sculptured in Paris, 1894

Bronze Horse

Arab Stallion

Small bronzes sculptured in Paris, 1895–97

General John A. Logan

By Augustus Saint-Gaudens; horse sculptured by A. Phimister Proctor
Grant Park, Chicago, Illinois

General William Tecumseh Sherman with Figure of Victory
By Augustus Saint-Gaudens; horse sculptured by A. Phimister Proctor
Central Park, New York City

Puma

Bronze model for one of pumas at entrance to Prospect Park, Brooklyn. The sculpture also stood at the entrance to the Paris Exposition, 1900.

Bronze pumas
at the entrance
to Prospect Park, Brooklyn

Quadriga

Victory drawn by horses

Colossal plaster group atop American exhibit building, Paris Exposition, 1900. Also displayed at the Pan-American Exposition, Buffalo, New York, 1901.

Trumpeting Elephant
Small bronze, 1900

Lion

One of two large bronzes for the Frick Building, Pittsburgh, Pennsylvania

Griffin

Model for copper statue for
Louisiana Purchase Exposition,
St. Louis, Missouri, 1904

Louis Jolliet

Large bronze for Louisiana Purchase Exposition, St. Louis, Missouri, 1904

The sculptor at work on decor for the elephant house, Bronx Park Zoo, 1908

Decor for elephant house, Bronx Park Zoo, 1908

Detail over the entrance to the primate house, Bronx Park Zoo, 1908

COURTESY OF BUFFALO AREA
CHAMBER OF COMMERCE

McKinley Monument

Buffalo, New York

The four large marble lions at the base of the monument were sculptured by Proctor.

One of four large bronze tigers on the Sixteenth Street Bridge, Washington, D.C., 1908

Tiger

Small bronze model for one of the Princeton Tigers

COURTESY OF DEPARTMENT OF PUBLIC INFORMATION, PRINCETON UNIVERSITY

Princeton Tigers

Large bronze statues before entrance to Nassau Hall, Princeton University, 1909

Lion

Marble, for Pratt Institute, Brooklyn, New York, 1910

One of two large tigers at the entrance to the Herbert L. Pratt Estate, Glen Cove, Long Island, New York

Pony Express

Bronze plaque for stations on Pony Express route between St. Joseph, Missouri, and San Francisco, California

Pony Express station, Gothenburg, Nebraska, with Pony Express plaque in place

Bear's Head

Bronze bas-relief, the "mascot" of the Boone and Crockett Club, 1909

One of four large bronze buffaloes on Q Street Bridge, Washington, D.C., 1912–14

Tarpon

Small bronze, 1914

William Hanley

Bronze bas-relief, 1915

Indian Pursuing Buffalo
(Also called *Pursued*)

Small bronze, 1916

Jackson Sundown
(Also called *Indian Chief*)

Small bronze bust, Stanford University, Palo Alto,
California, 1916

The sculptor displaying the buffalo head, the bronze cornerstone for Arlington Cemetery Bridge, Washington, D.C. The cornerstone was commissioned about 1908, installed about 1917.

The sculptor at work on the model for *Pioneer*, large bronze, University of Oregon, Eugene, Oregon, 1917–18

Broncho Buster

Large bronze, Civic Center,
Denver, Colorado, 1918

On The War Trail

Large bronze, Civic Center,
Denver, Colorado, 1920

Top: The sculptor at work on the model for *The Rough Rider*

Below: Pointing up *The Rough Rider* from the model

The completed *Rough Rider*, ready for casting in bronze, 1920

The Rough Rider

Roosevelt Park, Minot, North Dakota
A duplicate of the originally commissioned statue,
which stands in Portland, Oregon

The Circuit Rider
Salem, Oregon, 1922

Til Taylor

Model for large bronze, Pendleton, Oregon, 1926

The Pioneer Mother
Kansas City, Missouri
1923–27

The Pioneer Mother

Kansas City, Missouri

1923–27

Two of the bas-reliefs around the base of *The Pioneer Mother*

Indian and Trapper

Model for large bronze, McKnight Memorial Fountain, Wichita, Kansas, 1932

Gifford Pinchot

Bronze bas-relief, 1932

Irving Hale

Memorial bronze tablet, West Point Military Academy,
New York, 1932

The sculptor at work on the model for *Pioneer Mother* for the University of Oregon, Eugene, Oregon, 1934

The sculptor at work on the model of *General Robert E. Lee and Young Soldier*, 1935

COURTESY OF WIDE WORLD PHOTOS, INC.

General Robert E. Lee and Young Soldier

Dallas, Texas

The working model for *Mustangs*, in progress at King Ranch, Texas, 1938

Below, right: The sculptor at work on the model

Mustangs

University of Texas, Austin, Texas, 1948

APPENDIX

THE MAJOR SCULPTURES OF ALEXANDER PHIMISTER PROCTOR

1885–88	Small bronzes:
	    Fate (fawn)
	    Bear Cub
	    Cub and Rabbit
	    Stalking Panther

1891–93	*Equestrian Indian* *Cowboy* Animals for bridges and buildings at the World's Columbian Exposition, Chicago, 1893

1894–97	Small bronzes
	    Dog with Bone
	    Horse
	    Panther with Kill
	    Indian Warrior
	    Puma
	    Arab Stallion
	    Buffalo Hunt
	Horses, five-foot bronze, for Augustus Saint-Gaudens's statues of General John A. Logan in Chicago and General William T. Sherman in New York
	Pumas, two bronze, for Stanford White's pedestals at entrance of Prospect Park, Brooklyn, New York

1898–1900	Colossal *Quadriga* for the American Building at the Paris Exposition, 1900
1900–1904	*Trumpeting Elephant*, small bronze Lions, large bronze, for Frick Building, Pittsburgh, Pennsylvania Griffin, copper, for Louisiana Purchase Exposition, St. Louis, Missouri, 1904 Louis Jolliet, large bronze, for Louisiana Purchase Exposition, St. Louis, Missouri, 1904 Decor for elephant and primate houses, Bronx Zoological Gardens, New York City Groups and *Quadriga* for Pan-American Exposition, Buffalo, New York, 1901 *Oxen Plowing*, small bronze, for Agricultural Building, Pan-American Exposition, Buffalo, New York, 1901
1904–1908	Lions, four large marble, for McKinley Monument, Buffalo, New York

ALEXANDER PHIMISTER PROCTOR

	Finish decor for elephant, primate, and aquatic-bird houses, Bronx Park Zoo, New York City
1908–12	Tigers, four large bronze, for Sixteenth Street Bridge, Washington, D.C.
	Tigers, two large bronze, for steps of Nassau Hall, Princeton University, Princeton, New Jersey
	Lion relief, Portland, Oregon
	Lion, marble, for Pratt Institute, Brooklyn
	Tigers, two large bronze, for entrance to Herbert L. Pratt estate, Glen Cove, Long Island, New York
	Pony Express plaque, bronze, for stations on route between St. Joseph, Missouri, and San Francisco, California
	Plaque, bear's head mascot, for Boone and Crockett Club
1912–14	Buffaloes, four large bronze, for Q Street Bridge, Washington, D.C.
	Tarpon, small bronze
1914–17	*Indian Pursued*, bronze
	Buffalo Hunt, bronze
	Indian Pursuing Buffalo, small bronze
	Jackson Sundown, bronze bust, for Stanford University, Palo Alto, California
	Martin Biddle on Horseback, small bronze, in Portland, Oregon
	William Hanley, bronze bas-relief
	Tom Allen, bronze bas-relief
	The Buckaroo, small bronze
	Broncho Buster, small bronze
	On the War Trail, small bronze
1917–24	Buffalo head, bronze, for cornerstone of Arlington Cemetery Bridge, Washington, D.C.
	Pioneer, large bronze, for University of Oregon, Eugene, Oregon
	Iron Tail, small bronze bust
	Indian Maiden and Fawn, large bronze, for Maytag family, Newton, Iowa; medium-size, for Brooklyn Botanical Gardens, Brooklyn, New York; medium-size, for Senator James Phelan's "Montalvo," Los Gatos, California; and medium-size, for Campbell Church, Eugene, Oregon
	Slim, small bronze bust
	Little Wolf, small bronze bust
	Dr. K. J. McKenzie, small bronze
	Frank Wiggins, bronze bust, for Chamber of Commerce, Los Angeles, California
	On the War Trail, large bronze, for Civic Center, Denver, Colorado
	Broncho Buster, large bronze, for Civic Center, Denver, Colorado

APPENDIX

	The Rough Rider (Theodore Roosevelt), large bronze, for Portland, Oregon, and Minot, North Dakota
1924–27	*Pioneer Mother*, large bronze, for Kansas City, Missouri *Howard K. Vanderslice*, bronze bust *Til Taylor*, large bronze, for Pendleton, Oregon *Cavalryman*, Goodyear Trophy
1927–36	*Indian Fountain*, large bronze, for Lake George, New York *Indian and Trapper*, large bronze, for McKnight Memorial Fountain, Wichita, Kansas *Pioneer Mother*, large bronze, for University of Oregon, Eugene, Oregon *The Circuit Rider*, large bronze, for Salem, Oregon *General Robert E. Lee and Young Soldier*, large bronze, for Dallas, Texas *Irving Hale*, memorial bronze tablet, for West Point, New York; Princeton, New Jersey; and Denver, Colorado *Gifford Pinchot*, bronze bas-relief
1936–39	Bas-reliefs, bronze, for Portland, Oregon; Lewiston, Idaho, and Des Moines, Iowa
1939–41	*Mustangs*, large bronze, in University of Texas, Austin, Texas
1941–50	Rough model of Jason Lee and John McLoughlin (of Oregon) for Statuary Hall, Washington, D.C. (finished by son Gifford MacGregor Proctor) Small clay model of idea for longhorns Small plaster model of Indian and cowboy

MEDALS AND AWARDS

Columbian Exposition, 1893
Rinehart Scholarship (to Paris, France), 1894–98
Medal and Prize, Academie Julien, Paris, France, 1894
Gold Medal for Sculpture, Paris Exposition, 1900
Jury Member for Sculpture, Paris Exposition, 1900
Bronze Medal for water color, Pan-American Exposition, Buffalo, New York, 1901
Member, Jury of Selection of Awards and Sculpture, Pan-American Exposition, Buffalo, New York, 1901
Gold Medal, Louisiana Purchase Exposition, St. Louis, Missouri, 1904
Member, Jury of Selection for Sculpture, Louisiana Purchase Exposition, St. Louis, Missouri, 1904

Gold Medal of Honor, Architectural League, New York, 1911
Gold Medal, Panama-Pacific International Exposition, San Francisco, California, 1915

MEMBERSHIPS

American Watercolor Society
Architectural League
Bohemian Club, San Francisco, California
Boone and Crockett Club
Camp Fire Club of America
Century Club of New York
Committee for Promotion of Roosevelt Ideals of Roosevelt Memorial Association
National Academy of Design
National Council, Boy Scouts of America
National Art Club of New York
National Sculpture Society
New York Art Commission
New York Zoological Society
Roosevelt Pilgrimage
Society of American Artists
Sons of Colonial Wars
Sons of the Revolution

INDEX

Note: Page numbers in italics refer to illustrations of works by Proctor.

Académie Julien (Paris): 125, 136–37
Adams, Herbert: 128
Adams, Ike: 48–49
Akeley, Carl: 123
Alaska: 109
Alden, Ike: 99
Allen, Tom (cowboy): 172
American Academy (Rome, Italy): 192
American Water Color Society (New York): 108, 131
Amsden, Billy: 125
Antelope: 32–33
Antelope Jack (hunter): 15–17, 22–23, 31, 41, 47; at Grand Lake, Colo., 49–52; in Grand County, Colo., feud, 60–63, 67–68, 70
Arab Stallion: 131, *213*
Arapaho Indians: 42
Art Students' League (New York): 25, 97; Proctor attends, 86–87

Baker, Jack: 18
Baker, Jim (scout): 22
Baker, Mr. and Mrs. Rhodes: 193
Baltimore Museum: 138
Barker, Burt Brown: 191–92
Bartlett, W. H.: 141
Barye, Antoine: 137
Bear's Head (Proctor's mascot for Boone and Crockett Club): *233*
Bears: 27–29, 32, 34, 39–41, 89–91; in Alaska, 109; Proctor's model of polar bear, 115–16, *210*
Beckwith, James Carroll: 86–87, 116
Biddle, Martin, statuette of: *163*

Big Beaver (Indian model): 180–82
Big Frank (hunter): 43–44
Bitter, Karl: 141
Blackfoot Indian Agency (Montana): 132
Blackfoot Indian Reservation (Montana): 132, 134, 180
Blackfoot Indians: 132
Blizzards: 50–51, 54, 56, 84, 106–107
Bobtail Mine (Colorado): 83
Boone and Crockett Club: 1, 118, 131–32; Proctor's mascot for, 118, *233*
Booth, R. A.: 183
Bouché, Alfred: 136
Boulder, Colo.: 43
Boyle, John: 116
Broncho Buster (Denver, Colo.): *175*, 178–79, *240*
Bronx Zoological Gardens (New York): 144–45, 152
Bronze cornerstone (Arlington Cemetery Bridge, Washington, D.C.): 182–83, *238*
Bronze Horse: *213*
Brooklyn Institute (New York): 145
Browning, Mont.: 132–33, 180
Brush, George de Forest: 128, 148–49
Buckaroo, The: *168*
Buffalo: 32, 115ff., 154
Buffalo Bill: *see* William Cody
Buffalo for Q Street Bridge, Washington, D.C.: 154, *233*
Buffalo soldiers (Negro army unit): 45
Bulldogging: 164, 166
Burnham, Daniel H.: 116, 118
Butler, Ed: 56–57

Camp Fire Club: 51
Central City, Colo.: 43, 83–84

Century Club: 52, 96, 131, 153, 181
Century Magazine: 23
Chandler, William Astor: 131
Chandler, Winthrop: 118
Cheyenne Indian Reservation (Montana): 158–62
Chicago, Ill.: 113–14, 119, 122, 124, 127, 132
Chicago Zoo: 115
Circuit Rider, The: 183, *244*
Clark, Al: 50–51, 63
Clark, Galen: 76
Clemens, Jeanne (daughter of Mark Twain): 149
Clinton, Mich.: 6, 86
Cody, William (Buffalo Bill): 119, 121; statue of, *174*
Coe, Dr. Waldo: 182
Coffin, Al: 49–51, 53; in Grand County feud, 60, 62
Coffin, Lon: 50; in Grand County feud, 60, 63, 67, 72
Cole, George: 185
Colorado: 9, 20–21, 88–89, 94, 99, 124; Utes, Arapahos in, 42–46; mining in, 59–60
Colorow, Chief (Ute): 45–46
Columbian Exposition, 1893 (Chicago, Ill.): 112–23
Contini, Attilio: 188
Cook, Sheriff Dave: 9, 23–24
Corbin, Austin: 143
Corydon, N. H.: 143
Cousins, Billy: 43, 143
Cox, Kenyon: 116
Craig, Rev. Bayard: 23, 84–85, 89; hunting at Lost Lake (Colorado), 99–100

261

Cravens, Jess: 175–77
Crazy Head (Cheyenne): 160
Cripple Creek, Colo.: 59
Crow, Mont.: 158
Cub and Rabbit: 208
Cummings, Sir Gordon: 17, 31–32, 47
Curran, C. C.: 87

Dallas, Texas: 192–93, 196
Day, Barney: 70–72
Dead Bill (outlaw): 68, 70
Deakins, Edwin: 81
Dean, Capt. (Union Army officer): 62, 65, 70, 71
Deer: 28–32, 90, 103
Deering, Charles: 118
Delenbaugh, Frederick: 23, 96
Deming, Thomas: 128
Deming, W. W.: 97
Denver, Colo.: 8, 12, 21, 23–24, 26, 50, 71–72, 75, 83, 93, 106–107, 110, 174–75
Denver Post: 9
Des Moines, Iowa: 7, 83
Dobie, J. Frank: 197–200
Dodge, William: 116
Dog with Bone: 212
Drake, Edward: 23
Draper, Dr. William: 132
Dumond, Frank V.: 97
Durth, Henry: 97

East, Tom: 198
East Oregon Journal: 163
Eddy, J. R. (Indian agent): 158–59
Egeria Park, Colo.: 89, 101
Elk: 17, 32, 36–38, 103–105
Elliot, John: 89
Equestrian Indian: 175

Evarts, William F.: 129
Everett, Wash.: 110

Fate (fawn): 94–97, 125, 207
Finn, Mike: 53–54
Firearms: 26, 28, 35–37, 42–43, 48, 60–63, 66, 84, 89, 110, 131; Proctor's, 28, 32–33, 49
Flat Top Mountains (Colorado): 75; hunting in, 89–92
Fleming, Arthur: 156
Fort Garland, Colo.: 45
Fraser, George: 192
French, Daniel: 116
Frick, H. C.: 153
Furlong, Charles: 164

Gardet, Georges: 137
General Robert E. Lee and Young Soldier: 197, 253
Gibson, Jake: 63, 67
Gifford Pinchot: 250
Glacier Point (Yosemite, California): 76–77
Grand Canyon: 23
Grand County, Colo., feud in: 59–73
Grand Lake, Colo.: 12, 18–19, 32, 75, 84, 99–101; hunting at, 29–31, 35–42; Indian harassment at, 42–46; hunters, trappers, settlers at, 47–58; feud at, 59–73
Grand Lake, Colo. (village), in county-seat rivalry: 60, 70
Grand Lake Mine (Colorado): 60, 63
Grand River (Colorado): 14, 17–18, 28, 44, 59
Grasshopper (Cheyenne): 161
Gray Eagle (Blackfoot): 180

Great Northern Railway: 110
Greeley, Horace: 7
Griffin: 143, 221
Grinnell, George Bird: 118, 132
Guilder, Richard Watson: 23
Guns: *see* firearms

Hale, Irving: 9, 85
Half Dome (Yosemite, California): 76–81
Hands Up: 23&n.; Proctor's etchings for, 24, 25
Hanley, William: 171–72, 175
Harper's Weekly: 96
Hartley, Jonathan: 97
Hawkeye Bill: 68, 70
Hensell, Charley: 57–58
Holbein Studios (New York): 97
Hornaday, Dr. William T.: 151–52
Hot Sulphur Springs, Colo.: 31, 43–44, 57, 59, 66–67; in county-seat rivalry, 60, 70, 71
Hoyt, Judge (Grand County, Colo.): 50–51
Hoyt, Mrs. (wife of Judge Hoyt): 67
Hutchinson, James M.: 81

Indian and Trapper: 193, 249
Indian Maiden and Fawn: 183
Indian Pursued: 159–60
Indian Pursuing Buffalo: 138, 148, 173, 235
Indians: 6, 134–35, 180; settlers harassed by, 42–46; in Buffalo Bill's "Wild West Show," 119–21
Indian Warrior: 134, 137–38, 141
Ingersoll, Ernest: 23
Inness, George: 97

INDEX

International Exposition of 1900 (Paris): 139, 141
Irving Hale: 193, 250

Jack, John: 114–15
Jackson Sundown: 168, 170, 237
Jardin des Plantes: 125, 137
Johnson, Charley: 52, 56–57
Johnson, Studhorse: 36, 40–41
Joseph, Chief (Nez Percé): 168

Kawamura, Gozo: 183, 194–95, 200
Kemeys, Edward: 115
Kendall, William Mitchell: 182, 187
Kentucky Johnny (hunter): 43–44
Kerr, Benjamin: 86
Kerr, Isabelle: 86
Kills-Him-Twice (Indian): 119–21
King Ranch (Texas): 198–99
Kinney, Jim: 68, 70
Knight, Charles: 98

Laban (Chief Little Wolf's father, Cheyenne): 160–61
Lasar, Charles: 125
Lawson, Dorothy: 9
Leadville, Colo.: 59
Lee, Dr. Bowling: 194
Lee, General Robert E.: 192–97, 252
Lee, Robert E. IV: 197
Let 'Er Buck (book): 164
Lewiston, Idaho: 168, 170, 177
Lion (for Frick Building, Pittsburgh, Pa.): 153, 220
Lion (for Pratt Institute, New York): 153, 230
Lions (for McKinley Monument, Buffalo, N.Y.): 144, 225

Little-Black-White-Man (Cheyenne): 161–62
Little Wolf, Chief (Cheyenne): 159–62
Logan, General John A.: 127–29, 214
Long's Peak (Colorado): 25
Los Angeles, Calif.: 75, 185, 187
Lost Lake (Colorado): 99–100
Louisiana Purchase Exposition of 1904 (St. Louis, Mo.): 143
Louis Jolliet: 143, 222
Low, Seth: 144
Lowrie, Lee: 114
Luxembourg Museum (Paris): 137

McCartney, Alex: 110
McClusky, David: 24
MacGregor, Anne Cantoch: 5
McKim, Charles: 116, 129
McKinley Monument (Buffalo, N.Y.): 144, 225
McKnight Memorial Fountain (Wichita, Kans.): 193
MacMonnies, Frederick: 141, 177
McNeill, Herman: 116
McQuarry, Jack: 62
Maring, Philip: 116
Marker, Sheriff (Hot Sulphur Springs, Colo.): 44
Martin, Gil: 72
Maynard, George: 116
Mayo Clinic (Rochester, Minn.): 173–74
Meeker, Nathan Cook (Indian agent): 44–45
Melchers, Gari: 122
Mellon, Sandy: 44, 46
Merriam, S. Hart: 155–56
Merritt, Gen. Wesley: 45

Metropolitan Museum of Art (New York): 108, 145
Meyers, Helen: 140
Middle Park, Colo.: 12, 22
Miller, Johnny: 121
Millet, Frank D.: 96, 114, 123
Mills, Commissioner (Grand County, Colo.): 71–72
Mills, J. Harrison: 21–22, 31–33, 84
Monte Cristo Park (Washington): 110
Montross, N. E.: 109
Moose: 211
Morey, Steve: 60, 62
Morris, Hank: 132–34
Morton, Levi Parsons: 109
Moses, Charley: 92–93
Munger, Dave: 60, 62, 66
Murphy, Charles: 145
Musgrove, L. H., lynching of: 11, 25
Mustangs: 197–200, 254–55

National Academy of Design (New York): 85, 97, 131, 145
National Art Commission (Washington, D.C.): 182
National Sculpture Society (New York): 131
Natural History Museum (New York): 98
Newton, Iowa: 6, 7
New York Art Commission: 145
New York City, N.Y.: 25, 51–52, 84ff., 89ff., 93, 98, 106, 118, 127, 134, 149; Proctor in, 84–87, 94–98, 108–10, 113, 128–30, 135, 141–43, 153, 181–83, 187
New York City Public Library: 145
Nez Percé Reservation (Idaho): 168, 179
North Park, Colo.: 32

263

Ogden, Ralph: 197–98
Old Avery (hunter): 18, 48–49, 58
Old Wounded Eye (Cheyenne): 161
O'Neil, Louis: 179
Ontario, Can.: 5, 6, 85–86
On the War Trail: 178–82, *241*
Oregon City, Ill.: 124
Ouray, Chief (Ute): 45

Paderewski, Ignace Jan: 116
Pan-American Exposition, 1901 (Buffalo, N.Y.): 108, 141, 143
Panther: in Flat Top Mountains, 91–92; model of, 96–97, 109, 125, *207*; bronze of, 126, 188, *209*
Panther with Kill: 148
Paris, France: 122, 124, 127–28, 131, 134–39, 141–43
Parker, Doc (Grand Lake, Colo.): 47
Pasadena, Calif.: 75
Patterson, Sen. Thomas M.: 23
Payne, Capt. J. S.: 45
Payne, Robert: 129, 178, 187
Pendleton, Oreg., roundup: 163–68
Pierre (renegade Ute chief): 43–44
Pikes Peak, Colo.: 25
Pinchot, Gifford: 108, 119, 186; bronze bas-relief of, 108, *250*
Pioneer: 173, 178–79, *239*
Pioneer Mother, The (Kansas City, Mo.): 184–91, *246–47*
Pioneer Mother, The (University of Oregon): 191–92, *251*
Platt, Charles: 128
Plummer, Bob: 54, 56
Polar Bear: *210*
Pollard, Len: 32–35, 44, 47, 71–72
Pony Express (plaque): *232*

Porter, Doc (Grand Lake, Colo.): 35
Portland, Oreg.: 162–63, 172
Potter, Bessie: 117
Potter, E. C.: 116
Powell, Maj. John Wesley: 23
Pratt, Bela: 137, 186
Pratt, George D.: 108, 153, 155–57, 173, 181
Pratt, Herbert L.: 153
Prellwitz, Henry: 128–29
Prichett, Henry Smith: 143
Princeton Tigers: 150–51, *227*, *229*
Proctor, Alden (son): 140, 148–49, 170–72, 188
Proctor, Alexander (father): 5, 6, 20, 83–84
Proctor, Alexander Phimister: on modern art, 3; parentage of, 5, 6; birth of, 6; early education of, 7; baptism of, 10–11; early art training of, 20–25; hunting at Grand Lake, Colo., 26–42; life of, at Grand Lake, 47–58; in Grand County feud, 59–73; in Los Angeles, 75; ascent of Half Dome at Yosemite, 76–81; in San Francisco, 81; mining venture of, 83–84; homestead sold by, 84; in New York, 84–87, 94–98, 108–10, 113, 128–30, 135, 141–43, 153, 181–83; visit of, in Ontario, Can., 85–86; attends Art Students' League (New York), 86–87; in Flat Top Mountains, 89–92; modeling of, 95–98; at Lost Lake (Colorado), 99–101; at White River Ute Reservation, 103–106; prospecting of, in Washington, 110; in Skykomish River country, 110–13; in the Cascades, 113; at World's Columbian Exposition, 1893 (Chicago, Ill.), 113–23; marriage of, 123; in Paris, France, 124–27, 135, 137–39, 141–43; near Windsor, Vt., 128–29; hunting in Montana, 132; at Indian Hill, N.Y., 144–49; at Stamford, Conn., 149; hunting in Canada, 151–57; at Cheyenne Indian Reservation, 158–62; in Oregon, 162–72; illness of, 173–74; in Denver, 174 176, in California, 178–82, 185; in Rome, Italy, 188–91; in Sarasota, Fla., 195–96; in Seattle, 197; at King Ranch (Texas), 197–99
Proctor, Alexander Phimister, works of: engravings for *Hands Up*, 23–25; painting of mountain snow scene, 85; prints of wild animals, 87; fawn, panther models, 95–97, 109, 125–26, *207*; *Trumpeting Elephant*, 98, *219*; painting of cougar, 108; bronze bas-relief of Gifford Pinchot, 108, *250*; painting of bull elk, 109; oil painting of panthers, 109; polar bear, 115–16, *210*; bronze bear's head, 118, *233*; buffalo-head models for White House, 119; *The Rough Rider*, 119, 182, *242–43*; mounted Indian, bronco buster at World's Columbian Exposition, 121–22, 167; bronze panther, 126, 188, *209*; *Dog with Bone*, 126–27, *224*; model of General Logan's horse, 128–29; *Arab Stallion*, 131, *213*; horse for statue of Gen. William Tecumseh Sherman, 129–31, *215*; *Indian Warrior*, 134, 137–38, 141; pumas for Prospect Park (Brooklyn, N.Y.), 135–37; *Quadriga* for International Exposition of 1900 (Paris), 139–41, *218*; standing puma, 141, *216*; models for House of Primates, Bronx Zoo (New York), 143; *Griffin*, 143,

INDEX

Proctor, works of, continued:
221; *Louis Jolliet*, 143, 222; lions for McKinley Monument (Buffalo, N.Y.), 144–46, 149, 225; *Panther with Kill*, 148; *Indian Pursuing Buffalo*, 148, 168, 173, 235; decorations for elephant house at Bronx Zoo (New York), 149, 223; *Princeton Tigers*, 150–51, 227, 229; tigers for Sixteenth Street Bridge (Washington, D.C.), 150–51, 226; water-color sketches in Canada, 151; tigers at entrance to Pratt estate, 153, 231; buffalo for Herbert L. Pratt, 153; *Lion* for Pratt Institute (New York), 153, 230; *Lion* for Frick Building (Pittsburgh, Pa.), 153, 220; Buffalo, Q Street Bridge (Washington, D.C.), 154, 223; *Indian Pursued*, 159, 163; statuette of Martin Biddle and pony, 163; *The Buckaroo*, 168, 171; *Jackson Sundown*, 168, 237; *William Hanley*, 172, 234; Pioneer, 173, 175, 178–79, 239; Mohawk Indian, 173–74, 181–82; *Equestrian Indian*, 175, 181; *Broncho Buster*, 175, 178–79, 240; *On the War Trail*, 178–82, 241; bronze cornerstone for Arlington Cemetery Bridge (Washington, D.C.), 182–83, 238; *Indian Maiden and Fawn*, 183; *The Circuit Rider*, 183, 244; *The Pioneer Mother* (Kansas City, Mo.), 184–91, 246–47; charging panther, 185; *Til Taylor*, 191, 245; *Pioneer Mother* (University of Oregon), 191–92, 251; *General Robert E. Lee and Young Soldier*, 192–97, 252, 253; *Irving Hale*, 193, 250; dry points of wild animals, 197; *Mustangs*, 197–99, 200, 254, 255; *Cub and Rabbit*, 208; *Polar Bear*, 210; *Moose*, 211; *Bronze Horse*, 213; *Tiger*, 227; *Pony Express*, 232; *Tarpon*, 234

Proctor, George (brother): 8, 9, 12, 17–19, 26, 58; hunting at Grand Lake, Colo., 28–31, 33–38, 40–42; prospecting in Washington, 110–13; in the Cascades, 113
Proctor, Gifford MacGregor (son): 171, 200
Proctor, Hester (daughter): 137–39, 171, 177–78, 188
Proctor, Jean (daughter): 149
Proctor, Joanne (daughter): 197–98
Proctor, John (grandfather): 5
Proctor, Mrs. Alexander (Tirzah Smith, mother): 6
Proctor, Mrs. Alexander Phimister (Margaret Daisy Gerow, wife): 117, 119, 122, 125, 127, 135–36, 141–43, 150, 154–55, 170–71, 173–74, 180–82, 187, 193, 200–202; marriage of, to Proctor, 123; in Paris, France, 124–27, 135, 137–39, 141–43; in Chicago, 132; at Cheyenne Indian Reservation, 158–60; in Pendleton, Oreg., 166–67; in Denver, Colo., 174; in Sarasota, Fla., 195–96; at King Ranch (Texas), 198–99
Proctor, Ona Mary (daughter): 149
Proctor, Phim (son): 148–49, 172, 175, 188
Proctor, William (brother): 113, 177
Prospect Park, Brooklyn, N.Y.: 135
Puech, Denys: 125
Puma: 141, 216

Quadriga: 139–41, 218

Rabbit Ear Range (Colorado): 32, 59

Red Cloud, Jack (Sioux): 121
Red Fox (Cheyenne): 161
Redmond, Bill: 51, 53; in Grand County feud, 60, 62–65, 71
Redmond, Bud: 66–67
Redmond, Frank: 63, 65
Redmond, Mann: 50, 53; in Grand County feud, 60, 62–63, 67
Reed, Robert: 116
Reinhart, Charles: 116
Rinehart Prix de Paris Collection: 138
Rinehart Scholarship: 135–36, 138
Rochester, Minn.: 173
Rocky Mountain News: 21
Rogers, John: 94, 119, 154
Rogers, Phil: 68, 70
Rogers, Mrs. R. V.: 192–93
Rolling Bull (Cheyenne): 162
Rome, Italy: 187–91
Roosevelt, Kermit: 188
Roosevelt, Pres. Franklin D.: 196
Roosevelt, Pres. Theodore: 118–19, 131, 174, 182, 188
Root, Elihu: 118, 132
Rouett, Gov. John L.: 23
Rough Rider, The: 119, 182, 242–43
Roundup Association, Pendleton, Oreg.: 163, 166–68
Royer, Sheriff Charley (Grand County, Colo.): 67–68, 70–72
Runyan, Charley: 170–71

Saint-Gaudens, Augustus: 116, 127–31, 141
Saint-Gaudens, Lewis: 131
St. Mary's Lake (Montana): 132
Salvatore, Victor: 188
Sampson, Alden: 46–47, 50–51, 81, 85,

153, 177; in Los Angeles, 75; ascent of Half Dome (Yosemite, California), 75–80
San Francisco, Calif.: 81
Schafer, Ned: 53
Seaside, Oreg.: 163
Seattle, Wash.: 113, 197
Sherman, Gen. William Tecumseh, statue of: 129–31, *215*
Simmons (painter): 116
Skykomish River: 110, 113
Smith, Capt. Jonathan: 5, 6
Smith, Charley: 85–86
Smith, Detective Frank: 8
Smith, Granville: 87
Smithsonian Museum (Washington, D.C.): 155
Snohomish, Wash.: 110, 113
Snyder, Bill: 98
Southern Women's Memorial Association (Dallas, Texas): 192
Speer, Mayor Robert: 174
Stalking Panther: 188, 209
Stamford, Conn.: 149
Steele, Wilbur: 9
Stimson, Henry L.: 47, 50, 119, 132–33
Stimson, Mrs. Henry L.: 133
Stokes, Jim: 62, 70
Stokes, Rebel: 43
Sulphur Springs, Colo.: *see* Hot Sulphur Springs, Colo.
Sundown, Jackson (Nez Percé): 168–70, 179; *237*
Sundown, Mrs. Jackson (Cecilia): 168, 170, 179

Taft, Lorado: 116–17
Tarpon: *234*
Taylor, Sheriff Til (Pendleton, Calif.): 167; statue of, 191, *245*
Teal, Joseph N.: 173, 175
Texas, University of (Austin): 197, 200
Texas Centennial Exposition of 1936 (Dallas): 196
Texas Charley (outlaw): 31
Texas Jack (cowboy): 92–93
Thayer, Abbott: 108
Thomas, Seymour: 87, 136
Thompson, Gid: 66–68, 70
Thompson, Jim: 171
Thornburg, Maj. Thomas T.: 45–46
Through Fire and Flood: (painting by J. Harrison Mills): 22
Tiger: *227*
Tigers at entrance to Pratt Estate: 153, *231*
Til Taylor: 191, *245*
Traveller (Gen. Robert E. Lee's horse): 193
Tregoning, John: 83
Troublesome Creek (Colorado): 31–32
Trumpeting Elephant: 98, *219*
Tyler, Rev. (New York minister): 84–85

Ute Bill (saloonkeeper): 31
Ute Indians: 17, 32, 46, 89; in Colorado, 42–46; of White River, 44–46; troops ambushed by, 45–46

Vanderslice, Howard: 185–86
Van Horne, Sir William: 109–10
Vivian, Sir Henry Hussey: 17, 31, 47

Wadsworth, Austin: 118
Waldron (developer at Grand Lake, Colo.): 52–57

Walker, Horatio: 130
Warner, Olin: 115
Warren, Antelope Jack: *see* Antelope Jack
Washington, D.C.: 118; *see also* Alexander Phimister Proctor, works of
Water Color Society (New York): 108, 131
Watrus, Harry: 145
Webber (outlaw): 60–62, 71
Weir, Alden: 16
West Point Military Academy: 193
Westcott, J. L.: 18, 28–29, 32, 41, 47, 49; skirmish with Old Avery, 48–49; in feud over townsite, 52–53; at wedding celebration, 57–58; in Grand County feud, 60
Weston, Edward Payne: 7, 8
Whipple, William D.: 118
White, Stanford: 129, 135, 137
White River (Colorado): 44, 101, 106
White River Indian Reservation (Ute): 46, 101; hunting at, 103–106
Whitman, William: 87
Wiggins, Carleton: 87
Wilbur, Dr. Ray Lyman: 182
William Hanley: 172, *234*
Wilmarth (art teacher): 85
Wilson, Pres. Woodrow: 150–51
Woman's Leggings (Cheyenne): 161
Wood, Col. Charles Erskine Scott: 163
World's Columbian Exposition, 1893 (Chicago, Ill.): 113–23

Yosemite Valley (California): 76–81

The pattern of Alexander Phimister Proctor's life suggests an interplay between his rustic background and his formal sculpture, and the design of this book attempts to express the same interplay.

The sketches scattered throughout the text are Proctor's own, some drawn especially for this autobiography in the sculptor's later years, and others done at the times the events of the narrative took place. They offer a striking contrast to Proctor's finished sculpture, of which a "gallery" is pictured starting on page 205.

The typefaces used in the book were designed by two of Proctor's contemporaries, both Americans: W. A. Dwiggins and Frederick W. Goudy. The text was set on the Linotype in eleven-point Caledonia, a typeface designed by Dwiggins and selected for its simplicity and vigor. Chapter titles are handset Forum Title capitals, designed by Goudy from formal Roman inscriptions.

The book was composed in metal type, proofed for reproduction, photographed, then printed by offset lithography on paper which bears the watermark of the University of Oklahoma Press and which has an effective life of at least three hundred years.

UNIVERSITY OF OKLAHOMA PRESS

NORMAN